Marquesan
Encounters

Marquesan Encounters

Melville and the
Meaning of Civilization

T. Walter Herbert, Jr.

HARVARD UNIVERSITY PRESS
Cambridge, Massachusetts
London, England
1980

Copyright © 1980 by the President
and Fellows of Harvard College
All rights reserved
Printed in the United States of America

*Publication of this book has been aided by
a grant from the Andrew W. Mellon Foundation*

Library of Congress Cataloging in Publication Data

Herbert, Thomas Walter, Jr., 1938–
  Marquesan encounters.

  Bibliography: p.
  Includes index.
  1. Melville, Herman, 1819–1891. Typee. 2. Marquesas
Islands in literature. 3. Nuku-hiva Island—History.
4. Civilization—Philosophy. 5. United States—
Intellectual life—1783–1865. I. Title.
PS2384.T83H4   813'.3   80-15979
ISBN 0-674-55066-8

To my wife
Marjorie Millard Herbert

| *Preface*

IN *WRITING* this book, which is concerned with the problem
of social boundaries, I have been aware with some uneasiness
of taking up issues that are conventionally the province of scholars in specializations other than my own. In the course of my academic training in literature, I sometimes came across the work
of social scientists who ventured to speak about literary matters,
and almost always responded with annoyance, only to find myself in later years returning to the same works with great admiration. On such occasions I was led to admit somewhat sheep-
ishly that my earlier irritation had resulted from the necessary
vehemence with which neophytes embrace the principles of the
group to which they seek entrance, in my case principles of historical literary scholarship. Whether such territorial impulses
subside with the completion of schooling is perhaps doubtful;
yet some increase of patience and generosity must take place if
intellectual issues are to be considered on their merits.

I hope someday to attain the patience and generosity that has
been shown toward me in the course of my work on this book. I
have been assisted at every stage by anthropologists who have
led me to crucial resources as well as sharing their own expert
knowledge and talking over theoretical questions. I am especially
grateful to James Boon, Megan Biesele, Michael B. Collins, Jack
Hunnicutt, John T. Kirkpatrick, Gwen Neville, Harry L. Shapiro,
Robert C. Suggs, and Annette Weiner. My work has also been

greatly aided by scholars who have read the manuscript and offered me their criticisms. Without wishing to implicate them in the shortcomings of the result, I want to thank Megan Biesele, Lee Andrew Elioseff, Francis G. Hutchins, Charles Rossman, Warwick Wadlington, and Annette Weiner.

The study undertaken here would be wholly impossible without the achievements of specialists in Melville studies who have placed before the researcher a wealth of reliable information and avenues to further information, covering the whole range of Melville's life and work. The notes will indicate specific points at which debts are owed to this tradition of scholarship. Beyond these local references there is a debt to the tradition itself as set forth in the following: Leon Howard, *Herman Melville: A Biography* (Berkeley, 1967); *The Letters of Herman Melville*, ed. Merrell R. Davis and William H. Gilman (New Haven, 1960); Charles Roberts Anderson, *Melville in the South Seas* (1939; rpt. New York, 1966); Jay Leyda, *The Melville Log*, 2 vols. (New York, 1951); *The Recognition of Herman Melville*, ed. Hershel Parker (Ann Arbor, 1967); *The Writings of Herman Melville*, ed. Harrison Hayford, Hershel Parker, and G. Thomas Tanselle (Evanston, 1968–).

This project was first undertaken on an NEH Younger Humanist Fellowship, and its completion was made possible through research grants from Southwestern University. Several institutions have offered indispensable assistance: the Houghton Library at Harvard University, the Peabody Museum of Salem, the Alumni Archives of Princeton Theological Seminary, the American Museum of Natural History, the Perry-Casteneda Library and the Humanities Research Center of the University of Texas at Austin, and the Pacific Collection at the University of Hawaii. With its remarkably complete and well-catalogued collections, the Hawaiian Mission Children's Society Library, Honolulu, should be better known as a resource for the history of American missions in the Pacific; and I am particularly grateful for the kind and expert assistance of Lela Goodell and Mary Jane Knight, the librarians there. I am also indebted to Dorothy Secor and Michele Secor, who painstakingly typed and retyped the manuscript.

Contents

Illustrations

Marquesan Encounters

1 | Characters in Search of an Audience

*I*N 1918, while he was enduring the trials of his pioneering fieldwork in the Trobriand Islands, Bronislaw Malinowski momentarily visualized the possibility of a "New Humanism" that would supplant the study of literary classics with a "new plan in which living man, living language, and living full-blooded facts would be the core of the situation."[1] This observation was committed to a diary in which Malinowski recorded a psychological tumult that was kept private as he sought to establish anthropological study as a social science; the idea was not followed up in his own work and remained unpublished among his papers until after his death. In the larger course of his career Malinowski tried to separate anthropology from humanistic concerns, fixing boundaries within which the fledgling discipline could thrive without disruptive interference from outsiders. The publication in 1967 of his *Diary in the Strict Sense of the Term* created a considerable stir within anthropology because of the marked contrast it revealed between the scientific self-possession that Malinowski displayed in his formal self-representations and the acute obsessive turmoil in which his own formative work was conducted.[2] Before he called forth a new community, to which others could wholeheartedly devote themselves, Malinowski first formed a new self; and as his "contribution" to anthropology has been critically assessed, only one of its features has remained unchallenged: his spiritual authority as a mighty ancestor. The charismatic force with which he affected colleagues and disciples is witnessed by the ambivalence visible in commentary on his work; it is also visible in the professional identities of those who provide the commentary.[3]

Malinowski's role as a founder of anthropology attests to the deep correlation that exists between the processes of individual and communal self-definition, and to the vigor with which such processes are informed by conceptions present in the culture at large, in this case "science" and "humanism." His example stands fittingly at the head of this study because it reveals two dimensions of a process with which we will be occupied on every page: first, the way in which a model of the self that is keyed to a compelling vision of the world sets boundaries within which persons can focus their energies in a coherent program of collective activity; and, second, the cauldron of uncertainties in which such programs are formed and tested, where at least momentarily larger possibilities become visible, more generous conceptions that are excluded when the formulated collective program gets under way.

In the broadening curriculum of study that Malinowski helped to inaugurate, there is increasing support for a conception of anthropology that has analogies with the traditional literary concerns of the humanities. The contention that human flesh and blood can replace "the classics" as objects for study suggests the thesis that writers such as Clifford Geertz, Victor Turner, Mary Douglas, Claude Lévi-Strauss, and James Peacock have in various ways elaborated: human beings and human activities embody systems of meaning as inherent constituents of their being human; knowledge of flesh-and-blood humanity is now seen as cognate to knowledge of literary texts.[4] This premise underlies a burgeoning enterprise that draws together cultural historians, literary critics, and anthropologists in an investigation of meaningful form not merely in myth and ritual, but also in such ostensibly nonsymbolic arenas of activity as politics, commerce, and sport.

The branch of this enterprise with at present the greatest influence on literary studies takes its point of departure from the structuralism of Lévi-Strauss. Having attained recognition as a presence on the intellectual landscape, structuralist literary criticism is now a subject of vigorous controversy, from which several themes have emerged that will help us to set in relief the project undertaken in this book. As Lévi-Strauss has noted, structuralism takes up from the linguistics of Saussure a commitment to looking upon its subject matter as a timeless self-contained system.[5] This commitment, immensely fruitful in linguistics and in the work of Lévi-Strauss, accounts for the similarity between structuralist literary criticism and the "new criticism" where an individual text is considered as a circumscribed unit that generates and sustains an inwardly coherent pattern of meanings. Excluded from such an approach is the fact that any utterance, whether in speaking, in primitive myth, or in literature, has a context; and the linkages that connect the text to the occasion in which it occurs give it meanings beyond those contained in its own interior logic, or that of the lawful system it exemplifies. As Paul Ricoeur explains, an individual utterance may well be taken as an example of the underlying system of language, but it also exists as a "saying something of something" and likewise as a saying "by someone to someone."[6]

It is a commonplace of literary study that there are limits to be placed on the effort to read a work of art strictly "in its own terms." As James Boon has shown, the structuralist school of thought is akin to the symbolist movement in poetry, where one finds works that do appear to present themselves as idiosyncratic codes to be broken, so that the aesthetic experience is constituted by the transactions among a specific set of images as they evoke possible totalities of meaning.[7] Yet even here, as Boon also shows, questions of historical context are pertinent to the meanings of poems; and in the general harvest of understanding that the old "new criticism" brought forth, the subtlest appreciations were achieved by critics who sought to answer questions about what a work of literature means in itself by attending simultaneously to questions about what it means as communicated between an author and an audience, and what, further, it has to say about love, or gardens, or murder, or the charge of the Light Brigade, or whatever its subject may be.

An approach is now developing within anthropology that differs from structuralism in seeking to elucidate the meanings present in occasions of significant activity by considering their particularities of context and reference, as well as by scanning them for evidences of internally consistent general structures. Holding that human activity "says" things, Clifford Geertz and Victor Turner find in it a rich interactive texture like that of the drama, where issues of general import are entertained among parties to a common circumstance. Comprehending such a communal discourse is not a matter of finding a timeless law to account for it, but of grasping how particular occasions, employing a distinctive cultural idiom, illuminate the ongoing interplay of meaning-laden action and make sense within it. In Geertz's essay on an abortive Javanese funeral, for example, as in Turner's on Thomas Becket, very small snippets of activity are seen under intensive examination to embody structures of meaning that reach out to embrace, and to comment upon, the concerns of an entire society.[8]

Suggesting a new appreciation of the place of imagination in social experience generally, such interpretive anthropological study offers distinctive resources for enriching our understanding of the historical contexts of literary art and thus of gaining a more exact understanding of the specific terms upon which works of art (like selves and societies) do indeed live their magical inward lives.

The investigation presented in this book, after shifting camp several times in search of fresh waters, has at length pitched its tents, perhaps illegally, in this newly emerging space, where an interpretive social science can be joined with literary criticism. What began as a pursuit of historical sources for Melville's *Typee* has become a sociodramatic analysis in which the essential metaphors and themes are seen to pervade action as well as writing.[9] And the specific circumstances under study are remarkably slight in comparison to their import: I take up three brief episodes in which early nineteenth-century Americans confronted the inhabitants of Nukuheva, one of the Marquesas Islands in eastern Polynesia, and find in those encounters a subtle and profound debate on the meaning of civilization.

It is well known that the idea of civilization was of momentous significance in America's early national period. As the new nation departed from its European origins and established itself on this continent, a series of generally shared cultural myths developed within which the American experience was seen to be meaningful by those who were living it. A corresponding series of distinguished scholarly studies has detected the presence of such general conceptions in the literature of nineteenth-century America; their titles—*Virgin Land, The American Adam, The Machine in the Garden*—evoke the powerful simplicity of ideas at this level of cultural significance.[10] Yet none of these comprehensive orderings of the American experience had the authority and scope enjoyed by the idea of civilization. That America was thought of as a "civilization" does not need to be detected in the writings of the period; it is proclaimed on every hand and has retained currency into our own time.

In present-day usage, however, the term has lost the specificity that it had for the early nineteenth century, as well as its glamour as the name for an inspiring social program. We now use the term "civilization" loosely as a sign of respect for the distinctive qualities of any culture, and find no strain in speaking of the civilizations of Polynesia or of the ancient Near East. In its earlier sense, however, the word carried a full charge of the dynamic significance now attached to terms like "progress," "development," and "modernization." Human history was seen as a process in which superior social forms superseded their less advanced rivals. In some parts of the world this process had moved farther than it had elsewhere, so that all human societies might be placed on a scale that ran from barbarism up through intermediate states to the highest form of all. Civilization was not merely the name for the highest form, however; it also denoted the process of advancement itself, the "making-civilized" that generated all the human felicities and achievements not given by nature. The nations deemed civilized, accordingly, were seen not merely to have progressed the most, but to have the greatest potential for further advance. It was of the nature of a civilized nation continually to improve itself and also to have a beneficial effect on those with whom it had dealings.

Charles and Mary Beard identify this inspiring idea of civilization with "the American Spirit" itself; they find the origins of the concept in Enlightenment philosophy and trace its myriad applications in succeeding American epochs. Ernest Lee Tuveson has

revised and enlarged this thesis: he shows that Christian millennial theory long before the Enlightenment envisaged human history as advancing through stages of progressive improvement,
and demonstrates that this religious tradition fundamentally
conditioned the American consciousness. In *The Savages of
America* Roy Harvey Pearce has opened another vista, showing
how the idea of civilization was adapted to the necessities of explaining the white confrontation with the Amerindian through
extensions of the companion concept of savagery.[11]

These studies canvass a vast literature, finding primary and
ancillary spokesmen for the concept of civilization in its various
transformations. The range of materials they are able to amass
gives authority to a shared claim, namely that the idea of civilization was something more than a literary curiosity or an item of
learned debate. The Beards, Tuveson, and Pearce all insist that
the idea was alive in the mentality of those who espoused it. It
was an idea that entered directly into action; it had the power to
organize other ideas; it was enshrined in mythic and symbolic
formulas; it was given ritual enactments; it was a world view that
afforded working conceptions of the self and the social environment.[12] Yet the immense documentation that these studies bring
forward does not permit us to see this fascinating aspect of the
notion actually at work. Treating the idea of civilization principally as a phenomenon that appears in formal treatises, they dis-
connect it from the living full-blooded facts that gave it reality.

In *Fathers and Children*, Michael Rogin has advanced this discussion along new and promising lines. He observes that "the
contrast between 'savagery' and 'civilization' dominated the
ante-bellum American imagination," as the energies of national
expansion were balked by the Indian and his distinctive way of
life.[13] Rogin's searching treatment of the destruction of the Indian uncovers psychological complexities that are not explored
in earlier studies; yet the idea of civilization (like other nineteenth-century ideas) is seen to act principally as an ideological
cover for psychosocial dynamics whose essential processes he
defines—often quite compellingly—in Freudian terms. The
trans-historical abstractions of Freudian theory, such as infantile
rage, oral frustration, and the anal stage, are not securely corre-

lated with the wealth of historical particulars that convey so immediate a sense of the conflicts Rogin describes. His effort to make the correlation, to join depth psychology and historical analysis, gives the book its extraordinary penetration, its power to get at certain disturbing truths that were not apparent to the historical figures in question, and which we have continued to conceal from ourselves. Yet the discrepancy between psychoanalytic universals and specific historical occasions remains, as it must always remain so long as unconscious processes are thought to be governed essentially by timeless forces—and this discrepancy sets a problem well worth addressing.

Is it possible to locate a circumstance in which the idea of civilization itself can be seen at work as a structural element of the American identity?

To say that an individual's words and actions exemplify an idea does not mean simply that he believes the idea to be true, but rather that it is axiomatic for his way of being. Jerome Bruner has observed that a cultural mythos informs character by providing a "library of scripts upon which the individual may judge the internal drama of his multiple identities."[14] A person whose character is informed by the conception of himself as civilized is not a mere robot, programmed to act out the requirements of that particular doctrine in every situation he confronts. On the contrary, his sense-of-self as "a civilized person" will be evoked on occasions that happen to engage this particular option as against other options in his repertoire of roles. The civilized person may also be a physician, a New Englander, and a parent, and will enact these other roles as occasions call them forth.

Confronting the Marquesans of Nukuheva, Americans were put on their civilized-person mettle. Tattooed bodies of men and women, and their sexual alacrity, thatch-roofed dwellings and vast ceremonial plazas, chronic warfare and human sacrifice and cannibalism, earplugs with intricately carved tiki-faces whose outlines could also be found in the massive religious statuary and the heads of warclubs, the drumming and the dust, the flies, the murmur and clamor of unintelligible voices, crowds of naked children in the surf, smells of cooking from the cooking houses and smells of coconut-oil skin ointments and hairdressing: all of

this surged in the foreground of consciousness as Americans encountered Marquesans, prompting them to steady themselves
against reliable tokens of their own reality and its meaning.

The Americans I treat found themselves perforce enacting a
civilized role. Returning home to put before the public an account of their doings, they provide instances in which the conception of civilization can be seen at work in psychosocial identity, strongly engaged as a way of coming to terms with the
interior and exterior landscapes that it had the power to characterize. This routine indeed, in which an individual voyages outward beyond the presumed borders of the civilized community
in order to bring back a report on the savage portions of mankind, is a typical gesture of the civilized self.

Individuals who engage in this activity are not merely following a private impulse; they nominate themselves at least provisionally as candidates for the role of exemplar. Just as a pilgrimage to a sacred shrine is a profoundly communal gesture, made
with the purpose of attesting and refreshing communal values, so
the journey of the civilized man into the domain of the savage
may take form as an effort to confirm the meaning of civilization
by giving it a typical enactment, an enactment that is completed
as a bid for exemplary significance when the actor makes his
story public: when he asks, that is, for an audience.

The three Marquesan encounters that are the subject of this
study involve men who wrote books promoting conceptions of
civilization that represent rival schools of early nineteenth-century American opinion: Captain David Porter was a spokesman
for the Enlightenment, the Reverend Charles Stewart was a Calvinist, and Herman Melville's views were Romantic. Yet while it
is possible to locate passages in each of these books that provide
thumbnail definitions of civilization and corresponding definitions of savagery, what strikes us in reading them is not a pattern
of argumentation with matters of fact brought in for support.
What we find in each case is a coherent story organized by a
consciousness that is itself organized by ideas of what constitutes
civilized life. The teller of the story does more than advocate his
version of the idea of civilization; he embodies it. And the true
substance of the debate among the three becomes apparent as we

grasp the ways in which these embodiments take form and are made to jostle against one another.

Captain Porter came to the Marquesas in 1813, in the course of his South Pacific operations during the War of 1812, and took possession of the islands in the name of the United States. His *Journal of a Cruise Made to the Pacific Ocean* (1815) portrays this undertaking not only as a significant conquest but also as an achievement of science, since it permits him to report on hitherto little-known peoples. Consider, as a sample of the figure he cuts, Porter's way of treating a situation that greeted every Western visitor to the Marquesas, the sexual availability of Marquesan women.

> The men repeatedly invited us to the shore and pointed to the women and the house near which they were standing, accompanying their invitation with gestures which we could not misunderstand; and the girls themselves showed no disinclination to grant every favour we might be disposed to ask; and to render themselves the more attractive, they retired and soon appeared clad in clean, and no doubt, their best attire, which consisted of a white and thin paper cloth, which enveloped their whole persons, with the exception of one arm and breast: and this simple drapery, when contrasted with the nakedness of the men, gave them an appearance of grace and modesty, we had little expected to find among savages. Finding that all their allurements could not prevail on us to land, the old chief directed the young girls to swim off to us: but on the appearance of reluctance, the young men led them toward the water, where they were soon devested of every covering and conducted to the boat amid the loud plaudits of the spectators on the shore. On their entering the boat, the seamen threw them their handkerchiefs for covering, with which they carefully concealed those parts which modesty teaches us should not be exposed: and after making them some small presents and delivering them one for the old chief, I found more difficulty in getting them out of the boat, than they had made in coming off to her; and one of them actually shed tears because I would not consent to their going on board ship.[15]

We find here a clearly articulated sequence of moves and counter-moves as Porter probes the intentions and character of the Marquesans. Porter sets the erotic materials within a pattern of cautious negotiation, suggesting that the "allurements" of the

women may have been a stratagem to get him to come ashore;
and considerations of prudence also determine his refusal to take
them in his boat to the ship. The presence communicated by this
passage is of a shrewd and observant man, fully equal to the uncertainties of the moment, and indeed eager to encounter new
experiences and to learn new things. Describing the women's
garments in exact detail, Porter emphasizes that his preconceptions were surprised by the "appearance of grace and modesty,
we had little expected to find among savages." And the passage
concludes with an incident to excite further curiosity, the seemingly unaccountable weeping of one woman on being rejected.

The passage works as a self-contained unit and delivers a coherent experience. Yet its equilibrium has a rhetorical edge, inasmuch as Porter was entirely aware that there were readers who
would not accept a picture of Polynesian women covering their
genitals with sailors' handkerchiefs as an illustration of modesty.
Exponents of the Enlightenment might do so, but not Calvinist
missionaries.

The Reverend Charles Stewart visited the Marquesas in 1829
as chaplain aboard the USS *Vincennes,* and in *A Visit to the South
Seas* (1831) he presents his account of the prospects for a Christian mission there and pleads that one should be sent. In the six-
teen years that had elapsed since Porter's visit, it had become the
custom for the men and women to swim out to meet visiting
ships.

And we had scarce let go our anchor, before scores of both sexes
came swimming in all directions from the shore, soon surrounding
the ship, sporting and blowing like so many porpoises. They were all
received on board; and we quickly had noise and confusion in
abundance. Many of them, both men and women, were entirely
naked, though most of the latter brought with them a *pau* or *kihei*
(petticoat or mantle) tied up in leaves or native cloth, and elevated on
a short stick, which they held above their heads with one hand, while
they swam with the other. Till they gained the deck, however, and
had time to make their toilette there, they all stood à la Venus de
Medici—an attitude which many, from an entire deficiency in their
wardrobe on this aquatic excursion, were obliged to retain. I should
think the number thus on board amounted to at least one hundred
and fifty, or two hundred . . .

On entering the harbor, a white flag had been hoisted at the fore-top-mast head, as a signal that the ship was free of access to all who might choose to come on board. The captain informed them of the design in setting it, and told the chiefs that any of the people might come off whenever they saw it flying; but that the taking of it down would show that the ship was tabu till it should be hoisted again—that now it was to be lowered for the night—and all on board, men and women, must start for the shore.

This . . . [their chiefs] made known to the crowds thronging the decks . . . At first, little attention was paid to the order; but when Captain Finch repeated the injunction to the chiefs, assuring them that the ship must be cleared, they assumed a more authoritative and decided tone towards the people, and the men began plunging overboard amidst the confusion of a general chatter and exclamation. The ladies manifestly considered the order as referring only to the other sex, and very composedly remained clustered about, in the belief that, like all other ships probably that had ever visited them, the Vincennes was to be their home till her anchor was taken for sea again. And when, after repeated declarations that they too must go, they began to suspect the truth of the case, scarce any thing could exceed the looks of surprise and inquiry they cast on one another and on the ship's company. They seemed determined, by their dilatory movements in obeying the order, still further to test the reality of such an unknown measure; and it was not till we beat to our usual evening quarters, and the officers by their swords very courteously pointed out the steps at the gangway to them, that they too began, with many a "taha! taha!" to leap one after another into the water, and "pull away," as they have learned themselves to say, for the shore. The chiefs said laughingly, as they took their leave to enter their canoe, "This is a strange ship!" And I doubt not it is the first in which they have ever known any restriction to be placed on the grossest licentiousness.

After the vessel was thus cleared of noise and nakedness, and the perfumes of coconut oil and other strong odors, which had greatly annoyed and disgusted us, Captain Finch invited me to a seat in his gig in a row round the harbor, or rather that part of it within our anchorage.[16]

Stewart is eager not to appear a narrowminded prude. His way of forming this circumstance bespeaks a cultivated individual who is eager to treat the Marquesans with kindliness and generosity, and who is also prepared to appreciate their physical beauty and exuberance. His allusion to classical statuary, for example, permits him to talk with admiration about naked people while displaying his own learned attainments. Yet Stewart also indicates that behind the show of appreciation and refinement there are vehement moral convictions, and a firm intention to see them adhered to. The elaborate scene in which the Marquesan "ladies" are excluded from the ship portrays the gradual escalation of forcefulness that is called for by this interplay between gentility and unshakable purpose, until the officers at length show the way overboard "very courteously" with their swords. Stewart is also careful to underscore, once the decks are cleared of them, that the Marquesans had "greatly annoyed and disgusted" him. The whole passage, indeed, suggests an extremely considerate host who is willing to strain his patience to the breaking point because he feels a benevolent obligation toward guests who have no idea what a nuisance they are.

The version of the civilized presence that Stewart offers may seem rather stilted, but it is a clearly recognizable image that was ardently taken to heart by his readers. His account of the visit at the Marquesas was received so enthusiastically, indeed, that a missionary party was promptly dispatched to take up the business of displaying Christian benevolence toward them in earnest.

Forming wholes in themselves, these contrasting glimpses of Marquesan encounters form part of something larger. Like advertisements for rival products in a nineteenth-century newspaper, they have a distinctive pervading atmosphere. They are held together by minute details of a style that is not fashioned by the individual authors but arises from the coherencies of the lived events themselves. Porter and Stewart both write up the occasion of first contact with Marquesan women out of a sense of its drama that was present to their minds in the moment of encounter. I do not mean that these are direct transcriptions of experience, of course, as though Porter and Stewart could have spilled on the page an unmediated record of their total response. But in writing up the moment, they underscored and sharpened patternings that were at work as they passed through it, patternings typical of the culture that the two men shared.

Perhaps the clearest evidence of the shared response that is reflected in shared verbal devices is their chronic recourse to euphemism. Of course they use euphemisms with notably different flavors, inasmuch as one would not expect to find the Reverend Stewart's phrase, "an entire deficiency in their wardrobe on this aquatic excursion," in one of Captain Porter's sentences; nor would Stewart use a phrase like Porter's "gestures which we could not misunderstand." The style of pious benevolence and that of worldly curiosity remain distinct. Yet both men find themselves confronted by a circumstance that forces them into roundabout expressions. This shared response is a signal of the civilized identity.

Herman Melville came to the Marquesas aboard a whaling ship in 1842; and after many adventures in the Marquesas and elsewhere, he went home to inaugurate his career as a writer with an account of his Marquesan experiences in *Typee* (1846). His description of first meeting with Marquesan women points toward the connection I shall endeavor to establish between something so abstract as the idea of civilization, something so fluid as a moment of experience, and something so minutely determinate as a particular way of saying something.

Thus arrayed they no longer hesitated, but flung themselves lightly over the bulwarks, and were quickly frolicking about the decks. Many of them went forward, perching upon the head-rails or running out upon the bowsprit, while others seated themselves upon the taffrail or reclined at full length upon the boats. What a sight for us bachelor sailors! how avoid so dire a temptation? For who could think of tumbling these artless creatures overboard, when they had swam miles to welcome us? . . .

The 'Dolly' was fairly captured; and never I will say was vessel carried before by such a dashing and irresistible party of boarders! The ship taken, we could not do otherwise than yield ourselves prisoners, and for the whole period that she remained in the bay, the 'Dolly,' as well as her crew were completely in the hands of the mermaids.

In the evening after we had come to an anchor the deck was illuminated with lanterns, and this picturesque band of sylphs, tricked out with flowers, and dressed in robes of variegated tapa, got up a ball in great style. These females are passionately fond of dancing, and in the wild grace and spirit of their style excel everything that I have ever seen. The varied dances of the Marquesan girls are beautiful in the extreme, but there is an abandoned voluptuousness in their character which I dare not attempt to describe.

Our ship was now wholly given up to every species of riot and debauchery. Not the feeblest barrier was interposed between the unholy passions of the crew and their unlimited gratification. The grossest licentiousness and the most shameful inebriety prevailed, with occasional and but short-lived interruptions, through the whole period of her stay. Alas for the poor savages when exposed to the influence of these polluting examples! Unsophisticated and confiding, they are easily led into every vice, and humanity weeps over the ruin thus remorselessly inflicted upon them by their European civilizers. Thrice happy are they who, inhabiting some yet undiscovered island in the midst of the ocean, have never been brought into contaminating contact with the white man.[17]

Most evident here is Melville's knack of constructing the moment by playing off the way it had been constructed by others. He parodies Stewart's display of Christian good breeding quite explicitly by asserting that it would have been downright rude to thrust the women overboard, and he points to the limits placed on permissible verbal expression in his avowal that he "dare not attempt to describe" their dancing. Yet he succeeds in conveying the dance and what followed it by appropriating, paradoxically, the language of moral disgust.

Melville seems to be condemning the "riot and debauchery" aboard the *Dolly*, but his true purpose is to evoke it. The pounding emphases of pious denunciation and those of sexual arousal beat each to each in these phrases: "Not the feeblest barrier was interposed between the unholy passions of the crew and their unlimited gratification. The grossest licentiousness and the most shameful inebriety prevailed."[18] Thus Melville completes the escalation of erotic excitement that began as the women came aboard and increased when the dancing started. He achieves this climax by reversing the function of a verbal commonplace, which was also a commonplace of response, and in doing so he makes that commonplace explicit as an object for reflection.

It is on the strength of such an objectification that Melville moves into the mock-serious general condemnation with which the passage concludes. Here the "dashing and irresistible party of boarders" has been transformed into "poor savages," and the licentious sailors are transformed into "their European civilizers." The startling idea that an orgy on the deck of a whaling vessel might be equated with the work of civilizing the savage is here broached amid the exuberant reversals of convention that give this passage its vitality; it is hardly meant to be taken seriously. Yet as Melville continues to elaborate his Romantic response, he soon asserts with fury that civilization and degradation come to the same thing.

Like the other civilized writers, Melville uses euphemism. Yet he also points at the fact of using it, and uses it to suggest rather than to screen the forbidden erotic scenes. In doing so he implicitly draws attention to the fact that moments of experience are structured by conventional forms and that the forms prevailing in this particular moment, in the bay at Nukuheva, are connected to a basic theme, that of the transaction between "savages" and "their civilizers."

The idea of civilization is, after all, an idea. It differs from images and stories by making its initial appeal to conceptual susceptibilities rather than to the senses. The idea of civilization was certainly elaborated and attended by a series of images and stories; but it remains at bottom a social theory and was the subject of much learned debate in its heyday. I stress this point because it may seem odd to claim that individual selves can be profoundly shaped by something so apparently bloodless as an abstraction, and to claim further that communities can define themselves in its light. Yet ideas, like metaphors and stories, can be embraced at more levels than one. The difference between a passing joke and a primal anecdote that lies at the root of communal life resides in the power of the great parable to concentrate and exemplify a typical experience of the community. An image that is suitable for brightening a casual conversation is also different from one—like "the machine in the garden"—that captures a fundamental configuration of consciousness. The psychosocial role of an idea, too, is not the same as its interest or validity as a rational construct, but depends upon its power to render intelligible extended ranges of experience that are crucial to the life of a community.

We say that a good idea "casts light" on a subject, meaning that it shapes and delimits the objects under consideration, producing among them a pattern of salient interrelationships. It renders them negotiable both cognitively and in practical terms, giving the individual who possesses illumination the ability to make his way through his experiences with a trustworthy sense of direction. The most famous early European explorer of the South Seas, Captain Cook, was known popularly as "the great navigator" because of his ability to use a conceptual system he had mastered in England to find his way in unfamiliar parts of the world. The idea of civilization was taken to have an authority comparable to the astronomical and cartographic ideas that Cook made use of. It gave Americans confidence that they could likewise maintain their bearings in the social environment of Polynesia.

Logical arrangements of abstractions have, indeed, an extraordinary power to carry what Alfred Schutz called "the accent of reality."[19] When we take ideas to be fully adequate, they have an absolute transparency, seeming to bring us directly into contact with the reality of the thing deliberated. For this reason, it is entirely possible for an idea, like an image or a story, to have the symbolic function of establishing a communion between the mind and the thing represented. It is true that images and stories have a thick polysemous texture and can embody rich vistas and dimensions of indeterminacy; and it may further be true that they do justice better than ideas to the great mystery of things. But one sometimes suspects that, amid the clamor in behalf of noncognitive modes of expression as the fundamental shapers of human experience, there is a secret impulse to preserve the cognitive realm as a transcendent domain where in point-blank univocal definitive ideas we can characterize the behavior of the thoughtless.

This implication appears in the commonplace definition of a symbol as the concrete vehicle of a concept, in which the concept is flatly identified with the operative reality in question (the *meaning* of the symbol), and the concrete image is seen as a useful device for conveying it. Claude Lévi-Strauss gets beyond this faulty assumption when he discusses *bricolage* as a manner of thought in which concrete constituents of thought interact with each other in accordance with their nonlogical configurations. But in continuing his argument he exemplifies the trait I am here seeking to describe, claiming that the scientist resides in a world apart from the *bricoleur*, a world where abstractions and their logical relations denote the real.[20] And yet as the impact of great intellectual innovators always reminds us, it is entirely possible for individuals and communities to be bewitched by a concept. Powerful new ideas gain converts because they clarify problematical issues of thought and experience; but this clarity, and the exhilaration that comes with it, often results from the suppression of tremulous insights that later prove more perceptive than the bold schema that excluded them. The life of the mind is far more adventuresome and passionate than its finished products may reveal (as Malinowski's *Diary* attests) because ideas have a grip on the deepest levels of individual and communal being.

Lévi-Strauss's work as a whole, indeed, testifies to the presence of imperative cognitive needs in human beings, needs that are served by the creation of structures of intelligibility that are sometimes elaborated as of value in themselves, as well as providing material advantages. Instead of viewing primitive cultures as the creators of impressionistic, mythopoeic lore that may (or may not) make up in evocative power what it lacks in exactitude, Lévi-Strauss seeks to grasp the specific terms upon which such peoples create categories of thought that are notable for the fineness of the distinctions they permit, for the interior coherence they maintain, and for the specificity with which they come to terms with the subject matters they comprehend. And though Clifford Geertz objects to Lévi-Strauss's picture of the savage as excessively cerebral, he includes intellectual capacities together with ethical and emotional capacities in his summary of the innate human powers that must be given coherent form by symbolic systems. The conception of humankind and human intellectual powers that is proposed here differs from that advanced by Arthur O. Lovejoy in his commentary on "the history of ideas," in directing attention to the generation, maintenance, and transmission of schemes of intelligibility within social experience itself rather than to "primary unit-ideas" conceived as

chemical elements that show up in various philosophical com-
pounds.[21] Ideas, unlike elements, are social institutions: they are
human achievements.

To say that early nineteenth-century Americans thought of
themselves as "civilized" in their dealings with the Marquesans
is not to engage in sarcasm, holding some presumptively valid
concept of civilization over their heads. Nor is it my claim that
the idea of civilization is wholly devoid of appropriateness for
describing the differences between Western and Polynesian cultures, as though the civilized parties to this intercultural encounter were acting in some absolute midnight of error and obtuseness. Yet I will focus nonetheless on the maladies of the civilized,
their self-contradictions and ironies, their blindness and vexa-
tion, their unintentional and needless cruelties, their folly and
despair. This is necessary because it is precisely in such circumstances that an idea reveals its purchase upon the structure of the
self.

It is possible to entertain a conception objectively, as a hypothetical explanation for some puzzling feature of experience, and
then to accept confirmation and disconfirmation with a more or
less equal mind. In an objective investigation, ideally, encounter
with the anomalous disconcerts inquiry only to make it more interesting, since we then proceed systematically to question our
own questions. Yet, as Thomas Kuhn has shown, there are
anomalies of a special kind even in the practice of physical science that do not yield readily to further study because they disconcert the paradigmatic structures upon which investigation itself proceeds.[22]

For this additional reason, the Marquesan encounters provide
an opportunity to observe the idea of civilization as a structural
feature of the American identity. In the Marquesas early nineteenth-century Americans confronted a social reality that was
not merely alien to their way of being but incompatible with it.
This is not to say that Porter, Stewart, and Melville were wholly
mistaken in their estimation of Marquesan life: on the contrary,
the Enlightenment, Calvinist, and Romantic versions of the idea
of civilization permitted them to see various characteristics of
Marquesan culture very clearly indeed. One of the ways in

which these three schemes can be distinguished is in the particular beam of light that each throws upon the common culture apprehended by each. Not everything beheld is in the eye of the beholder. The three schemes can also be distinguished by comparing what the three exemplars did *not* see. What lay outside the awareness of the Enlightened believer in primal virtue comes to the center of the stage in a Calvinistic assessment. There were, however—and this is the critical point—perceptual blindspots shared by all: there were features of Marquesan life that could hardly be imagined within the conceptual system that the Americans had available. The reality of Marquesan life was in some respects incommensurable with the scheme of ideas that represented social reality to the Americans, a surd presence. As a result, the interactions between Americans and Marquesans, intelligible to a certain extent, nonetheless yielded a drumfire of anomalous occurrences that placed pressure on the constitutive paradigms of their experience, casting doubt not only over the enterprises in which they were engaged but upon the meaningfulness and intelligibility of their existence. An examination of the resources and maneuvers that the Americans called upon in this crisis will take us to the center of what it meant to them to be civilized.

What I will not be able to provide is a comparable interpretive understanding of what it meant to be Marquesan. They, like the Americans, found themselves confronting a surd presence as the white man intruded more and more into their lives. And if it were possible to describe the systems of meaning according to which they sought to negotiate such an irruption of strangeness, this study would have a valuable further dimension. But the opportunity to create such an understanding has almost surely been lost, since we lack vernacular Marquesan comment from the period in question and since the culture of that period no longer exists. The destruction of the Marquesan way of life—and of the Marquesans themselves—during the nineteenth century is one of the principal horrors of Pacific history, the population falling from an estimated 100,000 at its height to 4865 in 1882.[23] A good deal is known of that lost culture, as the result of careful ethnographic work in our own time, but the knowledge upon which to build an interior understanding of the Marquesans' response to the white man seems beyond reach. It is known, for example, that as depopulation advanced under French colonial rule, the Marquesans staged marathon feasts, strenuously recapitulating certain key rituals of their severely threatened way of being, in a manner reminiscent of the "ghost dance" of the American Plains Indians in a comparable plight.[24] Yet it is not known what these rituals were, or what they had customarily meant, or what they meant on such occasions, or indeed exactly what provoked them.

The Marquesans of necessity, therefore, figure in our story as a problem for the Americans, a living enigma that they sought to comprehend on the terms provided by the idea of civilization. The Marquesans thus became counters in a debate in which they did not directly participate. But by reason of their cultural integrity, leading life on their own terms, they at times disconcerted the debate and the debaters.

We are embarked, then, upon the interpretation of a circumstance having distinct levels of meaning: in confronting the Marquesans as "savages," the Americans engaged in dramas of self-definition by which they asserted themselves to be "civilized." Behind the idea of civilization as a rational form is a psychosocial process, a metabolism of meanings that has a life of its own. Yet in order to make certain that the profounder internal systems are not mutilated in the act of uncovering them, careful attention must be given to the realities amid which these persons lived and moved, the specific forms of their actions and thought. We will accordingly move in this book from manifest to latent issues, taking first of all at face value a series of conceptions and judgments that later will be examined for their subsurface characteristics. The claim that the completed identities of Americans as "civilized persons" rested upon processes that produce and maintain identity cannot be vindicated unless the resultant identities are themselves granted to exist as historical realities worthy of study in themselves. And to discuss the terms "civilized" and "savage" as elements in a dialectic of self-definition has significance only insofar as the flesh-and-blood selves defined that way are first of all appreciated fully and in detail from their own point of view. If the tradition of anthropological study has taught us not to take a condescending view of "primitives" and "savages," we should likewise refrain from superciliousness in discussing the "civilized."

A word must also be said concerning the order of treatment. Instead of beginning chronologically with David Porter, I present first the ill-fated mission project to the Marquesas Islands that was launched in response to Charles Stewart's plea. This permits me to place primary emphasis where it belongs, on the encounter between Americans and Marquesans, and then to take up the forms in which such encounters were represented in print to the American public at large. Since the mission project was an abortive affair, it did not recommend itself for publication and was not in fact written up until the end of the nineteenth century, and then only in cursory fashion.[25] The anomalous characteristics that made this mission difficult for its sponsors to comprehend, however, make it peculiarly adapted to my interests. Moving then to consider Charles Stewart's role in the sending of the mission permits me to discuss action and writing together as a "passage" of undertakings, an extended pious enterprise whose metaphors and narrative design contain a distinctive thematic structure. David Porter dominates the next such "passage," articulating an alternative version of the doings proper to civilized persons. The display of Enlightenment motifs and themes in his enterprise proposes a vivid contrast to the Calvinistic schema of the missionaries. With these competing systems before us we will be prepared to appreciate the significance of certain thematic patterns that bind them together as analogues, and to examine the psychosocial dynamics that lie behind them. Melville's response to the matter comes last, because it is enriched by his sensitivity to the process in which experience is taken up into the conceptual structures a community uses to define itself. Of the three exemplars of American civilization at the Marquesas, he tells us least about the Marquesans themselves, but most about what it meant for Americans to encounter them. As my title implies, Melville's way of probing the social dynamics of meaning provided an impetus for this study, even as it forms the heart of my subject matter.

It will be observed that the notion of drama is at work here in a double sense: not only do I use it as a basic paradigm for the analysis of the subject, I have also incorporated it into the structure of this book. Instead of a chronological presentation show-ing "development," what lies before you is a trilogy: three epi-sodes related to one another according to a protocol that compels their mutual relevance to show itself, three circles of light upon the darkness of a vast social experience. Within each circle is a passage of doing and utterance that is treated as a "text" whose meanings are interpreted by way of a detailed consideration of its formal characteristics. I have placed these texts within bound-aries as a way of enclosing something intelligible, but also as an instructive gesture of dismissal, such that the excluded vistas are invoked as a background of the concerns at hand. Against the background of American intellectual history, the circles invoke evangelical Calvinism, Enlightenment, and Romanticism; against the background of American social history, they postulate Mis-sions, Imperialism, and Popular Literature. The nonchronologi-cal structure that circumscribes the whole likewise excludes and sets in relief the notion of temporal progress, which is essential to the idea of civilization. And the texts thus circumscribed carry on a conversation among themselves in which a consideration of cognitive issues yields to a consideration of psychosocial dynam-ics. The missionaries, David Porter, and Melville disagree vehe-mently among themselves concerning the nature of civilization and the nature of the Marquesans, so that the explicit theme of the trilogy may be framed as a question: "What is American civilization?" But the latent theme is an affirmation that contains a justification for the whole procedure: our understanding of others will be no better than our understanding of ourselves.

I do not see the Marquesan encounters finally as a laboratory or as a microcosm. It might be argued that, as laboratory, the ex-perience tested under uniform Marquesan conditions a series of ideas about American civilization. But this metaphor, useful to a certain extent, shows its weakness when one reflects that the conditions of the three tests were not uniform, and that an ex-periment can hardly be said to exist where none of the variables can be controlled by the experimenter. As microcosm, the Mar-quesan experience might be seen as a representation in little of typical energies of nineteenth-century America, especially the relation of white Americans to those deemed savage who were living on the American continent. Yet it would be an error to assume that what I have to tell about these Marquesan experiences could be transferred by simple magnification (from micro to macro) to other social movements in America.[26]

No. These events are exemplary first of all because those who acted in them were determined to see them as exemplary. And they are made to be exemplary beyond such purposes because I have placed them in an arena where they are compelled to inter- act. I have arranged a pattern that allows key juxtapositions to speak for themselves, as they serve a progressive argument, so that the broader issues requiring consideration emerge naturally from the drama as the characters display the qualities of thought, passion, and deed that made them who they were. What we have at hand are provisionally self-nominated model figures, exem- plars of civilization, characters in search of an author.

They are also in search of an audience. It is the fate of such personages to act in a larger text that is bounded finally by the interest others are willing to show in what they said and did, so that the writing of this book is itself an expansion of the context of the actions it treats. The general cultural enterprise by which America comes to a sense of its place in the world has not ceased. It is a vast deliberation that originated in the sixteenth and seven- teenth centuries, informs the tiny occurrences I discuss here, and continues to implicate us all. By the act of reading this book you yourself become further involved and, by your own responses, help to form the drama.

Readers in various fields of specialization will find that parts of what I have to say touch familiar subjects. I have contracted an extended series of debts to students of Pacific history, Polynesian ethnology and archeology, and interpretive anthropology, as well as to specialists in American intellectual history, American church history, and Melville studies. Members of the mixed au- dience for whom the book is intended will find that I have sought to repay such debts by consolidating them into a central obliga- tion, the task of illuminating the agon of a specific social identity as it merges into the deeper and richer perplexities of human ex- perience itself.

There is a wisdom to be found in an enlarged conversation with humans both strange and familiar who are wrestling with the meanings that their society makes available to them. And because people are far more mysterious than any language of the self has ever captured, wealth of existence is attainable for selves that push into the mystery beyond the given roles. This book concerns a series of moments in which Americans sought to enact for each other an idea of what it meant to be human, and I seek to catch the movement between quotidian disarray and formal fulfillment. It is in the striving toward the enactment of a momentous role that the full pity and terror and glory become visible: the president waiting in the wings, the ballerina putting on her shoe, Malinowski dreaming and fuming among the Trobrianders—the moment where the exemplary action can be caught as it rises, begins to rise up, from the commonplace experience of which it is the apotheosis, summary, and degradation.

2 / City on a Hill

IN AUGUST OF 1833 a party of Americans came to the island of Nukuheva in the Marquesas Islands and planted there a beachhead of civilization. Backed by the American Board of Commissioners for Foreign Missions and having the blessing of the famous American mission in the Hawaiian Islands, they meant to bring a beacon of light and truth to a place whose savagery, they conceived, was absolute. Mr. William Alexander, the leader of the mission, kept a journal that he wrote in the form of a series of letters to Rufus Anderson, the secretary of the American Board. "Two weeks ago," he begins, "the *Dhaulle* weighed anchor & left us on these heathen shores, whose inhabitants for ages have sat in darkness living without God, devoted to the most bestial sensuality & perpetrating deeds of horrid cruelty."[1]

In coming with the purpose of exerting a moral and spiritual influence upon the Marquesans, Alexander's party acted out a deeply held conception of the meaning of America. When John Winthrop affirmed that the Puritan colony was to be a "City upon a hill," he had in mind the example that would be set on the North American continent for the decadent societies of Europe: the metaphor was meant to imply (as it implies in the New Testament) that the city would be visible at a great distance. And, as Rush Welter has shown, this conception of America was a central article of national faith during the early nineteenth century. Abram Maury asserted in 1847, for example, that the

American destiny was to become "a beacon and a landmark on the cliffs of time, to the nations of the earth—by whose light they may be guided in the reconstruction of their own defective forms of polity."[2]

Yet as Americans came to terms with their American situation, Winthrop's root metaphor developed a second meaning. It came to suggest that the hilltop city would radiate civilizing energies into its surroundings. It would not simply appear exemplary to other cities on distant plains; it would also confront the wilderness, and the peoples of the wilderness, with a demonstration of the enlightened community.

In a paragraph discussing the analytical power of metaphor, Perry Miller notes the connection between the Puritan sense of mission and the famous "frontier hypothesis" of Frederick Jackson Turner, suggesting that Turner's thesis is limited by unrecognized metaphoric assumptions.[3] Why should the North American forest and plains have been looked upon as a "frontier" by the Europeans who came to dwell on this continent? "Frontier," in the American sense, is not merely the name of a patch of territory that happens to be contiguous to one's own; it includes the notion of a dynamic interaction along a contested boundary. Deeper than the challenge and promise of the western lands themselves in the formation of the American character was the impulse to view those lands as challenge and promise.

This deep sense of "America" as a characteristic activity, that of giving form to a strange and recalcitrant environment, appears in the expansionist policies of the early republic, when it came to be felt that America could fulfill its destiny and maintain its character only through enlarging its dominions westward.[4] The idea of civilization was taken up as a way of expressing the meaning of this expansion, so that the increasing power of the new nation over continental territories was conceived as the "advance of civilization." The American Indian, standing in the pathway of this advance, was assumed into the regnant imagery as a denizen of the wilderness that must inevitably yield to the civilizing process. The logic of the confrontation between whites and Indians, as administered by the rationale that the whites brought to bear upon it, demanded that the Indian increasingly be governed by the standard prevailing in the hilltop city, or else be destroyed. "Civilization or death to all American Savages," a slogan Roy Harvey Pearce offers as the summary of this logic, neatly formulates the alternative roles of the savage as prototype and as antitype of the civilized. This doctrine may well have been pathological, as Michael Rogin argues, in certain of its inner meanings; and it was assuredly brutal in certain of its applications.[5] But it also provided sociological content for the dream that was implicit in Winthrop's original proclamation, the dream of America as the ideal society, providing a pattern of felicity for others.

The Americans in Alexander's party were bearers of this dream. They came to the Marquesas as self-conscious emissaries of light and order, intending nothing less than the transformation of Marquesan culture.

They were a party of six adults and four children when they arrived. Mr. Alexander and his wife had two sons, the younger then three months old. Richard Armstrong was also accompanied by his wife, who had a one-year-old daughter and a son of four months. Mrs. Armstrong was pregnant at the time of arrival and bore a child before the party left seven months later. The same was true of Mary Parker, the wife of the third missionary, Benjamin Wyman Parker. The *Dhaulle* brought them to Taiohae Bay, where Haape, a leader of the Teii tribe, had promised them hospitality.[6]

Haape made a sizable Marquesan dwelling available to the group, but thinking it unsuited to their purposes they set about persuading the Marquesans to build them a mission compound. The Marquesans, for their part, were not familiar with the sort of construction that the Americans desired, so Alexander, Parker, and Armstrong were obliged to supervise every step of the work. It was a vexatious and lengthy job, as Alexander noted more than once in his journal. The islanders' "habits of indolence" were very difficult to cure, he discovered; he found it necessary to offer jackknives, pieces of cloth, and other valuables practically every day in exchange for work on the houses. Yet the construction of the mission compound was an important and very rewarding feat. It was an image in small of the task that the missionaries had set for themselves, of reshaping the Marquesan environment into a civilized design.

When the compound was completed at last, Alexander described it at length in his journal. Each house was

> about 40 feet along & twenty wide—A description of mine would answer very well for the other two. The wall plates are coconut logs, each supported by four posts of breadfruit timber eight feet high. The ridge-pole is breadfruit supported by three posts of the same. The rafters are of the hibiscus peeled & soaked for several weeks in water to prevent worms from attacking them. Most of them are as straight as an arrow & from 2 to 3 inches in diameter, there are 250 on my roof—for shingles we have breadfruit leaves strung on rods about 10 feet long—The ends are enclosed in the same manner as the roof. The sides are made of the hibiscus timbers placed as close together as it can stand & thatched with braided coconut leaves. Leaving off the thatch my partitions are made in the same manner as the sides . . .
>
> Our houses are situated on the N. western side of the bay, & form a hollow square. That you may have a better view of them I will give you a platt of them.[7]

The "hollow square" in which these houses were arranged made it possible for the missionaries to keep each other in view and thus provided a measure of mutual protection. It also expressed the rectilinear moral order they planned to extend into the community beyond. The lumber in these houses was of breadfruit and coconut and hibiscus; but the design was civilized. The interior partitions, for example, afforded the individual privacy that was lacking in the dwelling Haape had given them on their arrival. This little city was not set upon a hill; it was on the shore of Taiohae Bay. Yet the idea that it embodies is one of moral elevation and moral influence directed outward and down at the surrounding wilderness.

When the missionaries looked beyond the borders of their compound, however, they discovered things that did not conform to this implicit imagery, and the Marquesans did not respond to their efforts in the ways they had anticipated. The definition of civilization and savagery they brought with them did not yield an effective program for the transformation of Mar-

'Our houses are situated on the N. western side of the bay, & form a hollow square. That you may have a better view of them I will give you a platt of them

A. The house & premises of
    Mr. Armstrong
B. The house &c of Mr. Parker
C. house &c of Alexander
a, b, & c. Cook houses
D. A taboo inclosure
E. A taboo pile of stone

The Bay

quesan culture. It did not, in fact, properly account for the relationship that actually developed between themselves and the
Marquesans. Before a year was out, the missionaries found
themselves enmeshed in difficulties so severe that they decided
to abandon the project. The completion of the mission compound, however, seemed a harbinger of larger successes and
provided Alexander some much needed encouragement. But on
the day the families moved into it, he voiced his persistent misgivings, and employed a sharply contrasting imagery: "We have
felt much as if we were living in the crater of some great volcano,
making eruptions on every side."[8] Instead of yielding to the
forces of order and light, the savage confusion of the Marquesas
seemed about to swallow them up.

Among the easternmost of the Polynesian archipelagoes, the
Marquesas is a group of ten islands extending northwest to
southeast for a distance of roughly 230 miles. The group is located eight to ten degrees below the equator, some 4200 miles
west of the coast of Peru. Tahiti lies 850 miles to the southwest,
with Hawaii 2200 miles to the northwest. The islands lie along an
area of ancient volcanic activity that developed upon deep fis-
sures in the Pacific floor. The island of Nukuheva, largest in the
group, was formed by two episodes of volcanic activity of which
the later formed a cone within the crater of the earlier and much
larger volcano.[9]

These nested cones were cracked across the middle along a
roughly east-west line corresponding to the fissure through
which the volcanos erupted. The southern half of both craters
has disappeared, leaving a rugged and irregular southern coastline interrupted by three large bays. Taiohae is the central bay; it
is semicircular and is enclosed by a steep amphitheater of mountains. Perched on the northwest coast of this bay, Alexander's
mission was, indeed, in the crater of the inner volcano.

The bays to the east and west of Taiohae stand at the outlet of
long valleys that curve inland toward each other, and thus tran-
scribe the semicircular cleft between the cone of the later volcano
and the crater of the earlier one. The eastern valley is by far the
broader and richer of the two. From the standpoint of the Mar-

quesans it was the most desirable valley on the island, because it
had the largest amount of arable land. The eastern bay is better
sheltered than Taiohae Bay and offers a superior natural port.
But Americans stayed away from that bay because it was controlled by the Typees, a notoriously dangerous tribe.[10]

The gross structure established by the volcanos was complicated by other features that developed because most of the present island was under water when the volcanic activity ended. The
sloping craters were subjected to a long period of marine erosion
during which the ocean cut away softer materials leaving the
more resistant rock in huge irregular configurations. Except for a
few of the highest peaks the ocean planed off the high ground of
the island. In the subsequent uplifting of the entire archipelago,
the leveled area on Nukuheva became a central plateau at an elevation of 2600 feet while the vast rock formations carved beneath
the surface of the ocean came up to form a complex of precipitous ridges separating narrow valleys, and plunging directly
down to meet the sea in a bold jagged coastline.

There are no springs of fresh water in the Marquesas, so that
all the usable moisture comes in from the southeast on the trade
winds. The amount of water these bring is sufficiently limited so
that the direction of the wind can be observed in the distribution
of wetness across the entire archipelago. Fatu Hiva, the south-
easternmost island, is relatively wet, while Ua Pou is quite dry
because the moisture is intercepted by islands lying south and
east of it. On Nukuheva the lushest valley lies in the southeast,
while on the northwestern side of the island there is a "barrens,"
which seems never to have sustained any extensive society. This
vivid pattern of wet and dry was imposed on the cycle of the
years as sharply as on the topography of the islands.[11] In the
years when the rains came, the island of Nukuheva was decorated by magnificent free-standing waterfalls, as the upland
plain was drained by rivers that poured over the high cliffs to ir-
rigate breadfruit and coconut in the valleys below. But there
were also years of drought, when the crops would not support
the population, and against these bad times the islanders prepared themselves by storing away large quantities of breadfruit
paste in communal pits.[12] When the drought extended over five

or six years, there were decimating famines. Between 1803 and 1813, it is reported, a time of scarcity wiped out two thirds of the population.[13]

The settlement of the Marquesas took place during or before the second century B.C. It was carried out deliberately, by voyagers who came fully equipped to establish a colony.[14] They appear to have come from Samoa, 2000 miles to the west, in a feat of open-sea navigation made all the more striking because they sailed the distance to their tiny destination against the trade winds.[15] No clear picture has been obtained of the cultural stock from which these earliest Marquesans came. They appear to represent a remarkably early stage in the development of South Seas peoples: Marquesan culture is predominantly Polynesian, but the presence of Melanesian traits has suggested a common Melanesian–Polynesian heritage lying behind these now quite distinct cultures.[16] By the time Americans and Europeans began to have an influence upon Marquesan culture in the late eighteenth and early nineteenth centuries, the Marquesans themselves had lived on the islands for two thousand years without consequential interference from the outside. The Marquesas are now viewed, indeed, as one of the major centers from which Polynesian culture was itself transported elsewhere. It appears that Marquesans carried out voyages of exploration across tremendous Pacific distances: to Hawaii in the northwest, to Easter Island in the southeast, and to New Zealand in the southwest, as well as to several central Polynesian areas.[17]

When Alexander and his mission party looked out across the perimeter of their compound, they saw a people who were living at the culmination of a slow and extended cultural development. The form of life that the Marquesans had developed can be known today only in part, because the ravages of contact with whites obliterated almost all of the original culture and reduced the population so sharply that, by the time anthropologists arrived in the late nineteenth century, there were very few remaining who could recall the earlier days and act as informants. Yet even slight evidences under careful study can be made to glow with possibilities of insight, yielding firm information together with tantalizing suggestions of what remains unknown.

A look at the business end of a Marquesan warclub presents

you, for example, with a strong impression of what was fearful, admirable, and enigmatic in the character of the aboriginal Marquesans. No surviving artifact is more expressive. It has two broad sides that seem at first glance like front and back, except they are identical in all but the finest detail. On both "fronts" of this Janus-faced design a broad band of intricate carving decorates the section where the shaft thickens and broadens into the club head itself, ending in a neat line beneath a polished horizontal cross-bar. Above the cross-bar the two broad surfaces rise in a double-concave manner, arching away from each other into paired semi-ellipses whose crowns form the top of the club and whose sides slope downward toward the cross-bar. The club attains its greatest thickness at the cross-bar and the top, so that maximum striking force is delivered along these graceful edges.

Looking directly at one of the fronts—as in the example given—you see an abstract of the human face. Within the concave surface above the cross-bar is a pair of knobs encircled by fringes of radiating lines, wide-open eyes beneath the solid brow of the crown; at the midpoint of the cross-bar is another knob suggesting a stylized nose set on a line between ears. A closer look reveals that the three knobs are themselves tiki-faces, that there is another stylized face along the topmost ridge, and another pair of eyes in the tracery beneath the cross-bar. It is a human head made up of heads, a face made up of faces, confronting you with a puzzling composite stare.

The question of what culture lies behind that stare can be answered only in part. Yet enough has been reconstructed to provide a far richer portrait than I will give in what follows, since my primary concerns are those elements of Marquesan life that disconcerted the missionaries and other Western visitors. I will address those issues about which the missionaries had most to say, while attempting to indicate something of their place within Marquesan culture itself.

Along the watercourses that ran down the narrow valleys, the Marquesan dwellings stood in clusters. Such a dwelling, called a *pae pae*, had a rectangular overall form, divided so that the rear half of the rectangle was occupied by a thatched building, while in front was a stone pavement. Some time around A.D. 1300 this basic design had been adapted to the steep sides of the Marque-

san valleys by way of a terrace that elevated the rear section from
the porch. By the eighteenth century *pae pae* were being constructed on a very imposing scale.[18] The ones Alexander saw
were elevated from the ground on all four sides, with the porch
in front standing as much as ten feet high and sixty feet long.
This porch was girded by two or sometimes three courses of immense stones carefully fitted to create a massive wall across the
front and down the sides. Facing on this porch there stood a large
shelter, thatched as were the homes of the missionaries with
breadfruit leaves; and at the rear of this was a large area of bed-
ding, running the length of the building, where the Marquesan
household slept.[19] In addition to this primary dwelling, a substantial household had a special eating house for the men, a
cooking house, and a sacred enclosure or platform for the observance of family rites.[20]

Marquesan families were structured in a way that baffled early
Western visitors; yet the Marquesans, not surprisingly, gave
great importance to family relationships and could articulate
their complexities with precision. Contemporary students of the
Marquesas, as of other societies, have found in kinship structures and kinship terms a major avenue toward understanding
the society as a whole. The critical importance of senior descent
lines, for example, according to which the eldest-born son receives the most *mana* (and in the Marquesas supplanted the father at birth as the preeminent member of the household), is reflected in the fact that older and younger siblings addressed each
other with reciprocal terms.[21] The Marquesan sense of kin relationship further observes a structural opposition between brothers and sisters such that cross uncles (mothers' brothers) and
cross aunts (fathers' sisters) are clearly discriminated from parallel uncles (fathers' brothers) and parallel aunts (mothers' sisters).
This distinction is reflected in the special terms signaling the relationship between a child and his/her cross uncles and cross
aunts. The child in this relation was referred to as *i-amutu* and the
adults as *pahu pahu*. *Pahu pahu* had special ceremonial duties in
relation to the *i-amutu*, and children who shared *pahu pahu* (that
is, cross cousins) were thought to be especially suitable as mates
for each other.[22]

The prominence of these cross relationships marks the antiquity of Marquesan culture and its role as a center from which other eastern Polynesian areas were settled. Although cross relationships have an important role in western Polynesian societies such as Samoa and Tonga, they are of greatly decreased significance in Hawaii and Tahiti, as elsewhere in eastern Polynesia.[23]

The pattern of family relationships that the missionaries encountered was rendered even more confusing by the multiplicity of sexual rights and obligations. In certain circumstances the brothers of a husband assumed his role with respect to the wife, and the husband himself was likewise situated with respect to his wife's sisters. This sharing of sexual access among the parallel uncles and aunts corresponds to the prohibition of marriage among parallel cousins and is likewise in keeping with the sacred quality of the cross relationships. The scheme of sexual relations was complicated further yet, however, by the system of *pekio* or secondary mateship, according to which individuals or couples might attach themselves as subordinate mates in the household of another.[24]

Indeed, as Keith Otterbein has observed, in analyzing Marquesan domestic relationships it is necessary to consider the household as the basic unit rather than the family.[25] Although familial lines were highly important, the accustomed Western pattern of one family per household did not obtain in the Marquesas. A well-to-do man might be the head of a household that included the families of his brothers and sisters, as well as numerous individuals and couples in a *pekio* relationship to himself and them. Many combinations are possible within this structure, all perfectly intelligible to the Marquesans but defying the categories with which the missionaries were equipped.

The Marquesan dwelling featured a large sleeping space at the rear where the members of the household slept together, and when the three missionary families were given such a dwelling they immediately set up inner partitions to give each family privacy. They concluded with reference to the Marquesans themselves that "the bond between husband and wife in this land is so feeble, that the marriage relation can scarcely be said to exist."[26]

The communal life of the Marquesans centered on the public ceremonial plaza, called the *tohua*. These, like the *pae pae*, had evolved from an early form to a high degree of sophistication.

They were very large rectangular courts up to 570 by 85 feet in size, which were used for dancing at festival times. Looking in upon the central floor were stadiums and verandas to accommodate spectators, as well as megalithic *pae pae* and other structures of ceremonial and domestic uses. Each great tribe, embracing the people of an entire valley, had its *tohua*, where tribal business and tribal observances were carried out. But the culture of the Marquesans also featured numerous subtribes, intermediate in scale between the family and the major tribe, which had certain degrees of independence and *tohua* of their own.[27] The social structure of the Marquesas, as evinced by the clusters of *pae pae* and the *tohua* of varying sizes, was not sharply stratified. Instead of a centralized hierarchical order, Marquesan culture was an interwoven network of groups at various levels of size and importance. There were, to be sure, important distinctions in political and social significance between large and small units, but a perceived identity among them is revealed by the fact that one term was applied to all. Both a household and a major tribe were referred to as a *hua-a*.[28] Early visitors noticed, moreover, that the chiefs of the Marquesan tribes appeared to have only a slight preeminence over the heads of the major households and subtribal groups. The people "laugh at his orders," Admiral Krusenstern observed, "and should he venture to strike anyone, he would infallibly meet with a like return."[29] The chief's regalia was limited to a special staff and a pandanus fan, and he mingled with his fellow tribesmen casually, without the stylized remoteness of high office.

In his discussion of Polynesian societies Irving Goldman describes the Marquesan social system as an "open" one, which is distinguished from "traditional" and "stratified" systems by the opportunity it presents for individuals of energy and skill to attain high rank. Access to power was not blocked by an ironclad commitment to seniority of descent (as in traditional societies) or by the existence of an exclusive class of rulers such as maintained control in Hawaii and Tahiti. The Marquesan term for chief, *haka-iki,* was given to every firstborn male, and while the firstborn of prominent men had better opportunities than others, the road to leadership was in principle open to all.[30] Gregory Dening has given a fascinating discussion of *haka-iki* who retained a highly significant sacral prominence even when others amassed more wealth and more political power. Charged with the *mana* of a superior descent line, and having the power to announce the occasions for major tribal festivals, these preeminent *haka-iki* were core figures, embodying values central to the society as a whole. The deference paid to the supreme *haka-iki* was consistent with the flexible power system in which less-honored figures struggled for advantage—his role in the settlement of disputes was not so much to impose a solution by force as to legitimate the solution that emerged by participating in its creation and accepting it once formulated.[31]

The power of the *haka-iki* as a political leader, however, rested on his ability to maintain a sizable following through the amassing and deployment of wealth, the making of favorable alliances, and success in war. But his subordinates, down to the weakest, were free to shift their allegiance to another *haka-iki*, so that his power was precarious and it was further limited by the power of other tribal officials. The *taua*, or inspirational priest, was regarded with greater awe than the chief himself. The gift of the *taua* was to fall into a state of possession in which a divine force seized him and made known its will, and because these supremely sacred utterances had considerable influence on the activities of the tribe, it frequently happened that the *taua* was a member of the chief's family. But an individual of low origins might also become a *taua* by virtue of exhibiting authoritative seizures. Others with an official role were *tohuna*, or master craftsmen, skilled in arts that varied from housebuilding and navigation to the chanting of genealogies and the performance of prescribed religious rites. The most powerful of these consulted with the *haka-iki* concerning tribal affairs generally and, since they were able to amass great wealth, were sometimes able to become major chieftains themselves. The Marquesan *tohuna*, unlike the Hawaiian craftsmen, never became formally organized into guilds; the mobility of the laborers whose work they directed, and the access they enjoyed to the chiefly role itself, discouraged the formation of a structure to advance their common interests. Another public figure distinguished by title was the *toa*, or leader in war, who was expected to inspire his fellow tribesmen in battle by spectacular displays of courage. The importance of the *toa* suggests how prominent a role bravado played in the conflicts among Marquesan tribes, since he had no administrative or strategic responsibilities but fulfilled his official function by fortifying tribal morale and seeking to intimidate the enemy.[32]

Economic, political, and military affairs were carried on in the Marquesas, therefore, by way of a scheme of offices in which responsibilities were portioned out in a way unfamiliar to Alexander and his fellows. Accustomed to a formalized governmental structure, the missionaries mistakenly concluded that the Marquesans had no government at all, and attributed the difficulty they experienced in writing sermons to this lack. "The language is so barren & our attainments in it so small that we communicate truth very vaguely. A very important class of words referring to government seems to be entirely wanting, for having no government they have no use for such words, they have no word for *law*, none for *because*, & a multitude which I might mention, for the want of which we feel greatly straitened when we sit down to write sermons."[33]

This comment, discerning to a certain extent, is notable chiefly for Alexander's assumption that a one-to-one correlation exists between the Marquesan language and English, as between language itself and the world of objective things. The "class of words" referring to government in his view forms a blank spot in the Marquesan vocabulary, like the blank spot in their social system, and the deeper reasons why they couldn't understand his sermons remain hidden.

The missionaries were hampered even further when it turned out that Haape, the *haka-iki* who had offered them hospitality, was not in a position to exert an influence much beyond his own household. The missionaries in Hawaii, by contrast, who attached themselves to Kamehameha II found it possible to impose their plans on the entire population by working through him.

The interworked multiplicity of the Marquesans' social relationships was reflected, and to a degree encoded, in their communal chants. The great genealogical chants that were recited at the birth of a firstborn son traced his descent from an ancestry in which all Marquesans understood themselves to share. An elaborate festival provided the setting for the recitation of such a chant: a month was devoted to the preparation of food, and members of the various branches of the family were reminded by messenger to prepare to recite their parts. When the festival was held, a professional chanter would commence with the earliest sections of the genealogy and bring it down to the ancestry of the family in question. At the appropriate points in the sequence, representatives of family units would take over the chanting and trace out the lineage of its various branches, while the professional chanter kept silence, waiting to resume his recitation of the central line. Since the names of tribes, subtribes, and other family heads were included in the genealogies, this process affirmed the relationship between the newborn and a vast system of communal relationships.[34] The genealogical chants proper were linked with creation chants, which connected families to a sequence of mythical forebears that extended back to the beginning of the world when Atea, a primal masculine figure, mated with One-u-i, his feminine counterpart.[35] The *pu-e* and the *vavana* were creation chants used on a large number of occasions, as the opening sections of a chant that was applied to the specific circumstance in question. There were festivals of chanting when a new *pae pae* or *tohua* was constructed. The making of canoes was likewise consecrated with chanting, as was the making of weapons, tools, and ornaments. It is not the case that every article of manufacture in the Marquesas was ushered into the world with a chant; but the Marquesans were equipped with chants that *could* be used to link the production of any particular object with the processes from which the world itself was generated. In principle, there was a detailed set of linkages that tied together individuals, groups, natural objects, fabricated things, and the origins of the universe. It is important to recognize that the form of this linkage was generative: it was the sexual bond.[36]

Sexuality had a conspicuous place in the social life of the Marquesans. Specific physical qualities of the male and female genitals were regarded as having special degrees of sexual attractiveness, so that there was a vocabulary differentiating penises according to various sizes and shapes. An extensive program of beautification was applied to the vagina, which began in babyhood with massages and exercises intended to increase its muscle tone. There was, in addition, a mild astringent that was applied

in an effort to decrease the production of vaginal fluid and to in-
hibit unpleasant odors. A ritual focusing upon these efforts
marked the passage of females into adulthood: first they were
formally examined to determine whether their labia were pale,
their pubic hair pliant and short, and to what extent other desirable characteristics had been achieved. Then they took part in
kioka toe haka, the festival of the clitoris dance, at which they displayed their genitals to the tribe at large.[37]

In adolescence and early adulthood, as they passed through
the course of instruction that prepared them for mature roles in
society, male and female Marquesans were called *ka-ioi*. During
this period they had apparently unlimited sexual access to each
other, and they pursued their opportunities with such alacrity
that early Western observers mistook the *ka-ioi* for a rollicking
band of pleasure seekers with no social obligations at all. Yet
they were expected to master a great deal of technical and traditional lore, and were required to assist with virtually all of the
communal festivals of the society, performing upon the great
dance floors of the *tohua*. The erotic excitement that their dancing
produced was not incidental to the meaning of the festivals; the
ka-ioi were expected to provide this highly important feature,
underscoring the continued sexual energy of the Marquesans.

The spiritual importance of the sexual impulse is evident in
the festivals that were held in honor of deceased *taua*. These were
the greatest of the Marquesan feasts, of such surpassing importance that warfare among the various tribes was suspended, and
months were passed in waiting until enough food could be collected to supply them. The festivals themselves contained elements that evoked the Marquesan's sense of his genealogical and
cosmic past, perpetuating the tradition of ancestor worship that
the earliest settlers had brought to the islands in the second century B.C. The deification of the departed holy man, which was
the spiritual achievement at which the festival was directed, was
simultaneously intended to celebrate and enhance fertility. The
ka-ioi contributed highly erotic dances to these celebrations.[38]

Sexual activity was abundantly manifest in the daily lives of
the Marquesans, greatly to the dismay of the missionaries. "The
scenes of licentiousness exhibited in our presence, and even in
our houses, were too shocking ever to be narrated by either pen

or tongue," Armstrong later observed. "Were we to give a *matter of fact* account of the common every-day talk of those islanders, our reader would cast the paper away from him as though his very fingers were polluted by it."[39] The Marquesans directed toward the missionaries' wives a barrage of appeals that prompted them for the most part to stay indoors. "Such confinement," Mrs. Alexander noted, "was not very good for my health, so I proposed a walk with my husband one day. We had not gone very far from the house, when the men followed us, and behaved in such a manner that we returned to the house." Instead of a staging area from which a civilized program could be mounted, the missionary compound had become in this instance simply a refuge. But as Armstrong had observed, the Marquesans did not perceive the compound as an inappropriate place for their demonstrative sexuality; even here the white women were confronted by disconcerting solicitations, when islanders looked in at the windows: "What was most annoying," Mrs. Alexander continued, "was to see their black faces peering at me. I dared not look at them for I would see a look that would fill me with disgust and horror."[40]

Alexander had an opportunity to glimpse something of the significance of sexual stimulation in the religious and ceremonial life of the Marquesans when he observed the funeral of Haape, the chieftain who had been his host. After a period of hideous wailing, Alexander relates, "the women dressed themselves in their finest white tapas, & decorated their heads with splendid feather caps—but this was only a preparation for a scene still more abominable, for they were no sooner attired than they mounted a platform in front of the house in which the corpse lay, carefully opened their tapas in front & folded them back until their nakedness was fully exposed; then turning their faces to the corpse they danced for some minutes. Then turning to the crowd they continued their shameless dance all day amid shouts of applause. This exposure of their persons they consider the strongest expression of affection they can make to their departed chief. When we expressed our abhorrence of their conduct they defended it most bravely & maintained that it was not only decent & honorable but so praiseworthy that to withhold such expressions of regard would be to pour contempt on their chief."[41]

Alexander's mission was severely hampered by the death of Haape. Not only did the missionaries lose the protection of his friendship; they also had to contend with Marquesans who asked why they had not been able to prevent him from dying. The missionaries were understood to be holy men, counterparts in some sense of the Marquesan *taua;* they had lost considerable prestige by their failure to heal their chieftain's illness. But the circumstance that led directly to their abandonment of the mission had its root in a major aspect of Marquesan life we have not yet discussed, the persistent warfare among the tribes.

The narrow valleys of Nukuheva are separated by high precipitous ridges, which made it very difficult to move from one valley to the next, so that valley tribes were isolated from each other. In consequence a pattern of continual parochial belligerency developed in the Marquesas; tribes inhabiting the several valleys were engaged almost all the time in skirmishes and raids against each other. This intertribal hostility at times involved coalitions of tribes and grew on occasion into full-fledged wars of extermination. But such large actions never resulted in the establishment of a centralized island-wide authority. The exercise of such authority would have been balked by the sheer physical difficulty of controlling the affairs of one valley from a headquarters in another. The islands of Hawaii and Tahiti, by contrast, are surrounded by extensive coral formations that created a broad margin of flat land between the volcanic mountains of the interior and the sea. When the nineteenth-century European explorers arrived, they found upon this easily negotiable terrain what could plausibly be called "kingdoms," though even here conflict among factions was extensive. In the Marquesas they discovered a system of feuding among relatively independent groups, a texture of hostile transactions that had meaning on many levels to the society as a whole.

Human bodies were required for the correct performance of a substantial number of ritual observances, and these were obtained by means of raids on neighboring tribes. In every tribe there were males who carried a revenge obligation because a member of their household had been kidnapped in such a raid or slain openly in battle. This obligation required them to kill or kidnap in return, and until it was discharged the warrior signified his grievance by shaving off half of his hair and arranging what remained in a special knot.[42] This hairdo was so commonplace among the Marquesans that early European explorers did not think it was connected to a specific obligation, but simply perceived it as the "normal" hairstyle.[43] The principle of revenge obligation can fuel an endless sequence of reciprocal affronts, of course, and seems to have done so through hundreds of years in the Marquesas.

The original settlers of the Marquesas were cannibals, though it is not known whether cannibalism was at that time associated with the completion of revenge.[44] By the nineteenth century, however, the obligation formalized in the hairstyle could not be completely discharged until people from the offending tribe had been eaten. This activity completed the vindication by annihilating the enemy altogether and absorbing his defeated essence into one's own triumphant self. In the ceremony of *tipi-te-e* the victim was divided into small pieces and shared by all the warriors of the tribe, a practice suggesting that the individual Marquesan, and by extension the tribe as a whole, was conceived (at least in part) as the repository of bested enemies.[45] The personal and social sense-of-self fostered in Marquesan culture depended on the presence of immediate opponents, acquired sharpness in conflict with those opponents, and was confirmed by conquering and absorbing them.

Intertribal hostilities were embedded in the ritual life of the Marquesans, so that fighting was routinely suspended when a major festival was in the offing, to be resumed again when the ceremonies were concluded. And fighting itself had a ritual aspect like that discerned by Karl Heider and Roy Rappaport in the battles among New Guinea peoples.[46] In most of the skirmishes that took place between patrols of enemy tribesmen, threats and taunts were vehemently exchanged but injuries were not extensive. Even large-scale conflicts between tribes were characterized by features which indicate that economic and political objectives were inseparable from considerations of prestige that had meaning within a Marquesan symbolic world that we cannot now reconstruct. Edward Robarts, who lived among the Marquesans from 1798 to 1806, recounts a three-day battle in which a total of four men were killed. The last day of the battle, he reports, "is more for mirth then war, every one making the best appearance he can. Their Allys meet them on the mountains, makeing a grand appearance of about 4000, evry party bringing their drums and conch shells. A very grand dance ensues: some is fighting, others danceing. At times those that was fighting would set down and talk with each other with as much composure as though they was friends and then rise again and renew the fight."[47] Forceful rivalry was simply endemic to the way of life that developed in the Marquesas, and it included proud antagonisms between sub-tribes and households as well, contributing a further reason for the absence of a stable centralized political authority. Western observers were struck by the characteristic bearing of the Marquesan male, which was bold and proud and direct, without the manners formed by conventions of deference or accommodation.[48]

The aggressiveness of the Marquesans was aroused when Alexander and his fellows condemned their religious beliefs. "I have not met with one," Alexander observed, "who when the folly of regarding Nukuhevan gods is urged, will not defend them—Even Haape, who appeared so ready to cast away his idols, clings to them as fast as any of the people. They say their gods are *motaki* (good)—but ours is *kikino* (bad)—Yesterday about a hundred assembled to hear Mr. Armstrong—after sermon one of our Hawaiian domestics conversed with Haape to make the sermon more clear to him, but he treated the whole subject with perfect contempt, said the gods of Nukuheva were *tiatohu* (true or genuine) but that Jehovah of whom we told him was *tutai* (dung)."[49]

The missionaries were put on their mettle by such offensive replies, so that the exchanges between them and their prospective converts occasionally became quite heated. "When we tell them their gods are no gods, that their tauas are men like themselves & nothing more, that their images are fit only for fuel & their deified fowls & hogs mere food, it is very common for them to apply every abusive epithet to Jehovah which their language will admit of—If we say we eat the fowls which are their gods, they reply 'we also will eat Jehovah.' " Reflecting on such spiritual obstinacy Alexander expressed his misgiving that deep troubles might lie ahead: "We have every prospect of having to wade through persecution."[50]

The anticipated persecution did not come. The real menace confronting the missionaries did not arise from the hostility that developed between them and the Teiis but from their apparent friendship. In the eyes of the other Marquesan tribes, Alexander and his party were allies of the Teiis, and hence were suitable targets for attack. Especially dreaded were the Typees, the most powerful tribal group on the island. On the day Alexander moved into the missionary compound, he recorded that the Typees had several times threatened to burn it down or to kidnap a missionary on one of their periodic excursions into the Teiis' valley in search of human sacrifices. The missionaries did not understand the character of the animosity that existed between the Typees and the Teiis, and correspondingly found it difficult to predict their own chances of survival. They noted, for example, that Typees were among those who brought hogs to the feast in honor of Haape. Yet within a week they found that the people of the bay were "in great terror dreading a threatened invasion from the united forces of the Typees and Taioans." The missionaries seized this opportunity to blame the Marquesan religion for its requirement of human sacrifice, and found the Teiis eager to agree. But within three weeks the terror, and their receptiveness, had disappeared. In late March of 1834 Alexander himself made a journey to visit one of the less feared of the Typee subtribes and encountered there an aged taua who calmly and firmly denied that the Typees ever sought sacrificial victims or indulged in human sacrifices. Only the horrible Teiis, he maintained, were guilty of such deeds. Alexander was also informed that within the next month a large feast was to be held, which had taken two years to prepare for. After this feast all barriers to full-scale hostilities between the Typees and the Teiis would be lifted, so that he and his group could look forward at best to being driven out of the valley.[51]

This was more disconcerting than any amount of persecution. The missionaries and their wives were prepared to withstand maltreatment that might be directed against them for being emissaries of truth. But to be killed as friends of the cannibalistic

Teiis was quite another thing. They had meant to maintain a civilized altitude above the social processes of the Marquesans, a hilltop position from which they could exert a civilizing pressure. Now they found themselves engulfed by those processes, the meaning of their presence undergoing a radical transformation as the Marquesans themselves came to terms with it. Within the basic imagery that informed their acts, the missionaries were prepared to undergo prodigious hardships; but events were unfolding in a way that threatened to dislodge that imagery, to transform the city on the hill into an incidental chip floating on the violent and unpredictable currents of Marquesan affairs.

They met on April 1, 1834, to discuss the state of the mission and concluded that it ought to be abandoned. It was a decision they had resisted from the earliest weeks, when their misgivings first began to multiply; and they did not make the decision now without a day of prayer and fasting. But once the decision was made, it had the effect of releasing anxieties that brought them to the verge of panic. They decided that the departure should take place "as soon as possible," and immediately made application for passage to Captain Coffin of the *Benjamin Rush*, a whaleman then in Taiohae Bay. As the captain temporized, the *Royal Sovereign* arrived at Nukuheva bringing supplies for the mission. Alexander then redoubled his appeals, pointing out that the *Royal Sovereign* could carry home a portion of their goods, and finally the thing was arranged.

As the mission compound was being vacated by the missionaries, it also suffered its last indignity at the hands of the Marquesans. This miniature version of the city on the hill, constructed at so great an expense of trouble, had simply not worked as a center from which transforming influences would flow expansively outward. The lines of force had soon begun to run in the opposite direction, in fact, as the women sought refuge in their houses from the erotic solicitations of the Marquesans. But the compound could not be maintained as a civilized environment even in this shrunken role. Increasingly after the death of Haape, it had been raided by thieves, who cut sharply into the missionaries' essential supplies. In the last month of their stay, Parker later explained, "scarcely a night passed without our houses being molested by thieves. We have waked in the night & found them at our windows with long poles & a hook attached to the end of them pulling out such articles of clothing as they could get. At other times we have awakened and found them pulling up the thatching and taking out whatever they could reach . . . We have known our houses to be surrounded by a gang stealing at the same time from different parts of the house. The windows directly at our bedside have been stripped of all the articles that hung near them. If we attempted to drive them away they would persist till they obtained the article they were trying for, or if they went away would soon return again to that or some other part of the house."[52]

This savage invasion culminated on the day of departure, bringing the missionaries' panic to a nearly unbearable climax. After working straight through the Sabbath to get things packed, the missionaries worked with carpenters from the two ships on Monday morning to build shipping crates. "By noon," Alexander relates, "we had every thing ready to send aboard. The crews of both vessels then laid hold with vigor & before it was dark had all our goods on board the two ships. Before we got it all aboard however, the natives grew almost furious with a desire to get it. Before Mr. Parker had succeeded in getting his removed they pulled down one side of his house & tore away all his partitions."[53] The women and children were taken to the ship between a double file of sailors, and "were quickly surrounded by a multitude of the savages, armed with spears and clubs."[54] "Oh what a sense of relief we felt," Mrs. Armstrong later reflected, "when we were all on board! It was a critical moment, for the natives were like friction-matches, ready to explode on the slightest provocation."[55] The city on the hill had been routed; it had become a one-way corridor leading out.

In his very extended account of the conference of April 1, Alexander makes scant mention of the violence of the Marquesans or of the dangers to which the mission was exposed. His essential argument for leaving the Marquesas is not that the mission is likely to be overwhelmed by an unmanageable multitude of savages, but that there are too few savages in the Marquesas to justify so large an undertaking as his mission represented. In the earlier stages of his ruminations on the subject, Alexander characteristically focuses his attention on the size of the population when other reasons for departure are on his mind. In his very first journal entry, where he discusses the great difficulties he encountered trying to get the houses built, Alexander makes the comparison that would ultimately serve as his reason to quit the effort. "The population of this island I suppose is not greater than that of Lanai, which the Hawaiian Mission considers too small to have even one missionary stationed upon it."[56] Before they met in conference, the missionaries made extensive and laborious journeys, to other islands as well as on Nukuheva, to determine the size of the population. Alexander's ostensible reason for departure is that struggling on in the underpopulated Marquesas makes no sense when much richer fields stand unattended in Hawaii. And yet he, like his fellows, was at least peripherally conscious of more salient reasons for not continuing.

The mission of 1833 was a virtual non-event, easy to brush aside as insignificant in comparison to the notable triumphs of the mission enterprise elsewhere. Yet it leads us to questions about the attitudes and motivations that lay behind more successful ventures and were lost sight of in the midst of success. What psychological processes, we may ask, generated the panic that assailed the missionaries so violently at the end of their stay? The conference of April 1 did not actually give them new reasons for leaving; they already knew that the population was smaller than expected. Yet the meticulous and laborious census they performed somehow gave them permission to act on a series of misgivings whose sources lay elsewhere. Their interpretive powers having been swamped, they vainly sought contact with reality by amassing quantitative data in support of a proposition already known to be incontestable. Yet this seemingly frivolous effort conferred an air of authority upon reasons that made at least some kind of sense within the rhetoric that they and their sponsors shared.

So obviously misplaced a rationale for departure clearly indicates that buried and unacknowledgeable anxieties are at work. The missionaries' refusal to invoke their fears for their own safety is not a matter of mere bravado, invoked for this occasion alone; nor is their refusal to acknowledge that the Marquesans simply were not amenable to the mission effort. The curious dislocation in their reasons for departure gives us a glimpse of the basic psychosocial processes at the heart of our drama. As a preliminary sketch of those processes we may observe that the missionary rhetoric that the Alexanders, Parkers, and Armstrongs shared with their official sponsors made these persons who they were. It articulated a system of meanings that informed their identities as individuals and as members of the society to which they belonged.

For the missionaries to admit that their personal misgivings deserved consideration as a reason for giving up the mission would be to invite a chain reaction of distresses: it would disconcert the scheme of values that brought them to Nukuheva in the first place, which would in turn trigger the really violent anxieties of disintegrating selfhood. The fear of fear itself may well be the best recourse when total disorientation threatens.

These were brave men and women, who were also quite intelligent; most of what was dangerous and unpromising in the Marquesas was known to them before they arrived. Yet they acted within a conceptual system that made it impossible to count those discouraging realities against attempting the mission, or to count them in favor of abandoning it. What version of the idea of civilization prompted them to engage in this seemingly incongruous activity? What idea of the city on the hill led them to attempt establishing one in the crater of a volcano?

3 | Liberating
Satan's Slaves

I HAVE PROPOSED Alexander's mission to the Marquesas as
the expression of an idea of civilization, taking a rather distant
perspective which presents that idea in schematic terms. Making
a more intimate investigation of the conceptions that lay behind
this undertaking will reveal something of the way in which they
worked in practice. The theory of the relationship between civilization and savagery that animated the missionaries was Calvinistic, and much of its practical bearing on their work is traceable
to the objective doctrines of that creed. But as they enter into
practice ideas reveal something more than their rational content;
they also show the grip they have on the minds of those who
profess them. The missionaries' idea of savagery was not based
upon their encounter with Polynesians; it was the form in which
they interpreted their encounter with Polynesians. Alexander's
mission stands before us as a program of activities ordered by a
set of ideas, ideas that gave intelligible form to the circumstances
amid which the missionaries worked to inaugurate the program,
to quell internal misgivings concerning it, and to give it purpose
and coherence in the day-to-day struggle at Nukuheva.

Alexander's mission to the Marquesas may be conceived as an
abortive offshoot of the spectacularly successful American mission in Hawaii; it certainly has been viewed in retrospect as a
trivial footnote to that famous story. Recent studies of missionary enterprises in Oceania have shown that, instead of a uniform

"impact," such efforts have had markedly different consequences depending on the specific social circumstances in which they took place.[1] But Hiram Bingham's mission to Hawaii seemed to vindicate a broad abstract definition of the relationship between civilization and savagery, with the result that a movement developed in America to apply this definition elsewhere in Polynesia. Even though they heartily embraced the definition, however, and saw themselves as having demonstrated its universal validity, the missionaries actually at work in Hawaii were very reluctant to back the mission to the Marquesas and made an effort to dissuade their American sponsors from undertaking it. One fact emerges clearly from the curious interplay of misunderstandings in which the Marquesan mission originated: the missionary definition of civilization had the power to coordinate diverse perceptions of this project and to stifle very sensible objections to it. We have spoken of the Marquesan mission as a non-event; to investigate the reasons why it was undertaken is to trace the development of a non-decision. It will be necessary to introduce the various parties to this process, so as to perceive the ways in which the shared idea of civilization shaped their purposes and their ambivalences.

When Hiram Bingham arrived at Hawaii in 1819 he did not find a patchwork of independent warring tribes; instead he managed to align the interests of the mission with those of a ruling group that found him useful. The "King" of Hawaii, Kamehameha II, was seeking to gain control of a government that had been established by his father, Kamehameha the Great, nine years before, after a sequence of struggles with chieftains in the several islands. On the death of Kamehameha the Great, just before the missionaries arrived, a power struggle ensued in which Kamehameha II outlawed the ancestral religion in order to consolidate his rule. The missionaries thus found the new rulers in need of assistance with the task of giving political and economic stability to their still somewhat fragile ascendancy.[2]

The missionaries quickly formed a close association with the king (and the ruling families loyal to him), and they worked to create a system of cultural dominion which reinforced Kamehameha II's control while it advanced their own civilizing purposes. They joined in condemning his recalcitrant enemies, who continued to worship secretly in the old way, and filled the ceremonial vacuum thus maintained with Christian observances. There were many hardships and difficulties along the way, to be sure, but by 1823 the missionaries were able to announce that the first Christian marriage had been performed, as well as the first baptism. The first Christian funeral, also performed in this banner year, was held for the queen, who had died a professing Christian, and it drew a very large and appreciative crowd. The king during this year permanently imposed laws enforcing the Sabbath, which attached penalties to an extended series of violations.[3]

The missionaries thus worked through the political and social power of the ruling class that had traditionally governed in Hawaii as they aided the new program of centralization. In 1824 leading chiefs met to frame a regular code of laws, using the Ten Commandments as their guide. The schools established by the missionaries had at first, by order of the king, been open only to Hawaiians of rank. When this restriction was dropped in 1825 enrollments soared from 2000 in 1824 to 37,000 in 1826, with further large increases in the years that followed.[4]

The missionaries in Hawaii were leading participants in a cultural revolution; there was hardly an area of life in the islands where their influence was not felt. They advised the rulers on the regulation of trade and on their diplomatic relations with European and Asian nations; they also insisted that the Hawaiians wear "decent" clothing.

The mission to the Sandwich Islands (as Hawaii was then called) was sponsored by the American Board of Commissioners for Foreign Missions, which had begun at Williams College in 1808 as a secret club of students concerned about evangelizing the heathen world. Transferring to Andover Seminary, where its members went for theological training, this group created an official organization, complete with a formal charter, in 1810. By the time of its tenth annual meeting the American Board was prepared to launch the pioneering mission to Hawaii.[5] Since this involved supplying twenty-two persons and paying for their passage, it is evident that the American Board was no longer a scholars' club, and when news of the early successes of the Hawaiian mission reached America, the constituency of the Board was vastly enlarged. A wave of enthusiasm for South Sea missions swept across American public life, as praises were lifted up in the popular media of the day.[6] The American Board had originated in the fervent commitment of conservative Congregational ministers; it was now becoming a national benevolence with well-known public figures on the board of directors.[7]

The happy news from the mission field arrived as American religious life was undergoing a fundamental alteration. Waves of immigrants to America with distinctive religious traditions were enlarging populations (especially in the cities) that had earlier been dominated by a few major denominations, even as the movement of settlers to the West placed large numbers of people beyond the reach of traditional religious organizations. As a massive result of this massive demographic change came the Great Revival of the early nineteenth century and the emergence of revivalism itself as a central feature of American Christianity. As revivalism spread it generated a series of tensions and conflicts which eventually pervaded the Protestant community as a whole and redefined the terms upon which it conducted its life. The churches that had dominated religious life in America before the evangelical era found their social influence decreasing, and also found themselves ensnarled in manifold theological disputes, contending on the one hand with spokesmen for revivalism and, on the other, with thoughtful souls within their own communions who wished to adapt inherited creeds in the light of evangelical triumphs. Yet while Congregationalists and Presbyterians confronted the threat of fragmentation, the denominations in the forefront of revivalist expansion, such as the Methodists and the Baptists, also struggled in the face of rapidly swelling numbers to maintain administrative and theological coherence. The danger of such widespread organizational dislocation was that it would hamper the work of securing a stable Protestant influence over the new urban and frontier populations. Accordingly there sprang up a series of cooperative benevolent societies in which members of sects and denominations that were hostile along an extended range of theological issues could work together in social causes.

This effort to maintain and extend the social power of Protestant Christianity was informed by a strong national consciousness, such that the term "American" was given to each of the major interdenominational societies: the American Education Society (1815), the American Bible Society (1816), the American Sunday School Union (1824), the American Tract Society (1825), and the American Home Missionary Society (1826). The cause of foreign missions thus forms part of a general pattern in which Protestants in America sought to assert a common Christian identity that was linked to the identity of the nation itself. Christians who could agree on little else could join in working to make America a Christian nation, by a common definition of "Christian" which linked it with social superiority and thus with the task of bringing the urban masses and the settlers of the "wild West" up to a civilized standard. The motive of social control that Clifford Griffin discovers in the domestic benevolences does not appear in foreign mission work, since the Polynesians posed no threat to social order in America; as a result the symbolic significance of the foreign mission effort stands forth more clearly. It was an embodiment of the shared conception of America as a civilized nation, whose nature required it to act as an agent of the civilizing process.[8]

The first book-length treatment of the Hawaiian mission was William Ellis' *Journal of a Tour Around Hawaii* (1825). Although he was orthodox theologically, Ellis struck the note that gave his work interest to a large general audience. Acknowledging that the conversion of the savage is an end in itself, he also saw it as essential to a general social advance. *"Christianity Alone,"* he affirmed, "supplies the most powerful motives and the most effective machinery for originating and accomplishing the processes of civilization."[9] Instead of being the province of grim sectarians, the Polynesian effort was seen to reflect the highest and best of what Americans had achieved. Ellis' book was widely reviewed and swiftly ran through three printings; but perhaps because Ellis was himself British, with a special interest in the London Missionary Society (LMS) project at Tahiti, the welcome accorded his book was slight in comparison to the excitement that greeted Charles Stewart's *A Residence in the Sandwich Islands* (1828). Stewart had been a member of the "first reinforcement" sent by the American Board to the Hawaiian mission and had returned to America after two years because of his wife's frail health. Drawing upon this experience he wrote an account that established him as the premier American spokesman for the work of missions in Polynesia.

When a domestic agency sponsors an undertaking in a remote area, chronic organizational strains typically develop because of differences of view between those who are doing the work and those who are paying for it. As the South Sea missions became a popular cause in America, they attracted supporters very different in character and outlook from the hardy evangelists in the field. As Ellis, Stewart, and countless lesser writers heralded the spectacular successes of Bingham's mission, moreover, it began to appear that the job of civilizing Hawaii was well in hand. Accordingly, in 1828, the American Board sent instructions to Hawaii that a mission should be fitted out for the Marquesas. This the General Meeting of the Sandwich Islands mission refused to do: "We are compelled to say we do not now see the way open for the immediate establishment of a mission at the Marquesas Islands."[10] Instead they formed a committee to obtain information about the Marquesas from the LMS mission in Tahiti.

Charles Stewart, meanwhile, had taken a position as chaplain in the Navy and had shipped once again for the South Seas with a commission as a special agent for the American Board. On this voyage the sloop of war *Vincennes* carried him to the Marquesas. On the basis of his report, the American Board took initiative directly and in November of 1831 dispatched William P. Alexander and Richard Armstrong with specific instructions to pursue the establishment of a Marquesan mission, subject to approval by the General Meeting in Honolulu.[11]

Charles Stewart's conception of civilization, and his way of applying it to the Marquesas, thus emerges as a critical element in the deliberations that brought the mission into being. The arguments that persuaded the American Board, as well as their general frame of reference, are embodied in a book he published shortly before Alexander and Armstrong sailed for the Pacific: *A Visit to the South Seas* (1831).[12]

Stewart's account is formed by his conviction that the achievements of civilized man are ultimately founded upon the power of God. Describing his work as a chaplain, he tells us that he delivered his sermons aboard the *Vincennes* from the capstan, which was covered by an American ensign, and that he secured a foot or two of elevation over his hearers by standing on a shotbox.[13] He presents this little picture in order to suggest that technological, political, and military force were centered in the sacred truth his sermons conveyed. To us it may appear that the theological and moral ideas Stewart had to offer were scarcely more than an ideological panoply whose real function was to advance and conceal the material objectives of the cruise and to make more bearable the material conditions in which it was carried out. To Stewart, however, the material and spiritual coordinates of reality were polarized in the opposite direction: the human capabilities and achievements represented by the capstan, the flag, and the shotbox had their validity and indeed their very being only insofar as they corresponded to the scheme that God had ordained, and would support, by his own supreme reality and power.

Stewart exemplified a Christian theory of civilization that had deep origins in the doctrine of the millennium and had been voiced in the late eighteenth century by the Scottish commonsense philosophers as well as by Samuel Hopkins and somewhat later by Horace Bushnell in America. This view held that God progressively unfolds his plans for the human race by way of a series of encounters in which those who are bearers of his truth come into conflict with the forces of darkness. The degree to which such historic progress could be peaceful and orderly, as opposed to requiring outright social conflict, was a question that was interpreted differently within the broad tradition of spokesmen for this view and in the myriad occasions on which it was invoked. But there was a firm consensus on the central judgment that we find Stewart setting forth, that Christian truth is not an ornament of civilization, but describes the spiritual processes that bring civilization into being.[14]

Correspondingly, Stewart felt that the impression created by civilized achievements might prepare the minds of the uninstructed Marquesans for the reception of Christian truth. As the *Vincennes* made its first approach, an enthusiastic crowd of Marquesans trooped down to the shore. "In the midst of the shouting and apparent importunity for us to land, Captain Finch ordered the music on deck; and the moment its full and animated strains reached the shore, the effect on them was most evident—they instantly crouched to the ground in perfect silence, as if under the influence of a charm. Nothing of the kind, it is probable, ever broke upon their ears before, and well might there have been a mingling of superstition in their minds with the sudden swelling on the breeze of sounds new and seemingly unearthly." Stewart found this incident profoundly inspiring, for it appeared to him a harbinger of the response that Christian truth would receive if it could be delivered at full strength. "It is probable," he continued, "that few ships, if any, have ever been so near to this little spot; and to its rude inhabitants, our beautiful vessel with her numerous crew in their Sunday dress of uniform whiteness—our floating banners, and our full toned band—must have seemed for the moment, like a vision of brightness from a better world. O that some far happier bark might speedily be seen from their shores, bearing to them that which is no dream nor 'cunningly devised fable,' but the wisdom of God, and the power of God unto salvation" (220–221).

Stewart portrayed the Marquesas as ripe for religious reconstruction, and he looked forward to the civilized amenities that would become possible once this reconstruction had taken place. He was impressed by the natural beauty of the islands; it reminded him of the goodness of the Creator and also struck him as providing a wonderful setting for the virtuous and refined life. The vile usages of "heathenism" formed a dismaying contrast to the morally inspiring natural environment; yet Stewart perceived them as rapidly decaying, offering only the feeblest obstruction to the process of social advance into which the Marquesans might enter. This three-way dramatic tension between the Creator's beneficence, the horrors of a decaying idolatry, and the promise of Christian refinement runs through passage after passage of his description. It offers a continuous invitation to the American reader which Stewart makes explicit when he calls for the sending of a mission.

The images are literally crumbling into dust and ashes. The decay resting upon them—rendered more conspicuous by their deformity—seems already to proclaim the approach of the period, when, with all the *'idols of silver and of gold, which every man hath made for him-self to worship,'* these too shall be cast *'to the moles and the bats,'* and be trodden underfoot in perpetual neglect and abhorrence. To me the sight was most gratifying, adding assurance to the impression al-ready received, that nothing more is needed, even here, than the dawning of the 'light of life,' to scatter the spiritual darkness resting on the land, like the vapors of the morning before the rising sun. (292)

In making this pronouncement, Stewart relies implicitly upon the legendary swiftness with which heathenism had vanished from the Sandwich Islands, which was taken by missionary in-terpreters as evidence of God's power. Stewart does not allude to the anxious labors of the missionaries or the contingencies amid which they worked. He presents the process as godlike and inev-itable, like the rising of the sun.

Having invoked the refining process as it burns away the mists of savagery, Stewart then portrays the moral beauties that are its triumphant end-product by describing a picnic he enjoyed in a nearby valley. He gives the reader extended descriptions of the natural loveliness of this valley and offers the picnic to show how human relationships can approximate the decorum of God's creation:

Seated on the grass in the edge of a grove, we partook, in true pic-nic style, of the ample stores furnished from the baskets of Johnston, our kind old steward. He is a steady and valuable friend on such occa-sions, and one we ought never to forget to toast, when with keen ap-petites and high spirits each seizes for himself, *sans fourchette,* what-ever comes uppermost of the cold roast fowls, nicely sliced tongue, beef, ham, cheese, and bread, he so snugly stows away for the time of need; with one tumbler only, however, from which, in common, to share a little of his best wine—having learned too well, from sad experience, the casualties to which, in such excursions, his cut glass is exposed, to be prodigal of the use of that luxury in this part of the world.

Surrounded by hundreds of the natives . . . we enjoyed all the honors of the *déjeuner ên public* of the Bourbon family;—with little of its forms, however—the group exhibiting all manner of attitudes, and a mixture of every character, in partaking the feast.

The dignitaries of the land, seated among us, nibbled and sipped, with becoming care and gravity, the strange articles of diet presented to them; while a cake of ship-bread, handed to some of the common bystanders, was quickly crumbled into a hundred pieces, and tossed to eager and noisy applicants on all sides, followed by loud laughter and various other expressions of delight. (292–293)

Stewart's concessions to the barbarous setting in which this feast takes place (his delicate admission that they had no forks and only one cut-glass tumbler) display his concern for the demands of genteel punctilio. They also underscore the larger thematic meaning of the vignette, which is that the picnic forms a beachhead of civilization in a savage land, a precursor of the refinement that awaits the Marquesans upon their reception of the "light of life." Embedding his description in an extended compliment to the steward, he reveals the exquisite good manners into which Christian morality can flower once the darkness of paganism has been scattered. The larger configuration of the scene is likewise instructive; it presents the civilized picnickers at the center, eating with the dignitaries of the land, while all around is an admiring throng of savages, eager to partake of the bread of heaven. It recapitulates the archetypal social design found at work in the consciousness of William Alexander: it is the city on the hill sending forth its civilizing energies into the surrounding wilderness.

"My heart sighed," Stewart concludes, "for the beginning of missionary instruction among them . . . [that] those good tidings be proclaimed to them, which, if received and embraced, would at once make their abode, not only what it is now by nature— one of the most romantic spots on the globe—but morally and spiritually *the happy valley* (295). This allusion to Samuel Johnson's *Rasselas* is part of Stewart's general effort to propose missionary activity as civilized and civilizing in the most refined available terms. His book is intended to exemplify the civilized attitude itself, according to which Americans should concern themselves with the savage parts of the world, and he openly acknowledges that civilized activities (such as his) in faraway places are performed largely for the sake of the sponsoring culture. "A principal fruit of these circuits of the globe," Stewart quotes from William Cowper on his title page, "seems likely to be the amusement of those that stay at home." This comment is not meant as a criticism of egocentric American Christians who

support missions merely to amuse themselves, but as the aegis
under which he asks for their attention and support. Missions,
he assures them, are not a painful obligation insisted upon by
narrowminded religious zealots; they are a natural and agreeable
extension of the civilized way of being.

Stewart's way of presenting the missionary effort, like William
Ellis', was highly gratifying to the American constituency of the
American Board. To missionaries in the field it was seriously
misleading. In the archives of the American Board there is a
thirty-nine-page manuscript "review" of Stewart's *Visit to the
South Seas* by a missionary in the Sandwich Islands, who maintains that Stewart's own Christian faithfulness has been corroded
by the "exquisite fondness" he had contracted "for the fashions
and recreations of the polite world." He scolds Stewart for failing
sufficiently to emphasize the "dark and sickening traits" of heathen character and warns that public support for missions will be
undercut by his rosy delusions, because they raise hopes that can
only be followed by a "painful and chilling disappointment."
The Board retained this document but did not preserve the name
of its author or the date of its receipt, which indicates something
of the uneasiness with which they sought to maintain a cooperative balance between Andover-trained Calvinists laboring in
Polynesia and wealthy Americans stirred by revivalist piety to
sponsor benevolent enterprises.[15]

The subsequent history of the deliberations leading to the
mission at the Marquesas reveals further aspects of this tension
and leads us to recognize the shared conception of civilization
within which it was contained. At the first broaching of the proposal in 1828 the missionaries had demurred by suggesting that
the London Missionary Society mission in Tahiti could more
easily supply the Marquesas (since it was 1300 miles closer) and
that the LMS itself might have a prior claim. When Alexander
arrived in Hawaii, the mission there requested that he make a
tour of inspection, covering the same territory Stewart had covered, and that he also interview the missionaries in Tahiti to determine whether they would be willing for him to establish an
American mission in the Marquesas. When the tour was concluded, Alexander's own mind was divided. His observations led

him to remark tartly that "Mr. Stewart has been even more faulty
in his fine paintings than Mr. Ellis," asserting that their works,
which purport to represent actual conditions, are in fact "religious novels."[16] He found that the English missionaries in Tahiti,
however, were quite happy to have Americans occupy the Marquesas. They themselves had no desire to extend their work into
that field, though they did ask Alexander to recognize that the
headquarters in London might be making plans for one. It was
the same pattern as with the Americans: the men in the field
shied away from the Marquesas while the sponsors back home
were poised for action. The misgivings of the English missionaries were based on a tour of the Marquesas they had made in
1829: "such was the impression made upon their minds by the
lawless and repulsive conduct of the natives, that they deemed
the establishment of a European mission at these islands imprac-
ticable."[17]

The issue of the "safety" of a mission to the Marquesas had
been mentioned by the Sandwich Islands group when they first
resisted the initiatives from the American Board, and it was very
much on Alexander's mind as he made this journey. And yet it
was a matter that the missionaries found hard to explain to their
domestic sponsors, and may indeed have found difficult to explain to themselves. The men in Hawaii and Tahiti had been
amply exposed to the physical risks of missionary endeavor and
had learned from ship captains as well as other missionaries that
the Marquesas was an incomparably more dangerous place. The
fundamental reason why the mission to the Marquesas was
doomed had to do with the character of the Marquesans themselves; yet the conceptual system that the missionaries used to
assess that character made it hard for them to include its more
frightening features among the reasons to stay away.

Charles Stewart may have littered his descriptions with literary allusions and polite mannerisms, but he had voiced nonetheless an encompassing conception of the relation of civilization
and savagery in which Boston and Honolulu ardently agreed. A
conception that recalled the stark Calvinist doctrines in which
the missionaries themselves had been trained, it echoed the central affirmations of revivalism: savagery, they all agreed, was
bondage to sin. Whether the power of God would lead the civi-

lized man to perfect his table manners, as Stewart implied, or whether his power aimed at more rugged forms of virtue, the first task to be performed in the process of moral advance is liberation. The Marquesans, Stewart affirmed, are "under the dominion of an iron-handed tyranny—the tyranny of superstition, over the darkness of minds and hearts lost in ignorance and sin" (266). All the moral deformities of the savage were conceived as originating in this essential spiritual condition, the condition he shares with Fallen Man everywhere.

The South Seas thus appeared to provide a laboratory in which the power of God to counteract original sin might be observed. It was generally agreed that the warfare between God and the devil was continuously going on, in the churches on Beacon Hill, in the camp meetings in Arkansas, in the hearts of believers and unbelievers and sometime believers everywhere. But in Polynesia the lines of battle seemed reassuringly easier to define. As Stewart journeyed aboard the *Vincennes* he set for himself the task of reporting the progress of this contest, comparing the "condition and prospects of immortal beings still in all the darkness of paganism" with those "upon whose characters and condition the enlightening and regenerating influences of Christianity have been made, in a greater or less degree, to bear" (213). In the Marquesas, where no mission had ever taken hold, Stewart found "pure heathenism—heathenism as it is before one ray of Christian light has beamed upon its darkness" (262). The behavior that repelled and frightened Europeans was by this argument drawn into the reason for attempting a mission project. Reflecting on his journey of reconnaissance to the Marquesas, Alexander counted these qualities in favor of his undertaking. "Contemplating the people thus debased & seeing how they are given to war & cannibalism & superstition, we see a field in which the laborer should have much faith in God & in which the gospel may work glorious triumphs ... Why should the American churches be still straitened in not sending them the gospel? Have they said hitherto, 'the people are fierce and bloody, we dare not go among them?' Tell them they are not straitened in the Lord, but in themselves, for He has opened a way of access, & we are ready to go with our families & dwell among the people, although still a race of cannibals."[18] It is not the Lord, Alexander affirms, who is afraid to confront the slaves of Satan, only his timorous servants. As his mission project was falling to pieces, Alexander returned once again to this consideration: leaving the Marquesans in their sin will "give infidels occasion to say the Gospel is not equal to the work of taming the rude savage of Nukuheva & Satan will exult when he finds he is left unmolested in his old dominions."[19]

This way of conceiving of the condition of the savage made it difficult for Alexander and others with firsthand experience to construe their misgivings as authentic. Yet Alexander's misgivings were strong enough, when he returned from his reconnaissance, to leave him undecided. The missionaries in Hawaii were likewise skeptical of the project, so that the issue was very much in doubt when whaling captains fresh from Nukuheva brought word that Haape, whom Alexander had met there, was building houses for the missionaries and was eagerly awaiting their arrival. Even so, at the 1833 General Meeting of the Sandwich Islands mission that finally authorized the project, there was vehement opposition, and five of the nineteen brethren voted against it. Ironically enough, word was then on its way from Boston asking that the project be halted, because the headquarters of the London Missionary Society had complained that the Marquesas should be left for English workers. By the time this information arrived, Alexander and his party had already set sail.[20]

On his arrival in Nukuheva, Alexander discovered that Haape had available for him a Marquesan dwelling in which the three missionary families were expected to live together as a single Marquesan household. Six weeks later he summarized the confusion that now threatened to overwhelm him. "The subject of this mission has been shrouded in darkness ever since I reached the Pacific; it was first undertaken on *the highly exaggerated reports of Mr. Stewart*, & when almost abandoned, the erroneous statements of sea captains at Lahaina turned the scale, so we came in darkness & we now sit down in darkness not knowing whether we ought to remain or return. May the Lord yet cause light to burst in upon us."[21]

Having coordinated the disparate official and private responses that resulted in their arrival at Nukuheva, the evangelical version of the idea of civilization enabled the missionaries to go forward in the face of severe anxieties by giving them terms in which to interpret their immediate daily experience. South Seas missionaries generally accepted sacred doctrine as a working model of reality, which guided their perceptions of the experiences through which they moved. It succeeded in giving their projects internal coherence amid the drastically strange social context that Polynesia provided, so that they retained the semblance of moral accuracy and validity even when, as at the Marquesas, they encountered deeper and deeper frustrations.

The stratagems adopted by the missionary have meaning as elements in a drama of liberation in which God's power demolishes the tyranny that holds the savage in thrall. Since a radical reconstruction of his character is necessary as the baseline from which civilizing progress can be made, his religion must be abolished and his immoralities suppressed in a program of wholesale renovation. Hiram Bingham conceived his achievements in Hawaii in these terms, and the missionary plans for the Marquesas were similarly defined. Pausing before an altar at Nukuheva, where sacrifices were laid out, Stewart describes the swarming flies and odor as an image of the spiritual filth that must be scrubbed out of Marquesan life. "How was it possible for me to gaze on such a scene, but in the devoutest prayer that God, in mercy to his creatures, would speedily prepare the way for an utter overthrow of this system of darkness and of death." A missionary in his proper role "is made the instrument of razing to the dust such altars of abomination and blood, and of erecting on the ruins humble chapels of adoration and prayer, where the only offering required is the sacrifice of 'a broken and a contrite heart' " (333). Alexander's frontal attack on the religious beliefs of the Marquesans was premised on his view that the right worship of God could only be performed upon the ruins of the existing system.

The missionary himself only represents the power of God; he is "the instrument" rather than the agent of redemption. Although he administers a revolutionary spiritual process, he does not control it. Alexander was led to reflect upon the workings of God's power when he learned that a plot had been laid to kill him during his reconnaissance visit the year before. While the missionary vessel had been in harbor a chief had sought unsuccessfully to organize a party to seize it and kill all on board. It made Alexander very uneasy to realize that he had learned nothing of this plot until he had brought his fellow missionaries with their wives and children to work at Nukuheva, and so was reminded of the superintendent knowledge and power on which his safety and prospering would depend. "How many dangers of a similar sort we have been saved from since we landed we know not, but Jehovah is our refuge, though we dwell on the territories of Satan & in what might well be called the suburbs of Hell—The man who conceived the plot . . . has been laboring faithfully for several days, hewing timbers for my house. The same grace which transformed Saul of Tarsus can transform him & others more vile than he into fellow citizens of the saints & of the household of God."[22]

Saul of Tarsus had likewise been the devil's captive, breathing out murder and vengeance against the children of God. Alexander believed that the moral renovation that had overtaken Saul on the road to Damascus could remake his own would-be murderer on the shores of Nukuheva. The power of God was a tangible spiritual force in Alexander's understanding of human experience, and he saw a hint of its working in the fact that this man was helping to build his house. For American missionaries in the South Pacific this was the essential motor of civilization, the power of God working to free the slaves of Satan and then to ameliorate their condition. The conception they held of their program was as intimate as it was compehensive, extending from the transformation of the human heart to the creation of decent and industrious communities.

They also believed that God had ordained speech as the primary means for the achievement of their objectives. Giving utterance to the truths of the gospel, they maintained, would bring those truths to life in the human world. As Stewart concludes his assessment of the spiritual needs of Nukuheva, he affirms his belief "that a knowledge of the 'light of life' is the most direct and sure means of ameliorating the condition of man—as it alone can secure the salvation of the soul." "The REVEALED WORD OF GOD and the PREACHING OF THE EVERLASTING GOSPEL are the only sure and effectual, as they are the only appointed, means of accomplishing this benevolent object and this glorious end" (356). As soon as they arrived in Nukuheva, then, Alexander and his fellows set about learning the language so that they could use it in preaching and instruction. Their purpose was not simply to communicate information, but to form a linguistic conduit through which a psychosocial force of supernatural origin could be transmitted. "I long to have my tongue unloosed," Alexander stated as he struggled with vocabulary and syntax, "that I may tell them plainly the glad tidings which angels rejoiced to publish."[23]

Alexander's mission presents us with an altogether remarkable picture in which there are two groups of people on an island some twenty miles long by five miles wide. The larger group, numbering some 15,000, had led their life at that place for two thousand years. The smaller group plans to revolutionize their culture by talking to them. The missionaries had excellent reasons to believe that the project might succeed, with the achievements in Hawaii as a precedent. They were perfectly aware, however, that more tangible forces than speech had an impact upon the attitudes and behavior of the Polynesians they worked with. The preaching of the gospel was merely the centerpiece of a whole system of causes through which God, they believed, was bringing about redemption, a divine ordering of things called Providence.

The extraordinary tenacity of the missionary theory of civilization is traceable in part to conceptual resources provided by the doctrine of Providence, which the missionaries applied in such a way as to coordinate economic, political, social, and military realities in a design that supported their own spiritual program. Reflecting on the successes in Hawaii, missionary spokesmen were well aware that the way had been prepared for them by the outlawing of the traditional religion, and that they themselves had had no direct hand in that. They further believed that the royal ambitions of Kamehameha II and the means he used to achieve them were not in themselves praiseworthy. And yet they were part of the Providential plan: "This unparalleled event did not result from the influence of Christianity, nor from any good motive; but it was an instance in which the wonder-working hand of God was displayed in overruling the basest appetites and the vilest passions of men, to accomplish his benevolent purposes."[24]

In the Marquesas, too, Alexander had encountered great eagerness to have the missionaries come, which he attributed quite sensibly to reports the Marquesans had received concerning the wealth and power that had come to other island groups along with the missions. "Their highest motive, doubtless, is that they may become great like the people of Oahu or Tahiti. Still, this eagerness for missionaries created in the Providence of God by whatever cause, is an indication that now is the time to enter & possess the land."[25]

The idea of God's Providence created connections between the ultimate purposes of the missionaries and the proximate causes that aided or impeded their enterprises. In cases of success, it was not difficult to gather the subordinate circumstances into a description of the larger divine plan. In the Marquesas, however, the system came under exceptional pressure and here revealed its tenacity. Instead of celebrating the assistance of proximate causes, the missionaries found themselves again and again coping with frustrations.

They were especially disconcerted to find that their preaching, the essential conduit of God's power, did not make a forcible impression on the Marquesans. The missionaries' expressions of alarm, and their yearning for the holy quiet of the New England Sabbath day, make apparent the symbolic character of the drama in which God's Word was traditionally delivered to the worshiping congregation: on a day when all worldly occupations were laid aside, Christian people assembled to listen to the voice of one man as he gave utterance to the truths of the gospel. The design of this moment, with its rapt silence and its sacred focal point, embodies a specific complex of attitudes about the relationship between God and humankind. In the Marquesas, the missionaries were staggered to discover, this pattern was raucously violated.

Armstrong commented, after services one Sunday:

The behavior of the natives was a severe trial to my feelings, as it commonly is whenever we attempt to preach to them. Some lie & sleep: some laugh and talk: some quarrel with what is said: and others mock, and mimic the preacher & endeavor to excite laughter in others. Here one sits smoking a pipe, there one sits twisting a rope, and often there is such confusion that the speaker can scarcely hear himself speak. When we request them to sit still and hearken to our words, they reply, "Yes, let us all sit still, and listen." One says to another "sit you still there," and makes a motion as though he would strike him or throw a stone at him; the other must retaliate: and this excites laughter. Thus the whole congregation is a scene of noise & confusion. Not infrequently the half of all present will arise and go off, laughing and mocking. This behavior is no small trial to our patience & faith: I am sometimes tempted to give way to doubt, and ask can such persons ever become civilized & christianized?[26]

Alexander discovered, moreover, that the islanders drew his statements about "God" into a context that effectively robbed them of the meaning they held for him. "Their ideas of a God are so exceedingly low that we find it very difficult to reason with them—Their gods hold about an equal rank with the *witches* of N. England in former times—Their *mana* or *divine power* consists in their boasted ability to kill people by conjuration, & to give fishermen success. Their ideas of *Atua* therefore are such that when we speak to them of Jehovah they at once consider him a Taua like theirs & the perfections we ascribe to him are to them unintelligible." Alexander's insight into the reason for his difficulty is notably acute, but it is embraced in a framework that prompted him to keep trying. The "power" of the Marquesan gods was like that of the witches; it was a manifestation of the power of the devil. This satanic power was bound up in Alexander's mind with its dialectical opposite, so that his concluding observation invokes the countervailing power of God. "No truth is more evident than this, that without help from on high we labor in vain & spend our strength for naught."[27]

The Marquesans, like Alexander, expected their gods to exert direct influence on the course of human affairs, and they were soon to notice that the white man's god seemed incapable of taking action against them. Alexander's contemptuous remark that the Marquesans expected divine power to destroy persons against whom charms had been uttered refers to a routine process of Marquesan life, whereby individuals in fact died as the result of violating a taboo or offending an individual who had the authority to pronounce a curse. The Marquesans showed a similar contempt when Alexander was unable to act through spiritual means against an islander who had stolen his ax. "Some of them tauntingly asked where is Jehovah's power of which we preached, saying 'let him kill the thief & we shall then know that he is a powerful God . . .' They ascribe no *moral* attributes whatever to their gods, & it seems almost impossible for us to communicate to their minds any idea of a being possessed of such qualities. They say every people have their Gods, that Jehovah is ours, but the *tauas* etc. are theirs."[28]

No Marquesan would steal an ax or anything else from a Marquesan *taua*. Because of the small size of Marquesan tribes, the ownership of personal possessions was common knowledge; theft, when it occurred, was a direct challenge to the power of the owner. The routine punishment for theft in the Marquesas was summary execution, carried out by the offended party, so that when the missionaries applied to Haape for protection from thieves they were told simply to kill them.[29] In the absence of comment from the Marquesans at this period it is not possible to be certain in what light they viewed this circumstance. But it seems likely that they quickly noticed the missionaries did not kill thieves, that they did not use physical force and were also unable to lay hold of the spiritual weapons that were available to the Marquesan holy man. A Marquesan *taua* was competent to lay on curses that would soon have destroyed a thief who made off with his belongings; but the white *taua* (as the Marquesans termed the missionaries) were altogether defenseless. Certain Marquesans seem at length to have felt no qualms about stealing from the missionaries, much less the devastating horror that stood ready to seize them if they violated the sacred powers active within their own society. Like the sailors who "hung up their consciences when they rounded Cape Horn" and indulged in sexual orgies with an alacrity they could not have mustered in Boston, some of the Marquesans seem to have become rough and ready cultural relativists, not denying the power of their religion but recognizing its limited scope. "Every people have their gods."

It was of the essence of the missionary creed, however, that Jehovah suffered from no such restriction. Yet as Alexander continues to plead for "help from on high," it becomes evident that he knows the practical options are narrowing. To believe that God's power *alone* can bring the desired results may be taken in two senses; it can mean that all proximate causes are traceable to his Providence, but it can also mean that no proximate causes are visible.

The death of Haape was a severe blow to the prospects for Alexander's mission, because it occurred in a larger context in which the Marquesans found it impossible to acquire the power they anticipated would flow from the coming of missionaries. Hiram Bingham had prospered in Hawaii because of his association with the chieftains at Honolulu, who had achieved dominance through their association with whites. In the final battle where Kamehameha defeated his enemies, he was able to deploy an impressive array of Western military armaments.[30] The tribe of Haape (the Teiis) had also benefited from the white man's warmaking power. They still remembered with enthusiastic gratitude the visit of the American Navy Captain David Porter in 1813, who devastated the valley of their enemies, the Typees. But the Teiis had not been able to maintain supremacy after Porter's departure, so that the Typees had resumed their former position of ascendant power. When Stewart arrived in Nukuheva aboard the warship *Vincennes*, the Teiis greeted him with joy, anticipating a renewal of American military assistance. All American vessels, Stewart learned, were called "Porter's ships" by the Marquesans (227). This situation produced a sequence of occasions in which Stewart and then Alexander were obliged to sort out the relationship between God's Providence and the use of deadly force by whites.

In his discussions with the Teiis, Stewart found them quite receptive to his assertion that "all their gods, and all their religion and sacrifices were '*mea wahahe wale no*,' 'were altogether false,' and of no value." "I know Jehovah is a mighty God," a Marquesan *taua* commented. "I have heard of him from Tahiti, where the people have burned their images, and taken him for their God; and it might be well for us to do the same." The *taua* had concluded that Jehovah is "a greater God than any of ours," Stewart learned, "for he is the God of *thunder and lightning.*" The Marquesans had obtained this impression because they associated Jehovah "with the flash and report of cannon" (306–307).

Among the Teiis, American military technology had created an impression that played directly into Stewart's hopes. When he visited the Typees, however, he found it necessary to draw some distinctions. The *Vincennes* had been dispatched to the Marquesas partly in order to conciliate the Typees, to persuade them that Americans were not automatically their enemies. When they arrived at Typee Valley, the Americans found them busily throwing up a breastwork to repel an American invasion which the Teiis had assured them was imminent. Captain Finch of the *Vincennes* succeeded in persuading them, however, that his intentions were peaceful. "This is the first ship," they replied, "in which we were ever told, that it is wrong to fight: with Pota [Porter] it was all fight!" Captain Finch then informed them that "war was one of the greatest of evils; and pointing to the heavy guns of our battery—to the muskets, and cutlasses, battle-axes, and boarding-pikes of our well-guarded ship—assured them that all this array was not designed to promote bloodshed and war; but to secure peace, both at home and abroad" (314–315). Once the contrast had been established between Porter's action and the purposes of the *Vincennes*, a conversation took place concerning the evils of war itself which Stewart found deeply inspiring. The ultimate purpose of his spiritual mission became visible to him as the interview between Finch and the Typees took on symbolic proportions.

The scene exhibited was one of no ordinary character—a captain of a vessel of war, in the cabin of his battle-ship, surrounded by chieftains and warriors stained with each other's blood, unfolding the miseries attendant on the prosecution of violence and war; and importuning them to friendship and lasting peace, while they hang on his lips, seemingly with the delight of children listening to a new told tale. It was not a visionary thought that crossed my mind as I gazed upon it, that I had before me a proof, that the prophecy is not forgotten, which declares, that the period shall yet come, when all the nations of the earth, *"shall beat their swords into plough-shares, and their*

*spears into pruning-hooks; and shall not lift up the sword one against another,
neither learn the art of war any more."* (315)

Stewart's capacity to receive such an inspiration depends on
his faith in the intimate connection between the power of God
and the technical achievements of Western civilization. He believed that the superior armaments of the civilized parties to this
discussion reinforced the moral title that they held to give the
Typees lessons on the joys of peace. Taking a position outside
Stewart's system of beliefs we might ask how superior learning
in the "art of war" will hasten the day when that art itself can be
unlearned, or reflect that the Marquesans with their clubs and
slings appear a good deal closer to the promised ignorance than
was Captain Finch. Stewart, on the other hand, is eager to take
the impression providentially created by the military capabilities
of Americans as an occasion to drive home the advantages of
Christian faith, and to insist on the drastic reconstruction of
Marquesan life that it demands.

But Providence did not supply Alexander and his party the
advantages that other Christians were able to exploit; Alexander
proved unable to provide Haape and the Teiis any of the services
they had hoped for. Instead of making them great, as the missionaries had seemingly done for the people of Hawaii and Tahiti, the Americans had not even succeeded in preserving
Haape's life. The missionaries swiftly found themselves stripped
of the advantages inherent in the implicit alliance Porter had
created between the Americans and the Teiis, and of the prestige
that had accrued to the missionaries through their successes elsewhere. As a result, the thieving and harassments increased to an
intolerable level. The final turn of affairs leading to his decision
to abandon the mission can be traced to a discussion that occurred after a visiting ship's captain gave Alexander a gun: "a
fowling piece . . . not for the purpose of fowling, but to make
thieves stand in awe—The people are growing much more inso-
lent & much bolder in theft. Whether it would be proper to fire a
load of beans or salt at a thief we have debated & left undecided.
If we cannot maintain our posts without shooting with carnal
weapons it would seem that we ought to abandon them."[31]

Here Alexander invokes his commitment to the spiritual process he conceived to lie at the heart of civilizing the savage. The
means appointed to the missionary are spiritual means, no matter how God's Providence may quietly organize the material
causes of things. It is not for the bearers of the divine light to lay
their hands on "carnal weapons," although they may in good
conscience take advantage of the fact that others have done so.
This faithful invocation of the essence of his mission argued at
the same time, however, for an intelligent practical decision.
Given the combativeness of the Marquesans, the effort to cow
them with a single fowling piece would have been tantamount to
suicide.

There is a certain protection that is inherent in harmlessness,
which Alexander preserved by his decision not to use the gun.
The Teiis may have come to regard him as useless, but they were
not afraid of him and bore him no grudge. Alexander discovered,
however, that this was not true of the Typees. When he journeyed over the ridges to visit them, he found a reception very
different from the one that had greeted Charles Stewart. Instead
of finding the Typees glad that he was coming in peace, Alexander was compelled to plead his peaceful intentions in order to
dissuade them from taking revenge upon him for Porter's raid.
" 'Porter killed my father,' one of them exclaimed, Another said
'Porter killed my brother.' Another, clapping his hand on his
shoulder, said, 'Porter shot me here.' I replied that Porter & I are
different men, that my business was not to war but to prevent it
& teach all persons to live in peace."[32]

The frustrations of preaching, the increasing thefts, the death
of Haape, and the mounting physical threats could be interpreted
individually and thus faithfully experienced in keeping with
missionary doctrine; but taken together they presented a situation very hard to reconcile with the belief that God was working
through his Providence to effect the redemption of the Marquesans. This circumstance placed severe pressures on the missionaries' faith and called into question the validity of the task they
had undertaken to perform.

Even as they collected the census data that gave them the rationale needed for a speedy departure, they struggled with acute

misgivings. Drafting a joint letter that explained their departure
to the American Board, Parker concludes in sentences whose
slow and labored unfolding bespeaks the anguish he felt at having to confront the basic problem: What did the Marquesan mission mean in a world ordered by God's Providence? "We are unable to say why it is that who has said he will guide those who
ask him should have permitted the . . . [Marquesan] mission to
have been taken when it was so soon to be relinquished. We
know not what was the design of providence on how the time,
the property and prayers of the church expended on that mission
will promote the conversion of nations to Christ. We are told
that when we know not now we shall know hereafter, and we can
only leave this to be unfolded to us in that day when the secret
things of God shall be made known."[33] The missionaries thus
availed themselves of the ultimate conceptual resource within
the system that concerted their actions, the tenet which assured
them that God's plans are sometimes inscrutable to mortal men.
Because "the design of providence" is shrouded in divine mystery, faithful souls can continue to find guidance in it even when
the results are wholly unintelligible.

The severity of the psychological stress in which this faithful
utterance was penned becomes apparent in a private letter from
Armstrong to a member of the American Board, mentioning one
reason for the departure from Nukuheva that "could not with
propriety be mentioned" in the official joint declaration, namely
"the state of Brother Parker's mind." "Such was his disappointment and consequent dissatisfaction, accompanied with dejection of mind, and feelings of discouragement, that in our opinion
to have remained would have greatly abridged, if not entirely destroyed both his happiness & usefulness." Parker was not the
only one who was acutely distressed. "Indeed I never could
blame him a moment," Armstrong continues, "as I had often
similar feelings myself." Having taken the decision to abandon
the Marquesan field, Armstrong finds that the attendant conflicts
and uncertainties continue to plague him, and threaten to prevent him from pursuing his missionary calling. "This has
weighed so heavily on my mind at times as to entirely disqualify
me for business. My eyes have refused to sleep, and while reflecting on that whole undertaking and its final issue, I have

feared that I would never recover my accustomed courage & resolution. But through divine grace I hope to overcome this, and yet be able to do something for this benighted people."[34]

Alexander, Armstrong, and Parker were not permanently confounded by the Marquesan debacle, however; each survived its stresses and went on to long and distinguished careers as missionaries in Hawaii. Their conception of civilization and of the processes by which it can be brought about survived the disorienting pressures of this experience. Yet the Marquesan enterprise remained among the legends of the Hawaiian mission as somehow both heroic and perplexing, something that the brethren were not certain how to assess; and as the decades passed, surviving members of the mission were asked to record their memories of what had taken place. Parker's wife Mary gave a description fifty-four years later in which she reveals the lingering sense of anomaly. During the stay at Nukuheva, she says, it was difficult to keep track of time: "life was one episode, something thrown into life and still an unsolved problem, when I think of all that befell us, and our mission as wisely ordered, no doubt it was."[35]

The missionaries embraced a version of the idea of civilization which assigned to them the role of spiritual liberators. Holding that earthly affairs are regulated in conformity with a divinely ordained structure, according to which the human race is innately sinful and may be redeemed only by the power of God, they believed that the backward social system, primitive technology, and seeming moral squalor of the Marquesans had their origin in hearts and minds not yet illuminated by the glorious light of truth. The civilizing process leading toward superior social achievements thus depends upon an internal transformation that brings the souls of persons into line with the will of God. Before this radical alteration in his spiritual makeup has occurred, the savage is trapped in an endless cycle of depravity.

An alternative to the spiritual liberator is the political educator. Instead of assuming that the savage must be reconstructed before he can make progress, the educator seeks to cultivate the abilities displayed in the savage state. He uses institutional arrangements as instructional devices, instead of assuming that they flow from changes in the heart. The practical relations between the civilized and the savage are not kept backstage by the educator, as a domain governed by God's mysterious providence; they are central to the process by which he tries to move the savage up the line toward civilization.

Both the liberator and the educator devise programs of action aimed at eliciting and making use of savage responses, generating a scenario of interaction that will have a civilizing effect. In the missionary's model the city on the hill sends out energies that impose an order on the wilderness. The recalcitrance of the savage is part of the scenario, and the civilizer is ready with appropriate responses. Alexander, as noted, was prepared to "wade through persecution." The relation of civilized and savage is here a drama of spiritual conflict behind which the metaphysical drama of God's conquest over the devil may be glimpsed. In the educator's model, the city on the hill makes the most of the order that is already present in the wilderness. Instead of provoking opposition, the educator looks for promising aptitudes and areas of common understanding. He seeks to build his beneficial programs on mutual cooperation, friendship, and respect, dealing in conflict only where it is necessary to keep the relationship within bounds so that constructive activity can take place.

David Porter was a political educator. During his stay in the Marquesas he sought to apply this alternative version of the idea of civilization, meeting with no better success than the missionaries. In the later accounts of Alexander's mission, indeed, Porter's doings there are blamed for having made the savages even more savage. And Porter, for his part, looked upon the Calvinistic missionaries as religious fanatics, hardly less superstitious than the Polynesians themselves. Blaming each other for the failure to make the Marquesans civilized, Porter and the missionaries were actuated by a common frame of reference. The idea of civilization itself was present to all their thought and action as an unrecognized deep structure, whose true shape and functioning will become more apparent as we examine Porter's contrasting version.

4 | Educating Nature's Children

IN THE EARLY nineteenth century the term "civilization" had a more emphatic and limited significance than it has today; it was reserved for a state of society that stood at the head of a procession in which other societies had subordinate places. Yet even within this narrower definition the term could be taken in two senses: civilization could indicate the advanced condition itself or the process of achieving that condition. As a social arrangement, civilization represented a superior position toward which efforts should be aimed. As a dynamic process, civilization was the enterprise of shaping activities to reach that goal. These two senses of the term were interrelated in ways that vary with the specific content given to the term itself. For the missionaries in the South Seas, civilization as an achieved state was the outward sign of an interior process. The "arts" of civilized life, including law and commerce as well as technology, were the visible fruits of a spiritual renovation.

For Captain David Porter civilization was that state of society in which superior practical achievements are displayed. In his view, men are civilized when they exercise their inherent capabilities on an exalted plane. The essence of a civilized community is not hidden, therefore, in the hearts of human beings, where God's redeeming power is mysteriously at work; instead it is manifest in architecture, commerce, science, government, and technology. For Porter the process of becoming civilized is simply the mobilization of human capabilities for the purpose of bringing about a higher standard of achievement. Captain Porter did not think of America as an instance of civilization, but as aspiring to provide a new definition of it. The missionaries might invoke the blessings of American life as an example of what God's power can lead men to achieve, but for Porter the civilized state itself was the prime reality. He did not come to the Marquesas as a representative of the power of God but of the government of the United States; and he was sharply aware of his representative role. Porter has been called the first American imperialist, by those who identify imperialism with the claiming of territory not contiguous with the nation making the claim, because he took possession of the Marquesas Islands in 1813.[1]

He arrived in the Marquesas at the high point of his extraordinary Pacific campaign during the War of 1812. Placed in command of the frigate *Essex*, his original mission was to harass British shipping in the Atlantic, but he found occasion to reinterpret his orders and sailed in secret around the Horn. In the Pacific he operated without significant opposition for many months and virtually destroyed the British whaling industry, making room for an American dominance that continued until the industry itself collapsed because of the new coal oil. When he sailed into Taiohae Bay, Porter was at the head of a little fleet of his own: he had fitted out one of his prizes as a warship, which he called the *Essex Junior*, and had four armed whalers under his command that could be used for capturing yet further prizes.[2]

Efforts to understand the reasons for the War of 1812 usually include some notice of an American desire to vindicate the new nation as a member of the community of nations. It was important that Americans should feel that the United States was not a loose congeries of interests that would disintegrate at the first shock, but a vital and coherent presence in the world.[3] Porter was strongly aware of his position as an exemplar and spokesman of the American claim to full status as a civilized state. This nationalistic zeal is apparent in his truculent discussion of the "correct" name for the Marquesas Islands. What exasperates him is not that the American "right" to name them (which he claims by reason of prior discovery) has been challenged by the French and the British, but that it has been ignored. "Fleurinen in the discovery of this group claims for the French priority of the British, and in the discussion loses sight of any claim of ours: perhaps he has not considered us as rivals worthy of either of the great nations, and has attached to us no more merit than he would have given to one of the natives for being born there."[4]

Porter's conception of the qualities of a civilized nation reflect Enlightenment attitudes that were widespread in 1815. Charles and Mary Beard document fully the vogue enjoyed in the early republic by a version of the idea of civilization that is traceable to Condorcet, who argued that societies advance to higher and higher stages of achievement not through the mysteries of God's grace, but through the advancement of knowledge. American writers eagerly elaborated this theory, the Beards argue, coming like Thomas Jefferson to insist that rationality (attaining knowledge) was coupled with an innate moral sense (deciding how knowledge should be used) to form the twin engines within human nature that powered forward movement in society at large.[5] The concept of civilization embraced by the missionaries, by contrast, retained contact with its historic origins in the doctrine of the millennium, placing God and his historic actions at the center of the cosmic drama in which the human race advances from barbarity to refinement. In the liberal version, on the other hand, God has retired from his creation to permit the exercise of those rational and ethical capabilities with which human beings have been endowed. American Deists, as well as more moderate spirits, gained support for their arguments in behalf of man's natural faculties from the record of improvement they saw in human history. Calvinists, who insisted that all progress represented God's unfolding triumph over the inherent sinfulness of the human race, were looked upon by spokesmen for the Enlightenment as victims of the ignorance and prejudice that advancing knowledge would surmount.

The voyages of Captain Cook into the South Pacific were typical gestures of the Enlightenment spirit, and their results were drawn into the controversy between liberals and orthodox Calvinists. The account of Cook's first voyage, indeed, was written up in 1774 by John Hawkesworth, who decorated Cook's straightforward account with passionate declamations in favor of innate human virtue, based on Cook's favorable impressions of native character.[6] And while the account was greeted by a storm of protest from the orthodox, leaders of the Enlightenment in America were profoundly impressed by Cook's achievements. Benjamin Franklin, for example, was approached at the time of Cook's third voyage, which was scheduled to take place in the midst of the American revolution, by sponsors of the expedition who feared that American vessels might interfere with it. Franklin, then minister plenipotentiary to France, provided a special passport for Cook and informed American naval officers that he was to be given free passage because his voyage was for "the benefit of Mankind in general." Cook's successes prompted the governments of England and France to sponsor further voyages of scientific exploration, and the accounts provided by Vancouver and La Perouse received an enthusiastic reception when they were published in America in 1801.[7]

Yet as Henry May's masterful study has recently confirmed, the Enlightenment came to an end as a vital force in American life with the closing of the eighteenth century, surviving into the early decades of the nineteenth century principally as a didactic program.[8] During this terminal phase a version of Enlightenment principles was widely disseminated in college curricula, where such works as Guizot's *History of Civilization in Europe* became standard fare. Yet the confident rationalistic spirit of the revolutionary period, when it seemed to men like Franklin and Jefferson that human history was firmly in human hands, lost ground rapidly amid the vast and complex reshaping of American life whose religious expression was the Great Revival. Publishing his *Journal of a Cruise Made to the Pacific Ocean* in 1815, Porter exemplified Enlightenment attitudes just as the sweeping social impact of popular evangelicalism was creating the public temperament that would respond with enthusiasm to accounts portraying the South Sea islander as sorely in need of conversion. One telling evidence of the alteration of susceptibilities that was taking place even as Porter claimed public attention is the difference between the 1815 edition of his *Journal* and the second edition, published in 1822.

In the first edition Porter offers an extensive series of comments on sexual matters, written very much in the spirit of

Hawkesworth's version of Cook, where he adopts a mock-serious tone of enlightened tolerance toward the customs of the Marquesans and the American sailors' response to them. In the second edition all traces of this impulse to needle moral proprieties are carefully removed, even as his rationalistic commentary on questions of religious belief is allowed to remain intact. This expurgation suggests how fundamentally the age-long quarrel between liberals and the orthodox in religion was being modified by the new demand for moral earnestness—not to say prudery—as the focus of religious consciousness shifted in America from questions of right doctrine to the processes of moral regeneration. One of the ironies of Porter's Marquesan adventure, accordingly, and of the larger drama in which we find him, is that he declared America's right to a place among the "great nations" of the earth in a tone of cosmopolitan sophistication that Americans themselves were on the verge of repudiating.

In portraying his Pacific voyage Porter insists as strongly on its importance as a scientific expedition as upon its military successes. His treatment of the Marquesan sojourn includes lengthy discussions of the culture, illustrated by remarkable engravings in his own hand, and he compares his findings in detail with those of the internationally famous earlier explorers. Porter believed that voyages of discovery contribute to the splendor of a nation's reputation, and he also recognized the commercial and military advantages likely to flow from them. After the war, in fact, he proposed to President Madison that he be placed in charge of such a voyage into the Pacific; and he made this proposal in terms that reveal this aspect of his conception of national greatness: "To the voyages of Quiros, Mendana, and others the Spanish nation owes its chief fame, and the voyages of Cook Anson, Vancouver &c are the greatest boasts of England . . . All nations for La Perouse envy France."[9]

Porter does not argue that a successful voyage of exploration would bring greatness to America merely as an impressive feat, but because of its complex associations with economic and political interests. "We, Sir," he addresses President Madison, "are a great and rising nation. We have higher objects in view than the mere description of an island seen before by others . . . We possess a country whose shores are washed by the Atlantic and the

Pacific . . . Of its extent, its resources, and inhabitants, we our-selves are ignorant. We border on Russia, on Japan, on China; and our trade is now of sufficient importance there to attract the attention and excite the cupidity of an enemy." Porter argues that his voyage might open trade relations with Japan, which was then closed to all Western nations except the Dutch. He further argues that great improvements could be made in the American relation to China. While the American national territory ex-tended scarcely west of the Appalachians, in short, Porter had a vision of Pacific empire. He conceived a dominant international position for America as a leader in the advance of civilized achievement. "My views are general," he concludes trium-phantly, "and they embrace the whole world."[10]

Porter's voyage of discovery was never sponsored by the United States government, and his taking possession of the Mar-quesas Islands was never ratified. But his imperial conception of America has had a long train of successors that have provided a series of corresponding definitions of the meaning of America's relationship to nations conceived not to be civilized. During his stay at the Marquesas he sought to embody his idea of America as a great nation in a form that would bring the blessings of America's superior position to a people he thought well fitted to benefit from them. Porter "took possession" of the Marquesas in the name of the United States because he considered this an ap-propriate display of the greatness of America; but his definition of civilization also led him to believe that this action was suited to the character of the Marquesans, which he very sincerely ad-mired.

Porter measured the cultural state of the Marquesans by the scale of their practical achievements, and was vastly impressed. He marvels at the great *tohua:* These "places of feasting . . . are . . . . raised to height of six or eight feet on a platform of large stones, neatly hewn and fitted together, with as much skill and exactness as could be done by our most expert masons; and some of them are one hundred yards in length and forty yards in width, surrounded by a square of buildings executed in a style of elegance, which is calculated to inspire us with the most exalted opinion of the ingenuity, taste, and perseverance of a people, who have hitherto remained unnoticed and unknown to the rest of mankind." Porter takes note of the immense weight of the stones and the difficulty of transporting them and moving them into place; he also notices that the structures antedate the period when the Marquesans had access to iron, and realizes correctly that the neatly fitted blocks had been cut with stone. "Our astonishment is raised to the highest, that a people in a state of nature, unassisted by any of those artificial means which so much assist and facilitate the labour of the civilized man, could have conceived and executed a work which, to every beholder, must appear stupendous" (42–43).

Porter was uniquely well fitted to appreciate the Marquesans' skill in navigation, where his comments reveal admiration even more eloquently than the encomium above. He had no difficulty accepting the historical veracity of the Marquesans' legendary accounts, which identified the original settlers of the islands as having sailed eastward from Tonga. Contemporary scholarship has witnessed an extensive struggle concerning this issue, which has been resolved by a wealth of circumstantial detail confirming this ancient claim, which Porter believed on the spot. Porter pictures to himself the emotions of the early navigator who discovered Nukuheva, using terms that accord Polynesians the same impulses that lead white men to civilized attainments. "Months, nay years, must have appeared to him short while engaged in this pursuit, proud first of the honour of having proceeded farther than any of his countrymen, and secondly . . . of the glory of founding a new colony" (138).

Porter was aware that Calvinistic missionaries had visited the Marquesas, as well as other secular explorers, and that they had circulated reports of the savage degradation in which the Marquesans lived. Judging their character by his alternative definition of civilization, Porter came to the conclusion that they were not savages at all. "They have been stigmatized by the name of savages; it is a term wrongly applied; they rank high in the scale of human beings, whether we consider them morally or physically. We find them brave, generous, honest, and benevolent, acute, ingenious, intelligent, and their beauty and regular proportions of their bodies, correspond with the perfections of their minds" (62).

As an exemplar of the Enlightenment, Porter did not estimate
Marquesan character in the terms supplied by Calvinistic doctrines of human sin; on the contrary, he accorded the islanders a
full measure of the inherent human gifts of rationality and moral
awareness. Porter's denial that the Marquesans were savages
does not mean that he viewed them as civilized—only that nature
had granted them a large endowment of these essential human
qualities and that they had cultivated those qualities to good effect. The missionaries believed that the gulf between civilization
and savagery could only be crossed by way of a revolutionary
spiritual struggle. David Porter on the other hand believed that
civilization could be advanced among the Marquesans along a
scale of orderly development from their present retarded state to
higher and higher levels. He did not see them as moral monsters
to be reconstructed, but as promising neophytes to be sophisticated.

Porter employs this system of understanding in discussing the
Marquesan religion, which he found very perplexing. He could
see that it had major consequences in Marquesan social life; yet
its provisions appeared to him so capricious that he was brought
to credit the Marquesans with virtually omnivorous gullibility.
"They are not fond of trouble, and least of all, the trouble of
thinking. They are very credulous, and will as readily believe in
one religion as another. I have explained to them the nature of
the Christian religion, in a manner to suit their ideas; they listened with much attention, appeared pleased with the novelty of
it, and agreed that our God must be greater than theirs." But this
acknowledgment Porter perceived as merely the result of mental
slackness, which he saw as the essence of superstition. "Had a
catholic priest been with me at the moment," he observes, "he
might have made converts of every individual in the valley"
(117–118).

What was lacking from the Marquesan religious consciousness, then, was the mature individual assent to a reasonable
creed that Calvinists and Enlightenment Christians alike conceived to be absent from Roman Catholic piety. Instead of having
an intelligible core of doctrine, Porter found the Marquesans to
have a fantastic congeries of observances, convictions, rituals,
and traditions all somehow administered by what he called their

"priests and jugglers." But Porter does not find in this spiritual hodgepodge the menace and cruelty that his fellow Protestants perceived in Catholicism. On the contrary, his observations bring him to state explicitly a metaphor that operates throughout his account: he sees the Marquesans as intelligent but benighted children. When they ask if he would like to see their supreme deity, he braces himself for something truly impressive only to find that it is a little cloth figure that the islanders sing to and toss about. "In religion," Porter concludes, "these people are mere children; their morais [shrines] are their baby-houses, and their gods are their dolls" (119).[11]

But even so immature a religious rationality as that of the Marquesans, Porter implies, is sufficient to confound the theories of Calvinistic missionaries. He reports the account a chieftain's wife gave him of her conversation with one such worthy.[12] "He had informed her that our God was the only God that everyone should worship, that he made the island of Nukuheva and had sent down his Son to let us know that he was the true and only God. He ridiculed their gods as blocks, and stones, and rags, which . . . [said the chief's wife] was not right, for we did not ridicule his god, who, if he wished us to be convinced that we should worship only him would also send his Son to instruct us. We would not kill him, as did the tribe of which the missionary informed me; we would thank him for his good intentions and give him, as we gave the missionary, shelter and food while he remained among us. Our gods supply us with bread-fruit and coconuts . . . we are perfectly contented and we feel satisfied . . . you who reside in the moon come to get the produce of our island; why would you visit us, if your own gods and your own island could supply all your wants . . . The gods of the white man are intended for them alone. The gods of Nukuheva were intended solely for us" (134–135). It is hard to doubt that Porter has tricked out this "native" opinion in order to sharpen its resentment of Calvinistic intolerance, but as a fabrication it preserves the blend of primitive credulity and primitive rationality that he thought he saw in the Marquesans. The islanders may believe that white men live in the moon, Porter implies, but they can still see through the follies of Calvinism.

Even though the Marquesans had not elaborated their rational

Typee God

Ornament for the Neck

Womens Ear Ornaments

Mens Ear Ornament

W. Strickland del. & sc.

capabilities as civilized man had done, Porter did not conclude that their forms of life were irrational, much less depraved. What he saw in them were the rudiments of a healthy and flourishing state of society, not a carnival of corruption. This distinction becomes apparent in Porter's commentary on Marquesan sexual customs, which he stoutly defends as "modest." "Nakedness they cannot consider offensive to modestry. . . . for dress is not always a proof of modesty and virtue, nor is nakedness that of depravity and want of shame. I find no difficulty in believing, that an American lady, who exposes to view her face, her bosom and her arms, is as modest and virtuous as the wife of a Turk, who is seen only by her husband; or that a female of . . . [the Marquesas], who is seen in a state of nature, with every charm exposed to view, may be as modest and as virtuous as either. That they have a high sense of shame and pride, I had afterwards many opportunities of observing" (15). As for the many native women who made themselves available to the sailors, Porter observes that similar conduct is observable in any civilized port; but women of higher social rank, for all their relative nakedness, display that "sense of shame and pride" which is given refinement in civilized lands, sometimes to an obsessive degree as among the Turks, sometimes along a rational mean as in America. Porter himself encountered this unrefined but decisive natural reserve when his own advances were repulsed by a young lady of high position. If any blame is to be laid, Porter concludes, it must be laid against civilized whites who violate their own well-defined principles of morality and virtue. The islanders, he judged, acted in accordance with ancestral codes of hospitality.

Porter's confidence in the Marquesans' inherent moral consciousness was shaken, however, by the reports of Marquesan cannibalism. Since it "concerned the character of a whole people, who otherwise deserved to rank above the mere savage," Porter made special efforts to determine whether this practice was actually indulged in and concluded, quite mistakenly, that it was not. Although his native informants uniformly acknowledged that enemies taken in battle were sometimes eaten, Porter found this report impossible to reconcile "with the generosity and benevolence which were leading traits in their character" (45). Can-

Woman of Nooaheevah

nibalism further seems to him incompatible with the personal fastidiousness of the Marquesans, how they wash themselves three times a day and are cleanly in their manner of cooking and eating food. "How then can it be possible," he asks, "that a people so delicate, living in a country abounding with hogs, fruit, and a considerable variety of vegetables, should prefer a loathsome putrid human carcass, to the numerous delicacies that their valleys afford? It cannot be," Porter concludes, "there must have been some misconception" (45–46). Porter's rationalizations on this subject reveal the tenacity with which he clung to his Enlightenment conception of human nature, in which the intellectual and moral qualities the Marquesans displayed would appear to rule out "a practise so unnatural." But Porter had a further reason for not wanting to conclude that the Marquesans were cannibals: he wanted to establish a cooperative relationship with them by making them a "possession" of the United States. To find that they were cannibals would force Porter to conclude that the Marquesans lived in a state of utter savagery, so that taking possession of them would tend to demean, rather than glorify, civilized America.

Porter correspondingly stresses those features of Marquesan character that appear to reveal their aptitude for the arts of civilized life. What impresses him most strongly is the way in which they work together at communal projects, where they display an apparently spontaneous cooperation. "Nothing can exceed the regularity with which these people carried on their work, without any chief to guide them, without confusion, and without much noise; they performed their labour with expedition and neatness." What amazes Porter is that the Marquesans are able to work together in this way without the objective constraints that order civilized enterprises. He had perceived that Marquesan society lacked a formalized legal system and that the chiefs enjoyed very little preeminence over major household heads; and he incorporates this awareness into his tribute to their powers of cooperation. "It seems strange how a people living under no form of government that we could ever perceive, having no chiefs over them who appear to possess any authority, having neither rewards to stimulate them to exertion nor dread of punishment before them, should be capable of conceiving and executing, with the rapidity of lightning, works which astonished us" (66–67).

Porter's puzzlement at the spectacle of an intricately structured cooperation, working beautifully without rewards and punishments, prompts him to speculate on sources of virtue and rationality that lie deep in man's relationship to nature, deeper than calculations of advantage. "They appear to act with one mind, to have the same thought, and to be operated on by the same impulse; they can be compared only to the beaver, whose instinct teaches them to design and execute works which claim our admiration" (67). Instead of an articulated legal or commercial system, specifying the regulations by which affairs should be conducted, the Marquesans appeared in Porter's eyes to have arrived at a high state of competence by relying on the instinct they shared with unreflective members of God's rational and orderly creation.

So Porter felt it was entirely appropriate that the Marquesans should be adopted as junior members of the American polity. Their promising cultural childhood, with its unrefined yet egalitarian social systems, should win them admission "into the great American family, whose pure republican policy approaches so near their own" (83). Porter's "Declaration" of possession spells out the "considerations of humanity" which give it justification, anticipating "speedy civilization to a race of men who enjoy every mental and bodily endowment which nature can bestow, which requires only art to perfect" (84). In that formulation Porter captures the essence of his vision of the relation between civilization and the lower orders of men. Civilization is an achievement of "art": the elaboration of rational processes in technology, politics, religion, and all other human endeavors.

Porter sees Marquesans and Americans on a continuum of development in which an elemental human deposit of rationality and moral awareness is increasingly perfected through appropriate disciplines. The "pure republican policy" of the American nation stands at the most exalted end of the scale, in Porter's view, but it is inherently analogous to the ruder democracy of the Marquesan. It defines the goal toward which Marquesan culture will inevitably move as its capabilities are stimulated by the relationship with civilized men. Porter conceived that his possession-taking represented an important step in the long passage upward toward a fully developed civilization. "In order to encourage these views to their own interest and happiness . . . I have taken on myself to promise them they shall be so adopted; that our chief shall be their chief" (83).

Porter's relationship with the Marquesans moved through several stages before they asked to become members of the great American family, stages that Porter interprets in terms provided by the conceptual system that defined for him the nature of human society. As Porter describes his own actions it becomes apparent that this pattern of meanings guided him in the immediacies of a complex and at points highly dangerous situation. Like the missionaries, Porter did not look upon the idea of civilization merely as a source of rhetoric to be called upon in the language of formal document, but found in it the meaning of his actual experience.

We have noted already that Porter's ascription of Enlightenment virtues to the Marquesans led him mistakenly to deny that they were cannibals. In Porter's way of describing the practical steps that led to his taking possession, correspondingly, there is a pattern of discrepancies between Porter's explanations and the real character of the events. As with the missionaries, once again, Porter's preconceptions permitted him to see a great deal; but they also obscured certain important features of the human environment in which he acted. To watch Porter as he moves through the Marquesan experience is rather eerie, because of the number of highly salient developments that lie outside his awareness.

Porter sailed his fleet of prizes to the Marquesas because he wanted to refit the *Essex*. Though she had suffered no serious damage, her months in the Pacific had caused enough wear and tear to make the task of putting her in fighting trim a considerable enterprise. Porter needed to replace a large amount of worn rigging, replace his mainmast, build and fill new water casks, rid the ship of rats, and scrape the barnacles off her hull: for this purpose he needed to establish a little community of workmen on shore and secure it until the *Essex* would again be able to sail. He found what he as looking for at Taiohae Bay, on whose west-

ern side there was a level plain behind a sandy beach. Porter
learned that the islanders stayed away from this area because it
lay between the territories of the Teiis and the Happahs, who
were "at war" with each other.

It is highly unlikely that Porter could have remained any
length of time at Nukuheva without getting mixed up in the
feuding of the tribes. Yet his selection of this stretch of ground
has a symbolic value for us; it embodies Porter's ironical un-
awareness of the circumstances he was entering. That the Teiis
and the Happahs were at war meant to him that these two groups
were settling economic and political differences with which he,
of course, had nothing to do. Wanting to remain neutral, he felt
himself lucky to have located some neutral territory. He did not
conceive that the quarrel was meant to enact differences rather
than settling them, or that occasions of conflict were staged to
include ritual features that linked them to a fabric of meanings
pervading the society as a whole. It was quite possible, indeed,
that the plain where he set up camp was in fact designated as a
fighting ground between the two groups, which they occupied
when they wished to provoke each other.[13] But Porter assumed
he would be left alone; he had taken up a place nobody claimed
and had thus offered offense to none. He soon received a visit
from Gattanewa, the chief of the Teiis, who expressed great
pleasure in Porter's coming and proposed to exchange names
with him.

Porter recognized that exchanging names with Gattanewa
would be a formality of friendly relations, and so he agreed to it.
He did not realize, however, that it would be impossible to be on
friendly terms with Gattanewa and remain at peace with the
Happahs. When Gattanewa asked him for aid in the struggle
against the Happahs, Porter replied that he wanted "to be at
peace with all on the island," whereupon Gattanewa remon-
strated that having exchanged names, Porter should share his hatred of the Happahs because they had cursed the bones of his
mother, who was now Porter's mother. Viewing this rebuke as
mere "sophistry," Porter did not make a direct reply, but made
what he considered a generalized expression of loyalty to the
Teiis, saying that he would aid them against unprovoked Happah attacks. On the next day, a band of Happah warriors de-

stroyed a large number of Teii breadfruit trees without opposition from Porter. After the Teiis compelled them to retreat, the Happahs sent word that they considered Porter a coward, since they had entered Teii territory against Porter's will and he had not fought them. Soon, the Happahs informed him, they would come again and carry off Porter's sails, which he had confidently put ashore.

Porter looked upon this threat as morally wrong, as a violation of the Marquesans' own inherent instinct for virtue. To the missionaries, Marquesan immoralities were a sign of their essential spiritual bondage, to be corrected by spiritual regeneration through the grace of God. Porter, by contrast, believed that God had created a world of workable order, a great machine that could be turned to civilized uses once men understood its design. His application of this view to social relations is visible in his belief that the proper response to moral failure is not preaching, but a wise distribution of rewards and punishments. He determined that the Happahs should be given a course of moral instruction grounded on their aptitude for rational virtue. "The threat of the Happahs had somewhat provoked me," Porter states. "I did not view this people as mere savages, but as intelligent beings, capable of reason, and having proper ideas of right and wrong" (30).

Before using his military force against the Happahs, however, Porter tried to persuade them that opposition would be futile. Finding several Happahs near his camp he took the opportunity to "convince them of the folly of resisting our fire arms with slings and spears," and ordered his marines to show them how effective muskets are by shooting at discarded casks. After this demonstration, Porter drove home his appeal to their intelligence and moral awareness. "I directed them to tell their countrymen that it would only be making a useless sacrifice of their lives; that I had no wish to destroy them, but that my own safety and the security of the friendly tribes, whom I had promised to protect, required that they should be driven from the mountains overhanging the valley, where they had constantly kept their position, daily waving their cloaks to us to come up, and threatening us with their spears and clubs" (32).

Already persuaded that Porter was a coward, the Happahs were completely unimpressed by this display. They had their own views of moral worthiness and warmaking power, and having as yet little experience of Western firearms or Western conceptions of warfare, they felt they had no reason to discontinue threatening and taunting him. Porter soon found that Gattanewa's people were also beginning to view him as a coward and concluded that his whole establishment was in mortal danger. "Indeed," he declares, "it became absolutely necessary to do something" (33).

Porter's attack on the Happahs had results that suggest further elements of the growing discrepancy between his way of viewing the course of events and the Marquesans'. To the Marquesans the battle was an appalling and unprecedented slaughter, because five Happahs were killed. Gattanewa, now reduced to a frantic terror that Porter found amusing, stated that no single skirmish in his recollection had yielded so many dead. Porter's horrific eminence was further amplified because his men stormed a Happah fortification that all the islanders considered impregnable. The battle had been intended by Porter as a limited engagement with limited objectives and had resulted by his lights in a modest amount of bloodshed; but it revealed him as a supernatural destroyer in the eyes of the Marquesans. Porter, accordingly, proceeded to adapt his scheme of ideas so as to make sense of this new situation.

The day after the battle, Porter went to Gattanewa's house to arrange the terms of a peace with the Happahs and found there a large gathering of his allies, the Teiis. "On my appearance there was a general shout of terror; all fixed their eyes on me with looks of fear and apprehension. I approached the wife of Gattanewa, and required to know the cause of this alarm. She said now that we had destroyed the Happahs they were fearful we should turn on them: she took hold of my hand, which she kissed, and moistened with her tears: then placing it on her head, knelt to kiss my feet . . . It seemed that they had worked themselves up to the highest pitch of fear, and on my appearance with a centinel accompanying me, they could see in me nothing but the demon of destruction." Porter's way of describing his response to these gestures indicates that he had come to see himself not merely as an American Navy captain, Enlightened in religion, who is struggling through words and force to appeal to the God-given rationality of the Marquesans. He now assumes a loftier role, approximating that of the Supreme Being. Observe the stately biblical cadence and diction in which he defines the moral structure of his relationship to them. "If the Happahs had drawn on themselves our vengeance, and felt our resentment, they had none to blame but themselves. I had offered them peace; but they had preferred war; I had proffered them my friendship, and they had spurned at it. That there was no alternative left me. I had chastised them, and was appeased" (46).

Porter's language incorporates his judgment that he occupied a position of transcendent force vis-à-vis the Marquesans, but does not imply that he is prepared to use that force arbitrarily. On the contrary, Porter connects his use of force with a rational morality in two distinguishable ways. He claims that it was necessary to his pursuit of rationally defensible goals, in this case the goal of protecting his ship and crew. He further claims that it was "punishment," whose object was to arouse the Happahs to the consciousness of their morally defective position. He "chastised" them to make them realize that they ought to blame themselves for what they had threatened to do to him. In both senses, the use of force is aimed at rational goals that are communicated in words. The act of making war itself is not understood by Porter as a communicative act. It is merely an impersonal measure that reveals nothing new about the agent except the degree of his power and his willingness to "resent" infringements of rational morality. He does not make war to reveal his true self or to disclose his purposes; these are expressed and revealed in what he says. The use of force itself, for Porter, was morally neutral.

The missionaries had shied away from using force because they felt that it would be inconsistent with their essential purposes. Shooting with "carnal weapons" to secure a spiritual conversion would involve a contradiction that might invalidate their whole enterprise, causing the Marquesans to view them in a way that would render impossible the sacred task they wished to perform. For Porter, on the other hand, deadly force was available as part of the system of rewards and punishments that properly used could enhance the moral quality of a community's life. Its justification and its meaning were inherent in the purposes to which it was put.

It is quite apparent, however, that the Marquesans were far more impressed by what Porter had been able to do than by what he had to say about it. Their attention was captured not by the moral lesson Porter wanted to impart, but by the figure of Porter himself. The wife of Gattanewa did not kiss Porter's hand and moisten it with her tears, and then kneel to kiss his feet, because she was impressed by the moral error that the Happahs had made in threatening him. She did it because she viewed Porter as a "demon of destruction."

The Teiis were applying their own interpretive schemes to Porter in ways that we are not in a position to explicate. When Porter says that they saw him as a demon of destruction, he means it in a half-joking deprecatory way, certain that his own action does not sufficiently account for it. He asks Gattanewa's wife why the "general shout of terror" had gone up at his approach and concludes that the Teiis had "worked themselves up to the highest pitch of fear." He recognizes that their dread was something that they had generated on their own, but he does not recognize how deep an investment they had in the way of seeing things that underlay this response. Accordingly he believes that he can dislodge their impression of him as a dangerous god, or a demon of destruction, by making some explanations. Although their innate rationality may have been momentarily disconnected by this outburst of superstitious fear, Porter was confident that they could be restored to their senses.

He takes the occasion to explain a system of rewards and punishments that was meant to safeguard his own legitimate purposes, as well as providing advantages to the Teiis. "So long as they treated us as friends we would protect them against all their enemies; that they and their property should be secure, and that I should inflict the most exemplary punishment on such of my people as should be known to impose on a friendly native; but that should a stone be thrown, or an article stolen from me or my

people, and the offender not be given up to me, I should make
the valley a scene of desolation" (4647).

The relation of "friendship," which Porter here proposes to
the Teiis, quickly developed an additional dimension when he
discovered that they were bringing him "a large supply of hogs,
coconuts, bananas, bread-fruit, tarra [taro], and sugar-cane" (51).
Shortly after his arrival at Nukuheva, Porter had sought to trade
for foodstuffs, with the intention of keeping back his seastock
against the day when he would sail back into the war against the
British. At that time, however, he found the islanders unwilling
to trade and learned that they were recovering from an exceedingly serious drought. Now, however, the islanders were eager to
accept the pieces of iron that Porter had to offer and to give fruit
and hogs in exchange for them. Porter greeted the Happah chieftain on the following day with the proposal that the Happahs be
on the same terms of friendship with him as the Teiis and was
delighted to find the Happahs agreeable. His offer of pieces of
ironwork in return for a weekly provision of hogs and fruit was
accepted not only by the Happahs but by most of the tribes on
the island. "All agreed to the terms proposed," Porter declared;
"supplies were brought in by the tribes in great abundance, and
from this time for several weeks, we rioted in luxuries which the
island afforded. To the principal persons of the tribes I always
presented a harpoon, it being to them the most valuable article of
iron, and to the rest scraps of iron hoops were thrown, for which
they took much delight in contending" (60).

It is hard to contemplate Porter rioting in his luxuries without
a feeling of revulsion. Knowing that the food supply in the Marquesas was always precarious, so that large-scale famine threatened in periods of scarcity, we recognize that his requests put
pressure on an exceedingly sensitive area of the islanders' life.
His evident amusement at the Marquesans tussling over frag-
ments of hoops thus seems to add insult to quite a material injury. If we are tempted to call Porter's actions extortionate, it is
important to recall that his conception of civilization afforded
him a defense. Taking his cue from the initial offerings of the
Teiis, he characteristically terms the goods brought by the other
tribes "gifts" and relates that he gave gifts in return. This impli-

cation of unforced mutuality plays directly into the rhetoric of
"friendship," which is the name Porter gives to the mutually
beneficial side of his relation with the Marquesans. His purpose
as a civilized man in this place was to cultivate such relations, in
which he could stimulate the Marquesans to participate in arrangements that would school them to the nature of civilized life.
In addition to trading with them, Porter conceived himself as
having given them an even greater gift, namely a reign of peace
in the area over which he had influence. He observes that his
promise of protection had caused the ancestral wars of the Marquesans to cease, and reports that the islanders were grateful for
this improvement in their common life.

The true character of the Marquesans' attitude toward Porter
at this stage is very difficult to determine. At its bottom would
appear to lie a generalized alarm at the presence of a demon of
destruction, with the consequent mobilization of cultural resources to conciliate and exploit him. It is likely that in exchanging pigs for ironwork the Teiis and Happahs reached deep into
their symbolic resources in order to find terms on which a workable (or at least safe) relationship with Porter could be carried on.
Roy Rappaport's *Pigs for the Ancestors* recounts the intricate
meanings invested in pigs by a New Guinea society which, unlike the Marquesan, is still available for study; and though comparisons between New Guinea and Marquesan society are haz-
ardous, it would seem probable that a comparable significance
would obtain here as well. From the Marquesan side the exchange of foodstuffs for ironwork could hardly have appeared to
be gifts or trade in Porter's sense, as routines of an undisturbed
commerce. The Marquesans had been shocked quite profoundly
and now called upon central issues of their social existence in
making a response, seeking to get some symbolic and practical
leverage on Porter's otherwise unmanageable presence.

Porter tells us that the Marquesans began to call him "the
hekai" (59), which is the term (*haka-iki*) used for a tribal chieftain;
and since the *haka-iki* laid claim annually to the first breadfruit
crop, it seems possible that Porter's demand for food made some
kind of sense within an established Marquesan scheme of un-
derstandings. Or, since the foodstuffs were contributed by members of various tribes, the Marquesans may have conceived that

he had in mind sponsoring a great feast, of the sort in which customary intertribal hostilities were superseded in a great cooperative effort. It is likewise possible that Porter's giving of ironwork
corresponded roughly to patterns of exchange prevailing among
the Marquesans and may have been initiated by Porter in response to expectations that the islanders themselves communicated. It was customary, moreover, for a tribal *haka-iki* to preside
over a substantial complement of buildings; and Porter without
thinking to ask for it found the Marquesans offering to build a
village for him.[14]

On the fourth day after the battle, "upwards of four thousand
natives, from the different tribes, assembled at the camp with
materials for building, and before night they had completed a
dwelling house for myself and another for the officers, a sail loft,
a coopers' shop, and a place for our sick, a bake house, a guard
house, and a shed for the centinel to walk under." These buildings were fifty feet long and connected by walls four feet high
and twelve feet in length, so that the perimeter of the whole was
roughly five hundred feet. Taking possession on the evening of
the same day, Porter remarked that this delightful village "had
been built as if by enchantment" (66).

When one recalls the agonized months of struggle that the
missionaries endured in order to get their compound built, the
symbolic force of the two occasions becomes apparent. The missionaries intended to wedge their rectilinear compound into the
slovenly wilderness of Marquesan culture. The buildings themselves stood as a challenge to the heathen life all around, and the
struggle that went into their construction is a suitable figure for
the spiritual struggle that the missionaries were prepared to undergo in order to tame the savage heart of the Marquesan. Here,
by contrast, Porter's concept of a smooth continuum of rationality, ethical awareness, and technical skills receives physical embodiment. He takes up residence in buildings that the Marquesans build for him in their own way and after their own design.
He does not force upon them an alien conception of proper
lodging but accepts gladly what they offer as a gift. In Porter's
drawing, accordingly, the village occupies a key position in an
intelligible general environment.

To Porter the savage and the civilized are not antagonistic;

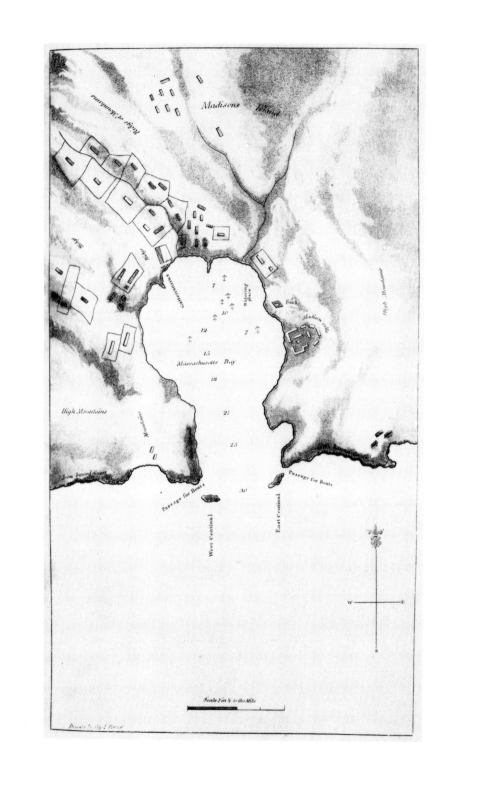

Madisens Island

Ridge of Mountains

High Mountains

Ridge

Ridge

Commissaries

Watering place

7

Fort

Madison ville

10

12

7

15

Massachusetts Bay

18

High Mountains

Mountains

21

25

Iron bound shore

30

Passage for Boats

Passage for Boats

West Centinal

East Centinal

W————E

Scale Fin's to the Mile

Drawn by Wm. I. Power

they are different points on a continuous scale of progress. He does not need to revolutionize their life in order to feel at home among them. On the contrary, he simply needs to make contact with those features of it which promise most strongly a swift advance to the civilized state. For him, the building of the village was preeminent among the considerations that led him to conclude that the Marquesans should be adopted as junior members of the great American family. It seemed a triumphant vindication of his vision of America as a civilization, and of himself as a civilizer who had made friends with gifted and promising children of nature.

Accordingly, Porter organized a ceremony of possession-taking, solemnly formalizing the relationship between the civilization that he represented and the Marquesans. He named the village "Madison Ville," and Nukuheva he named "Madison's Island." For the ceremony he ordered a salute of seventeen guns; then he read and signed a "declaration of the act of taking possession" and ordered one copy of it to be buried in a bottle. Porter takes care to point out that the purpose of this ceremony was explained more than once to the Marquesans themselves; he reports that they were very pleased to become "melleekees," and that they wanted to know whether their new chief, President Madison, was as great a man as Gattanewa (82). Yet when the Americans departed, Madison Ville was so completely demolished by the Marquesans that three months later nothing remained except a stone wall Porter had compelled his British prisoners to construct. The actions taken to conciliate a demon of destruction only prepare for the effort to eradicate every evidence of his power once that power has itself disappeared; and it was indeed customary, within the Marquesan understanding of the haka-iki as tribal chieftain, to signal his defeat by razing the buildings that were an emblem of his eminence. As for Porter's "Declaration," the Marquesans did not even bother to dig up the bottle; that was left for the British, who understood the civilized way of removing a spiritual contamination.[15]

For now, however, Porter was not aware of the structural shortcomings of the arrangement he had set up; his interpretation of it was consistent and in his eyes entirely reasonable. His effort to refit the ship, and to learn more about the customs of the Marquesans, now went on "with order and regularity" (70).

Before Porter formally took possession, he constructed a fort on a promontory that commanded the plain where Madison Ville stood, as well as overlooking Taiohae Bay. Porter's reason for building this fort and equipping it with cannon was not merely to control the harbor; he was also aware that Madison Ville might need protection against the Marquesans. Porter's vision of Marquesan character may have been excessively admiring, but he was not so deluded as to believe that the arrangement achieved through force could long be maintained without it. He pictures himself as a friend of the Marquesans, as a bringer of peace. But he was also aware of the military control he had attained, and of the fact that what he styled friendship was dependent upon his superior force. To conclude, on the other hand, that Porter's notion of friendship was a rhetorical pose intended to conceal the reality of despotic control would be to misread the situation.

To Porter the use of force and the relation of friendship were two sides of the same reality, the nature of man's innate morality. Motivated by rewards and punishments, man's rational nature could be led to improve itself if friendly guidance was supplied. Since rational morality is everywhere the same, Porter believed that his way of viewing the proceedings at Nukuheva were identical with the way the Marquesans perceived it in their moments of heightened insight.

After all, he had come asking only to be left alone so as to refit his ships. When this enterprise was threatened, he exercised the essential human right of self-defense. After the battle with the Happahs he had dealt mercifully with all parties, had not taken a single hog or piece of fruit that was not gladly proffered, and had given gifts in return. The resulting arrangement deserved the name of "friendship" since it was beneficial to all parties and was grounded, so Porter believed, upon the mutual recognition of a shared interest.

This pattern of ideas was coextensive in Porter's mind with the events that had taken place and the arrangement they had produced. He did not perceive any tension between his role as the man of war and his role as a friend of the Marquesans. When the inherent shortcomings of this system began to have practical effects, therefore, Porter perceived them as "disruptions," as irregularities instigated from outside the system. Porter noticed rather soon that one of the friendly tribes "had not been so punctual as the other tribes in sending in his supplies" (70), and he further noticed that other tribes were slackening as well. Upon investigation, Porter discovered that the supply trains had been harassed by the Typees.

The Typees were at this time the most powerful tribe on the island, inhabiting the most favorably situated of the valleys. In the age-old conflicts among the tribes of Nukuheva, the Typees had achieved an ascendance that made them unfriendly to the incursions of whites. The relatively weaker Teiis were more hospitable because they hoped to strengthen their position with Western assistance. But the white man's boats stayed clear of the bay that the Typees controlled, even though it was larger and better protected than Taiohae Bay. After spending several weeks at Nukuheva, however, Porter found it suitable to look upon the Typees as outsiders. He did not perceive himself as having intruded into a long-standing power arrangement, but as having set up a domain of order and peace which had every right to exist without annoyance from those who had not chosen to join in it.

Accordingly, Porter dispatched a messenger to the Typees to threaten them with "punishment" if they annoyed his allies further. His message employs the language I have analyzed, in which force and friendship are united in an appeal to rational morality. Porter stated that "we were strongly disposed to be at peace with all the tribes on the island; that this disposition did not proceed from fear, as I had strength enough to drive their united forces into the sea; but if they were disposed to be at peace, I was willing to meet them on the same terms as the other tribes, and only required an exchange of presents as a proof of their friendly disposition" (72).

The reply of the Typees, as Porter styles it, drives a wedge between the two sides of Porter's vision of his role, separating the language of friendship from the power relation to which in his mind it was rightfully joined. "They desired to know why they should desire a friendship with us? why they should bring us hogs and fruit? that if I was strong enough they knew I would come and take them; and that my not doing so was an acknowledgment of my weakness" (72). Trying to appeal further to the Typees' rationality, Porter reminds them of his victory over the Happahs; but the Typees redouble their defiance. "We had beat the Happahs," the Typees tell Porter, "because the Happahs were cowards; that as to myself and my people, we were white lizards, mere dirt; and as the most contemptible epithet which they could apply, said we were the posteriors and the privates of the Teiis" (73). Porter thus depicts the Typees as taking a position outside the domain of reasonable discourse. Their failure to recognize that his friendship is an authentic boon leads them to mistake it for armed robbery. The Typees' denunciation of Porter's benevolence only prepares for the outburst of irrational vilification to which they are reduced when Porter tries to bring them to reason. Instead of displaying a childlike rationality, the Typees confront Porter with savage obscenity.

Porter had claimed that the Marquesans were not savages, yet in describing his relations with the Typees he uses terms that suggest they had an intolerable contempt for civilized dealings. He presents the Typees as embodying a line of opposition to the conceptual structure he was using to construe his experience of the Marquesans, and his comments bespeak a disgust reminiscent of the missionaries. Porter's children of nature thus sometimes reveal savage features, especially where the Typee menace is concerned. Not only did their action tend to undermine his view of things; it also appeared to pose a serious threat to the practical arrangement he had set up. Porter was afraid of a coalition of the tribes and doubted that he could resist one. He had no reason to make war on the Typees, in fact, apart from his fear that they might trigger a chain reaction of defiance that could lead to an attack on his camp by the united tribes. As he temporized with the Typees, hoping to avoid a struggle, his relations with the Teiis became more and more ticklish. Porter's nervous awareness of his increasingly insecure position is revealed by his response to Mouina, the military leader of the Teiis, who took "rather a peremptory tone" in demanding immediate hostilities against the Typees and called Porter "a great coward." Enraged,

Drwn. by Capt. Porter   *Engraved by C. Goodman*

Mouina.
Chief Warrior of the Tayehs.

Porter thrust a musket into Mouina's face and threatened to kill him on the spot if he didn't apologize. In explaining this outburst Porter reveals the nature of his worry about the Typees. "My aim was to render all the tribes subservient to my views, and I thought it necessary to check the manner of Mouina, lest it might become contagious, and I should find a difficulty in keeping them in that subjugation by which only we could render ourselves secure" (73).

Porter's situation became even more precarious after he made an attack that the Typees successfully repulsed. Sailing into the Typees' bay, Porter fought his way up their valley under a punishing shower of spears and slingstones, only to be halted and pinned down before a stone breastwork that the Typees had erected across the path. Aware that the battle was being watched by members of the other tribes, Porter extricated himself from the trap by executing a feigned retreat that drew the Typees from behind their cover, where his men succeeded in killing two and wounding several others. In the ensuing confusion Porter made good his retreat in earnest and arrived on the beach to discover that the friendly tribes were descending from their points of vantage in the hills all abuzz with the observation that "the Typees have driven the white men" (96).

Porter met this situation with notable address. "Assuming the air and language of a conqueror (although I must confess I felt little like one) I directed one of the ambassadors to proceed to the Typee fort to tell them that with a handful of men we had driven them into their fortifications, that we had killed two and wounded several of them, and had now a force sufficient to drive them out of the valley; that I did not wish to do them further injury, and still offered them the terms I had first proposed" (96). Porter's effort to strike the pose of a conqueror was intended to maintain his credit in the eyes of the friendly tribes as much as to sound out the feelings of the Typees. When the Typees replied in terms that revealed they had not been intimidated, Porter's anxieties increased once again; so he promptly set sail for Taiohae Bay with the belief that a decisive blow would have to be struck against the Typees without delay.

The language in which Porter frames the Typees' reply reveals an element in his way of viewing them that becomes increasingly

problematical as his account of the subsequent hostilities unfolds. It is apparent that Porter was genuinely impressed by the
Typees' skill at assessing their military powers and his own.

It was true, they said, we had killed two of them, and wounded many
others; but considering their superior numbers, what was this compared to the injury they had done us. They had men to spare, we had
not. If we were able to drive them from their valley, what could I
promise myself by telling them of it. I must know they would not
believe me until I had done it. They said they had counted our boats;
they knew the number that each would carry, and were as well acquainted with my force as myself. They knew their strength and the
numbers they could oppose; and held our bouhies [muskets] in more
contempt than ever, they frequently missed fire, rarely killed, and
the wounds they occasioned were not as painful as those of a spear
or a stone; and, they added, they knew they would prove perfectly
useless to us should it come on to rain. They dared us to renew the
contest; and assured us they would not retreat beyond where we
had left them. (96)

Porter's way of describing his war on the Typees thrusts the
two sides of his vision into contradiction, revealing the weakness
of the premise on which they were unified. Porter's dealings with
the Marquesans are meant to stimulate their rational and moral
capabilities by rewarding displays of virtue and punishing vice.
But as Porter recognizes the intelligence of the Typees, he moves
into an awkward new position, from which the qualities that
should fit the Marquesan for the advance to civilized status at the
same time make him dangerous to the agent of civilization in
their midst.

This contradiction becomes even more apparent as Porter describes the communal achievements of the Typees, from the
vantage point of a ridge from which he mounted his second attack against them. "Villages were scattered here and there, the
bread-fruit and coconut trees flourished luxuriantly and in
abundance; plantations laid out in good order, enclosed with
stone walls, were in a high state of cultivation, and every thing
bespoke industry, abundance, and happiness" (102). When he
had fought his way to the farther end of the Typees' valley, he
came to the fortification that had checked him on his first attack

and, on inspecting it, concludes it would have permitted the Typees to resist him indefinitely had he attacked again from that direction. After finding that his men cannot throw down the massive stonework, he leaves it "as a monument to future generations of . . . [the Typees'] skill and industry" (107).

Porter's conception of the relation between himself as civilized man and the Marquesan aspirants to civilization controls the description of his march of destruction through the Typees' valley. He insists upon viewing the march as a punishment; yet his way of framing the matter points at an uneasiness that bespeaks the contradiction we have noted. "Never in my life did I witness a more delightful scene, or experience more repugnancy than I now felt for the necessity which compelled me to punish a happy and heroic people" (102). Porter found himself in the awkward position of destroying what was most promising in the cultural achievements of the Marquesans in order to stimulate them to higher achievements. Porter's logic had reached a pitiful inanity to which American policy returned in Vietnam; it had become necessary to devastate the Typees in order to civilize them. Trapped in the processes of his own reasoning, Porter gives a series of descriptions that contain this wretched paradox. We "met in our way several beautiful villages, which were set on fire and at length arrived at their capital, for it deserved the name of one. We had been compelled to fight every inch of ground, as we advanced, and here they made considerable opposition; the place was, however, soon carried, and I very reluctantly set fire to it. The beauty and regularity of this place was such, as to strike every spectator with astonishment, and their grand site, or public square, was far superior to any other we had met with; numbers of their gods were here destroyed" (105).

Porter does not recognize that he is engaged in an action that exposes the contradictions inherent in his conception of civilization; instead, he interprets the repugnancy that he felt as further evidence of his cultural superiority. Porter insists that the success of his venture gave him no personal satisfaction; on the contrary, he was performing a duty in which personal feelings had to be sacrificed to higher purposes. The sorrow he feels at this necessity is part of the burden that the civilizer must bear. The Teiis and the other "friendly" tribes, by contrast, are filled with glee at the destruction of Typee Valley and thus all the more reveal the relative humanity of Porter's own spirit.

Porter gives a second panoramic view of the valley after he had wasted it, which drives home this threefold distinction between himself, the admirable forlorn Typees, and their unseemly Marquesan brethren. "When I had reached the summit of the mountains, I stopped to contemplate that valley which, in the morning, we had viewed in all its beauty, the scene of abundance and happiness—a long line of smoking ruins now marked our traces from one end to the other; the opposite hills were covered with the unhappy fugitives, and the whole presented a scene of desolation and horror. Unhappy and heroic people! the victims of your own courage and mistaken pride, while the instruments of your own fate, shed the tears of pity over your misfortunes, thousands of your countrymen (nay, brethren of the same family) triumphed in your distresses!" (108). Between Porter and the triumphant tribes there is the moral gulf defined by the distance between his tears of pity and their shouts of pleasure; the distance between Porter and the Typees is contained in the single word "mistaken." They had believed they could defeat him, and were mistaken; their fault lay in tactical intelligence, so far as Porter could see, a shortcoming of strong but undeveloped rationality.

Porter's moral calculus is invalidated by his description of the way he pursued it, as its inherent error generates a series of contradictions and ironies. Viewing himself as a civilizer who uses the arts of civilized life to perfect the qualities of intellectual and moral virtue with which nature has endowed the Marquesan, Porter finds himself destroying the highest evidences of those qualities. He now ranks his opponents, the luckless Typees, higher in the scale of social achievement than the tribes that had accepted his friendship. Most profound among Porter's misconceptions was his confidence that the moral system he employed could reduce the use of force to a neutral implement of his purposes. Burning down a series of buildings and religious statues did not appear to Porter as a communicative act, revealing something of the essence of his relationship to the Marquesans. On the contrary, he felt that the nature of this relationship was contained in what he said about it. The difficulty he experienced in working the situation into his moral system did not trouble Porter for long, since he found it possible to include his misgivings among the evidences for his own virtue. Herman Melville, in commenting on Porter's march, provides an instructive contrast. Echoing Porter's language, Melville observes that "long line of smoking ruins defaced the once-smiling bosom of the valley, and proclaimed to its pagan inhabitants the spirit that reigned in the breasts of Christian soldiers."[16] In Melville's recasting of the incident the ruined valley itself reveals the interior of Porter's soul, speaking louder than his explanations.

Devastating the Typees did not increase Porter's anxieties about flaws in his system of understanding; it obliterated them. He had succeeded in destroying the anomalous element, reducing it to a position where it need no longer be feared. The threat of the Typees, originating outside the scheme of civilized order he had established, had now been swallowed up in the supreme civilized achievement: Porter had extended the realm of peace and friendship to include the entire island. He soon found himself so abundantly supplied with hogs that he regretted not having salt available to cure the meat for use at sea after his departure, so he directed that the hogs be marked in order to have them reserved for him in case he needed to return to Nukuheva at a later time.

The friendship that produced this abundance of supplies was less momentous in Porter's eyes than the renovation he had effected in the intertribal relations of the Marquesans. Porter was convinced that he had secured to his Marquesan friends the gift of peace, enabling them to transcend the wasteful conflicts in which they had engaged before.

Peace now being established throughout the island, and the utmost harmony reigning, not only between us and the Indians, but between the different tribes, they mixed with one another about our village in the most friendly manner, and the different chiefs with the priests came daily to visit me. They were all much delighted that a general peace had been brought about, that they might now all visit the different parts of the island in safety; and many of the oldest men assured me that they had never before been out of the valley in which they were born. They repeatedly expressed their astonishment and

Drawn by Capt. Pierce.   Engraved by W. Strickland

Windimerville in Massachusetts bay — Essex & her Prize.

admiration that I should have . . . been able to extend my influence
so far as to give them such complete protection, not only in the valley of Tieuhoy [of the Teiis], but among the tribes with which they
had been at war from the earliest periods, and had heretofore been
considered their natural enemies. (110)

A man who has deceived himself will deceive others, sometimes with a tentative awareness that he is doing so. The exact
degree of conscious cynicism we should ascribe to Porter, as he
makes his moral claims, cannot be determined for certain. Yet
we can be sure that he himself believed in what he was saying to
quite a considerable extent. He does not tell his readers that the
Marquesans were enthusiastic about the establishment of peace
with the personal belief that they resented it; nor does he describe his relations with the Marquesans as friendly with the
conviction that they hated him. To some degree he may have had
internal misgivings as to the validity of these claims, misgivings
he may have chosen to suppress in order to give an impression of
more certitude than he felt. Yet it is evident that he felt he had
grounds for the claim that emerges consistently and centrally
from his entire account—that he had read Marquesan character
correctly and had founded upon that reading a way of dealing
with them that had created a morally admirable and reasonably
stable system of relations. He had constructed a social order that
reflected his conception of the relationship between a civilized
man and a Polynesian native; while he had used force to construct this order, he believed that it was more than a mere subjugation and that its moral qualities would aid in sustaining it. Porter's confidence in the premises of his action was reinforced, as
we have seen, by the outcome of the battle against the Typees,
and it is given further testimony by the fact that two weeks later
he sailed away from Nukuheva leaving a small party behind to
care for the management of things.

He ordered Lieutenant Gamble, whom he left in command, to
remain for five months and then to depart if he himself did not
return. But Porter was hardly out of sight when the system of
order he had constructed began to disintegrate in ways he had
not expected. Gamble actually succeeded in hanging on for the
specified five months and survived to report to Porter on the general collapse. If he had not survived we would lack some instruc-

tive evidence concerning Porter's systematic blindness, because Porter himself wrote up the account of Gamble's experience in the tones of a man who hardly knows what to make of what happened.

Porter notes that the Marquesans soon began to steal the pigs he had marked as his own, and that they appeared to show no shame at doing so. "One of them, in the afternoon, even within sight of the encampment, ventured to carry away a pig. What were their real motives for this strange conduct, it is hard to conceive. Lieutenant Gamble had used every effort within his power to conciliate their esteem, and given them the strongest assurances, that he would pay for the coconuts, bananas, and everything else he received from them."[17] Porter's amazement at this behavior emerges from his confidence in the reciprocal justice of the trade relations he had set up with the Marquesans, and in their understanding of that justice. The theft of a pig in broad daylight implied not merely that the thief himself was indifferent to the moral requirements of the situation, but that the Marquesans in general cared nothing for them. Porter might have understood how a single Marquesan could fail to obey the laws of conduct that he considered universal, but it did not seem possible to him that the community at large could be so obtuse. Like the missionaries, Porter finds himself startled by the Marquesans' lack of shame, their failure to give emotional acknowledgment to the moral scheme he believed applicable to them. He supposes, accordingly, that this theft was a calculated act whose motives were obscure to him.

One of Porter's deeper premises was surprised when several of the men left under Gamble's command decided to make their home among the Marquesans. "It could scarcely be credited at first," Porter remarks, "that men, even of the lowest order in society, surrounded by savages, and without the possibility of reaching a civilized part of the world, in an open boat, could seriously think of deserting. But on a nearer investigation of the matter, such was found to be actually the case."[18] Porter's admiration for the Marquesans was held firmly within his certainty that they occupied a place far down the scale of societies from his own. His protest that they are not savages was not consistently maintained and was made in the confident expectation that

Western readers would assume that they were. He cannot understand that life among the Marquesans might look more ap-
pealing to an American than continued service in the United
States Navy.

Porter's actions in the Marquesas become virtually meaning-
less if the Marquesans are not equipped to recognize the moral
superiority of civilized life, since it is pointless to embody virtue
for the sake of people who cannot discern it. Yet if there are
Americans who do not see that Porter's society is superior to
Marquesan society, then the premise is subjected to an even
greater doubt. It is bad enough when the city on the hill is not
recognized as a superior form of life by a savage dwelling in the
circumambient darkness; but if a member of the superior culture
defects, then there is even greater reason for bewilderment and
alarm.

The deepest of Porter's miscalculations in fact concerns a
white man who had "gone native," a Britisher by birth named
Wilson who had been on the island for ten years, was well acquainted with Marquesan customs, and spoke the language
fluently. Porter had at first been shocked by the spectacle of a
white man covered by tattoos, but soon concluded that he was
"an inoffensive, honest, good-hearted fellow, well disposed to
render every service in his power . . . He became indispensably
necessary to us; and without his aid I should have succeeded
badly on the island." At the outset of his narration, Porter emphasizes the critical role that Wilson played in all his dealings.
"His knowledge of the people, and the ease with which he spoke
their language, removed all difficulties in our intercourse with
them; and it must be understood, in all relations of future inter-
views and conversations, which took place between me and the
natives, that Wilson is the organ of communication, and the
means by which we are enabled to understand each other: I shall,
therefore, in future, deem it unnecessary to say, I was assisted by
an interpreter; it must always be understood that I had one"
(20–21).

Wilson continued to act as an interpreter for Gamble, but as
early as the difficulties over the pigs Gamble began to suspect
that the Marquesans were receiving information he did not want
them to have. "Some villain had spread a report among the na-

tives, that the effective force of the whites amounted to only twenty men, and this, in a great degree, accounted for their rapacity and insolence." But it was not until four months later that Gamble began to believe that the malefactor might be Wilson.[19] Moving behind the protection of Gamble's faith in him, Wilson played a central role in the collapse of Gamble's command. He coordinated the Marquesans and the growing number of deserters to mount an attack on Gamble's force, and nearly succeeded in destroying it outright. As Gamble, badly wounded, sailed his undermanned and leaking vessel out of Taiohae Bay, Wilson was feverishly trying to work the guns that Porter had mounted at Fort Madison.

This demonstration of Wilson's readiness to act against Porter's interests leaves us with an unanswerable question. We cannot tell to what extent he may have influenced Porter's judgments along the whole line of his dealings with the Marquesans. To what extent, one wonders, might Wilson actively have sponsored the fight between Porter and the Typees? By Porter's own admission, Wilson acted as an interpreter at every stage of his dealings with the Marquesans; he was a filter through which all the verbal communications between them passed.

Wilson thus takes on a figurative significance for this study, the emblem of a process that would have taken place if he had not been there at all. Porter's experience of the Marquesans, as it came to him moment by moment, was structured in part by an interpretive scheme of whose operations he was not aware. Just as the trusted Wilson made a series of representations concerning the Marquesans which Porter accepted at face value, so also did Porter's conception of civilization and the correlative idea of savagery. The idea of civilization that Porter brought with him to the Marquesas was not merely a more or less accurate description of a social arrangement; it was a frame of mind. The concepts of rational morality, of rewards and punishments, of the scale of societies were elements of an organization of consciousness that minutely structured Porter's encounter with the Marquesans.

Wilson serves us as a figure for certain problematical features of this aspect of Porter's situation, as of the situation in which the missionaries were placed. His role in Porter's story indicates that the application of interpretive schemes to practical occasions may bring about circumstances that embody the unsuspected anomalies those schemes carry within them. The civilizers we have examined encountered situations that tended to undermine the systems of interpretation they were using. Self-conscious representatives of America as a city set on a hill, they faced circumstances suggesting that America was one of many cities on an uncertain landscape. As Wilson trains Porter's cannon on Porter's lieutenant, he emerges as a symbol of an irony at the center of the transaction between "civilized" men and "savages" in the nineteenth century; a circumstance in which the force of a practical model of social reality is turned against itself.

More frequently, to be sure, the guns are pointed in the other direction. As in the case of Porter's raid on the Typees, Western warmaking power usually served to eliminate the causes of hesitation: the doubts of civilized men washed away in the blood of savages. But this little scenario, however exceptional, is nonetheless instructive. It recalls the uncanny retributions of classic drama, in which the hero is confounded by a nemesis that strikes right through a perceptual blindspot inherent in his character, the gods making mad whom they plan to destroy. Instead of ascribing such occasions to supernatural intervention, or pretending that they don't take place, we are led to consider whether such an ironic fate is not formed by the individual (or nation) it appears to befall.

5 | Heart of Darkness

A CONTINUOUS INTERPRETIVE activity is essential to human life, as necessary and automatic as breathing. Lacking the minutely controlled instinctual patterns of animals, human beings guide action in accordance with information about the world that is not genetically transmitted but is itself a human creation. Clifford Geertz has argued that human culture is a symbolically encoded system of meanings that permits coherent action by rendering experience intelligible. It supplies programs that bridge the gap between the diffuseness of humankind's genetic imperatives and the specificity of the worldly tasks that we must perform in order to exist. "Undirected by culture patterns," Geertz observes, "man's behavior would be virtually ungovernable, a mere chaos of pointless acts and exploding emotions, his experience virtually shapeless."[1]

What we think of as "experience" is hence essentially noetic. It is not an assortment of raw data but a stream of happenings that become available to thought as they are processed by an interpretive activity which filters and selects them, which places a meaning upon them before we consciously begin to ask what they mean. Our experience is charged with meaning: what we seem to know firsthand as "the world" is in actuality a representation or portrait determined by the interpretive process that always intervenes between consciousness and the sensory interaction we have with our surroundings. We lead our conscious lives upon internal and outward landscapes whose contours receive definition from the system of meanings that we use to find our path across them.

As experience is noetic, so perception is constructive. The mind is not a passive *tabula rasa*, receiving the impress of facts that have inherent connections with each other as they stand ontologically immaculate as constituents of reality. It has an active and creative engagement with its materials, always to a degree forming the reality it perceives. The facts it deals with have an implicitly symbolic character, since they bear upon the conceptions according to which the world is being interpreted.

Kai Erikson has observed this in commenting on the social interactions through which a society formally identifies its deviant members. He points out that a courtroom procedure is one in which a high degree of symbolic significance is attached to carefully selected bits of behavior drawn from a life pattern that is preponderantly conventional.[2] The acts defining "the murderer" are only a tiny fraction of the total activity of his life, and yet they are made to give him an identity. Killing another person, if it takes place in circumstances that make it forbidden and when it is duly ascertained by the institution suitable to do so, affixes to the individual a socially recognized definition of what he is in himself, and how others should stand in relation to him. People who find themselves in the role of "murderer" may remark on the ironical disproportion between the symbolic value placed on these behaviors by society and the amount of space they occupy in the individual life. Yet that process of definition is awesomely powerful, inasmuch as the legal and ethical conceptions embodied by it are inherent in the responses that our culture trains into us, responses that are consummated in the ritual of the courtroom but that also act outside such formal settings as a pervasive condition of experience. Failing to condemn a murderer threatens not merely the public peace but also the coherence of our mental lives. The mild panic that spreads in a community when a murderer remains at large—or the mild nausea that is felt when a wealthy murderer obtains a verdict of innocence—reflects very little a concern for our physical safety; it bespeaks instead the restless need to reassert our bearings amid the social reality through which we move.

The interpretive systems that are brought to bear in cases of murder are programmed by the values, well established in our culture, by which we condemn it. There is a connection, that is to say, between the cultural traditions that give us pictures of reality and the ongoing process of navigation by which we make our way through daily happenings. If we believe that life (like liberty and the pursuit of happiness) is an inherent right, independent of any grant or ascription by another, then we will determine the real nature of what takes place around us in light of that belief. Living cultural traditions are thus working principles of thought and action, which are built into the interpretive process that relates man to the world.

The concept of civilization had such a role in the minds of Americans in the early nineteenth century; it was an axiom not merely of thinking and debate but of being-in-the-world. Before the latter half of the eighteenth century, Americans generally did not think of themselves as standing upon a level of human development that had emerged from a series of lower levels in the past. But the belief swiftly gained adherents because it incorporated a habit of thinking in hierarchical terms that had deep roots in occidental antiquity and strong representation in the centuries before the idea of civilization was itself born. Hellenistic and medieval schemes of thought that envisioned the entire universe as an hierarchical structure reaching from God downward were absorbed during the Renaissance into the idea of the "great chain of being." "There is in this Universe a Stair," said Sir Thomas Browne, "or manifest Scale of creatures, rising not disorderly, or in confusion, but with comely method and proportion."[3]

This general conception of a scale of creatures was given an extended application in the seventeenth century as Europeans through exploration and trade began to have increased contact with non-European peoples. In particular, the human segment of the universal scale was differentiated into levels that assigned certain humans, such as African pigmies, a position close to the animals while others were located in ranks approaching the angels.[4]

In the late eighteenth and early nineteenth centuries the static scale of human states was transformed by its merger with a doc-

trine of even greater traditional depth, that of the historical
drama in which the God of the Bible was working out a redemption for his chosen. Ernest Lee Tuveson has shown that biblical
teaching about God's activity in human affairs lay at the heart of
a Western mode of thinking in which the notion of significant
temporal development was innate. He has traced the course of
this historical consciousness in Christian doctrines of the millennium, where the present condition is seen as preliminary to a
grand transformation in the future, and he has further traced the
gradual integration of this optimistic view with conceptions of
natural law in the early eighteenth century that made such an advancement in the human condition seem inevitable.[5] In the late
eighteenth century these two traditions, of millennialist improvement and the chain of being, coalesced in a vision of historical
advance through graded steps of progress, a dynamic process of
development from the rude to the refined, the backward to the
advanced, the savage to the civilized.

This powerful and exciting new idea was distinctively summarized in the term "civilization." An evidence of the fundamental shift in perspective that took place during this time is
Boswell's amused report that Dr. Johnson refused to admit the
word "civilization" into his dictionary, insisting that the correct
term for expressing the opposite of "barbarity" is "civility," sig-
nifying urbane refinement.[6] "To civilize" had originally been a
legal term, denoting the transfer of jurisdiction over a case from
a criminal to a civil court, and it also had uses suggesting the ac-
quisition of learning and superior manners. But the new substantive, with the "ization" at its conclusion suggesting a
forward-driving historical process, was at that time a glamorous
neologism. Yet as the new way of thinking came to dominate the
consciousness of Westerners during this period, the neologism
became a commonplace. Swiftly disappearing as a subject of debate, the idea of civilization became the common ground upon
which debates were carried out. We have encountered proponents of its major versions: orthodox Christians (like Charles
Stewart) held that civilization took place through dramatic encounters where God's power overwhelmed the agents of darkness; spokesmen for the Enlightenment (like David Porter)
anticipated a smooth evolutionary development, as the increase

of knowledge and the improvement of social institutions permitted a fuller flowering of human virtue.[7]

Americans in the postrevolutionary period had powerful motives for using this term to interpret the historical circumstance in which they found themselves. Without probing the inner anxieties it embodies, Rush Welter has abundantly documented the chorus of American voices proclaiming that America was the climax of human history, fulfilling a destiny for all mankind that had been working its way to fruition for centuries and centuries past.[8] European culture and society, rich with the august and compelling symbols of an ancestral home, could be thus simultaneously retained and repudiated as a domain whose implicit promise was to be fulfilled in the American order of things, even as its shortcomings were decisively transcended. The concept of civilization gave substance and authority to this progressivist view and reinforced American self-confidence: if history were an upward passage along a stairway of social states, then America was arguably the next step for the human race. Instead of representing a temporary aberration in British colonial politics, the American venture could be looked upon as the advance guard of the caravan of history.

The idea of civilization also afforded a way of coming to terms with the gigantic American continent and with the varied social circumstances amid which human beings led their lives upon it. Looking out across the American territory toward the end of his life, Thomas Jefferson saw it as a vast chart upon which the stages of the civilizing process were represented.

Let a philosophic observer commence a journey from the savages of the Rocky Mountains, eastwardly towards our seacoast. These he would observe in the earliest stages of association living under no law but that of nature, subsisting and covering themselves with the flesh and skins of wild beasts. He would next find those on our frontiers in the pastoral state, raising domestic animals to supply the defects of hunting. Then succeed our semi-barbarous citizens, the pioneers of the advance of civilization, and so in his progress he would meet the gradual shades of improving man until he would reach his, as yet, most improved state in our seaport towns. This, in fact, is equivalent to a survey, in time, of the progress of man from the infancy of creation to the present day.[9]

In 1854 Representative John Perkins, Jr., of Louisiana likewise fixed his eye upon the continent as a whole and remarked upon the rapid advance of the Pacific states to a level of civilization equal to that in the East. "The grandest spectacle of the age is the gradual growth of the colonies along the Pacific Coast into free and independent States, received into this Union on an equality with those on the Atlantic. On looking back a little more than a century, to the first feeble settlements on our eastern shore, and then, from the standpoint of our present national greatness, forward into the future, at the spread of civilizaton and art, and the growth of towns, cities, and commerce, along our western shore, the mind is by turns awed and dazzled by the vision."[10] Perkins' somewhat jumbled syntax reveals that the concept of civilization could be made to work several ways at once to sort out geographical and temporal relations. Here "civilization" is something that has "spread" from the East to the West; yet it also apparently has taken place over time within the East and the West. Conceding that his mind is "awed and dazzled" Perkins gives us a statement that lacks the precision of Jefferson's, even as it omits mention of savagery altogether. The question of what to make of white dominion in North America is still a matter of confused debate, and a mind like Perkins', acting in accordance with great commonplaces, reached out instinctively to the notion of civilization in trying to make sense of it.

We have noted too that in the mid-thirties Charles Stewart explained social and political developments in Polynesia to the American public by means of a similar gradient of social states, differentiated by the degree to which the grace of God had been at work on the savagery of the islanders. Here, as with Jefferson, the image of a presumptive course of history becomes an image of the present moment: the historical scale embracing the "gradual shades of improving man" provides a set of meridians upon the map of an actual territory. Instead of a *terra incognita*, the land beyond the frontier—whether in North America or Polynesia—becomes pregnant with the possibilities whose realization is already visible elsewhere.

A mission compound or an American camp in the Marquesan environment made sense as an "outpost of civilization" because it completed the hierarchy. Representing the top of a scale on which the savage condition also stands, it creates a dynamic tension with its surroundings, exerting a pull in the direction of progress. Like a magnet brought to iron filings, it draws the environment into a prospective and yet visible order based on inherent properties that cannot be detected when the magnet is not there.

Providing images of America's relationship to the world, and of American actions in the Marquesas, the concept of civilization also provided Americans with images of their inner lives. The Renaissance antecedent of this temporalized stairway of spiritual levels taught that individual personality was structured as a microcosm of the grand hierarchy of the universe, so that individuals were called upon to struggle against parts of themselves that were beastly and to cultivate their higher faculties. The notion of civilization, in turn, sponsored a civilized self, which existed by virtue of its capacity to make the improved form of humanity prevail over the unimproved. Thomas L. McKenney, a leader in the formation of American policy toward the Indians, stressed the unwelcome moral effort required of the individual by civilized standards of behavior. "It is not in the nature of man," he affirmed, to give up "all the freedom" the Indian had enjoyed before the coming of the white man, so that he cannot be expected to "place himself, voluntarily, under the restraints which civilization imposes." In the absence of an internal character structure capable of undertaking the required discipline, the Indian can only be compelled "to endure the labor and toil that attend upon the civilized state" through the "stern law" of necessity.[11]

The city on the hill thus becomes also an image of interior striving, as the civilized person assigns ruling authority to parts of himself and requires them to subdue and transform other parts. As applied to psychological experience, the notion of civilization makes inner conflict intelligible as a program of personal growth and improvement whose objective is to become a civilized person. When he argued in *Civilization and Its Discontents* that internal disharmony was inseparable from the civilized condition, Freud recapitulated what moral teachers in the West had been insisting all along. The civilized self, as an organization of moral consciousness, exists by virtue of its triumph over antagonists that are primitive, primal, archaic, infantile, savage.[12]

There will always be savages, accordingly, so long as there are civilized men. The idea of the savage is not an invention of the civilized self, but a feature of it. It is the polar construct that gives the qualities of civilization visibility and sharpness. The Marquesans were seen by their American visitors as earlier forms of what the Americans themselves represented. In the upward progressive movement they represented a level beneath the white man and were deemed appropriate targets for cultivation and improvement. But they also represented those qualities that the white men felt obliged to fight against in themselves in order to maintain their own civilized identity.

A conception of the world provides a template by which selves are formed in a process that is never completed; self-definition is not a deposit laid down in childhood or a triumph of maturation. Nor can a society stand still upon an unchanging image of its life. Individuals and groups find themselves confronted by changing circumstances and (more profoundly) find that their apprehension of the values they take to be central somehow periodically goes stale in the absence of challenge and tangible reenactment. Insofar as Americans understood themselves to be civilized, they welcomed—and indeed required—confrontations with "the savage" in order to give substance to the principles of their own moral constitution.

It is now well understood that ritual has the function of preserving and reanimating values. The studies of Victor Turner, like others, have demonstrated connections between the features of a ritual observance and the webwork of symbolic meanings present in the society at large. Yet Turner has also pressed beyond ritual to describe social dramas of a less formal kind where transactions of meaning give a specific occurrence symbolic value that transcends the occasion itself. Such dramas take place, Turner observes, when the regular rhythms of communal life are interrupted by conflicts that cannot be resolved by established procedures. In the situation of crisis brought about by such a breaching of routine, patterns of loyalty and conviction that are hidden from view in the normal course of things suddenly become apparent. As the mask of formal order drops away, disturbing hidden realities find expression as they may, in symbolic role-taking and symbolic action, and the resulting course of events becomes a reference point in later times through which the root issues of the crisis can then be deliberated.[13]

Kai Erikson has discussed comparable circumstances of social crisis in which established ritual occasions are called upon to bear symbolic meanings beyond their usual load. When communal identity is shaken and needs to be reconfirmed, perhaps on different terms, symbolic dramas take place in the courts and elsewhere, in which selected persons are thrust into roles where they represent possibilities of existence that the community in general wishes to repudiate. Giving the community a new grip on its identity, such encounters define a boundary within which members of the community can take their bearings; they define what the community *is* by demonstrating what it *is not*.[14]

The savage is a figure in a drama of symbolic conflict that takes place outside formalized ritual settings and in the absence of social crisis. As a term of psychosocial self-definition for Americans in the early nineteenth century, the idea of civilization found enactment in circumstances of conflict and transformation, suited to the striving inherent in the idea itself, the agon between higher and lower levels of being. And the demands of this internal dialectic could best be lived out in encounters with peoples—like the Marquesans—who arguably embodied savage humanity. As a counterplayer against whom the civilized self can test its integrity and strength, the candidate for the role of savage may be an American Indian, a Polynesian, and even upon occasion a white man.

This notion of the savage as a testing ground for civilized virtue is present in the literary tradition of the "noble savage," where civilization is looked upon as having forsaken earlier virtues. Exponents of the noble savage had a polemical purpose, which was to declare that civilized man failed the test, having abandoned various desirable unsophisticated characteristics, such as generosity, physical health, moral rectitude, candor, and simplicity of life, in the pursuit of a civilized existence. Instead of celebrating the exclusion of savage qualities from the civilized order of things, the spokesman for the noble savage laments it;

yet the exclusionary process of civilized self-definition he tacitly reaffirms.

Evidence of the deep processes at work here may be found in James Baird's *Ishmael*, which discusses Melville in relation to a variety of primitivism where savage virtues are evoked not in order to scold civilized life but to redeem it. Baird discusses the power that is seen to be locked up in primitive symbologies when the regnant symbol systems of a civilized culture appear exhausted. Those banished realities of feeling and perception, repressed as savage in order to retain the coherent forms of the public self, are then welcomed into consciousness as a salvation from the sterility of those forms. The primitive then appears as more than a source of critical principles; it is a domain of wild, marvelous, and inchoate experience, experience that issues in new symbols with rich unrationalized meanings. Individuals, as Baird shows, can devote large portions of their lives to pursuing such experiences and their meanings.[15]

Yet symbols are never dead or alive in themselves, but only in relation to a community. To say that Christian symbolism had lost authority in the nineteenth century, and needed to be replaced, is to speak truly for Melville and others attuned to the social and intellectual developments undermining that authority. Yet for the sponsors and friends of the American Board of Commissioners for Foreign Missions, Christian symbolism was very much alive. Primitivism as a cultural movement may be a signal of the historical failure of a traditional symbol system; yet it also gives recurrent evidence of the psychosocial dialectic by which such systems live. Something of importance is *always* excluded from general consolidations of meaning, and in a civilized symbology those excluded things will be called savage. Whether the savage domain is seen as a mess to be straightened out, or as a fructifying mystery to plunge into, it remains a place of the mind. In either case, the lines of battle within civilized selves are projected onto the line of contact between persons of different cultures.

Porter and the missionaries were not conducting formal rituals in the Marquesas; they were engaged in living out the meanings that made them who they were as members of their society: their actions had for them and for their fellow Americans a symbolic tenor. And, like ritual, what they did had the effect of keeping these constitutive meanings alive and fresh, by taking actual occasions as the exemplary embodiments of them.

Thus the outpost of civilization is a figure in which the coherence of civilization itself is affirmed. The city on the hill is meant to give order to the wilderness, but it has also the latent role of maintaining the order of the civilized community by providing a model of its characteristic striving. Standing at the edge of a seeming confusion, it challenges an alternative model of reality that is already darkly familiar within the civilized community, an alternative humanity that is nearly overcome, but not quite.

Both David Porter and Charles Stewart use images of Roman Catholicism to evoke the cultural atmosphere that they detected at Nukuheva. Stewart viewed the massive rock outcroppings and was reminded of the ruins of medieval Europe, tottering under their own weight. Porter noted that the religion of the Marquesans was credulous and unintelligible, so that a Roman Catholic missionary might easily have made converts.[16] Exponents of sharply distinct Protestant versions of the notion of civilization, Porter and Stewart join in describing the savage environment as embodying an antagonist that is defeated in principle but not altogether abolished in practice. Roman Catholicism was for them, like savagery, a target against which to test their spiritual weapons. The "sin" in which the Marquesans languished, according to the missionary account, was likewise no stranger to the breasts of the missionaries themselves. They staked their civilized Christian identities on having received the promise of salvation from these very shortcomings. And the cluster of qualities that oppose moral enlightenment in Porter's schema—emotional self-indulgence, mental slackness, ignorant superstition—were capable of threatening his own sense of rational equilibrium.

Americans in the Marquesas, then, engaged in interactions with the Polynesians which reveal their effort to test and vindicate their own cultural identities. Viewed abstractly, as a principle of intellectual order, the concept of civilization may be seen to act like the jar in Wallace Stevens' poem.[17]

> I placed a jar in Tennessee,
> And round it was, upon a hill.
> It made the slovenly wilderness
> Surround that hill.
>
> The wilderness rose up to it,
> And sprawled around, no longer wild.
> The jar was round upon the ground
> And tall and of a port in air.
>
> It took dominion everywhere.
> The jar was gray and bare.
> It did not give of bird or bush,
> Like nothing else in Tennessee.

The jar will contain Calvinistic or rationalistic ideas, but as an ordering principle it acts in either case to give a point of reference from which the wilderness becomes a circle. The jar, taking dominion everywhere, is the emblem of a universal order which is valid merely by virtue of its presence as an invulnerable form in the midst of the sprawling wilderness.

The Americans at Nukuheva, however, were not jars. They were sensitive to episodes that tended to unsettle the schemes of order they brought with them. As their personalities were bound up with the concepts of civilization that impelled them, they recorded moments of severe disorientation in which their experiences threatened to stop making sense. These episodes of maximum testing are of great complexity and considerable revelatory power, because in them private experiences of dread are made to vindicate general cultural norms, even as the norms betray their interpretive inadequacies.

As this analysis has indicated, the savage is a source of testing by the nature of his meaning for the civilized self; he necessarily arouses and focuses certain anxieties. The dramas of trial our Americans describe have a thematic structure that assigns values to "the savage" which are manifestly the reflex of what is taken by the Americans to be "civilized." Joseph Conrad speaks of this in Heart of Darkness, when he observes that it takes your "inborn strength" to survive the confrontation with the wilderness without going mad or becoming a savage yourself.[13]

These moments of trial have a further element, however, in which their relation to the structure of the self becomes more apparent. They take place in circumstances where there is a discrepancy between the savage as visualized and the Marquesan as encountered. Programmed to meet the savage in his expected form, the American finds himself involved in a situation to which his expectations do not apply. Instead of challenging his civilized capacity to withstand savage energies or solicitations, the circumstance challenges the civilized-savage polarity itself. The American visitor finds it difficult to make sense of his experience of the Marquesans on the terms available to him.

Because of such stresses in the real experience of Americans in the Marquesas, we find them making passionate affirmations of the central values of civilization, affirmations that have the air of authenticity conferred by their setting in a living moment of extreme trial. Yet the source of the stress that is endured in this trial is precisely the lack of fit between the circumstance confronted and the principles affirmed. Typically presented in narrative segments that describe moments of acute anxiety, these tests have the paradoxical quality Victor Turner has noted in *The Ritual Process*, where principles that are essential to psychosocial structures are emphasized as axiomatic in exactly those situations where they appear not to be valid.[19]

At the core of the thematic structure of the test is the encounter in which the self interacts with the not-self, with the alien familiar against whom the self is defined.[20] This interplay of the self and the "other" is framed in the terms provided by the notion of civilization, so that in the climax of the test the participants have roles vividly defined as civilized and savage. The ostensible meaning of the occasion is that the civilized prevails over the savage. But the deeper meaning is that "self-other" survives a human arrangement that only partly corresponds to the "civilized-savage" pattern in which it is phrased.

What is presented in the narrative as a threat to the civilized self as a moral achievement is in fact a subtle defense of the civilized self as an organization of consciousness. Ernst Kris, in *Psychoanalytic Explorations in Art*, argues that great art causes the reader to relax his ego controls, so that the personality can regress into less fully integrated forms of psychic experience. But this regression is managed so as to permit the ego eventually to reassert itself in a stronger position than before, with a reinvigorated sense of its power to give order to the life of the psyche. This "regression in the service of the ego" is an analogue of the test we find in the accounts of the Americans in the Marquesas: the impulses given rein are just those that the civilized ego is equipped to rein back in.[21]

On the general issue of erotic arousal, for example, we have noted that the Marquesans viewed it as testifying to a primordial beneficent energy and evoked it on ritual occasions where spiritual reassurance was called for. The missionaries, on the other hand, looked upon it as testifying to the power of the devil. Their conception of the civilized self caused them to erect heavy psychic defenses against sexual feeling. The separate houses (with their interior walls) which they insisted upon building for themselves contrast instructively with the large communal beds of the Marquesans as an external expression of this difference in character structure. As persons the missionaries and their wives were equipped with patterns of avoidance and shame that were sharply provoked by the behavior of the Marquesans.

The "disgust" they felt for the Marquesans is a complex response. Since their repressive mechanisms were geared to sexual feeling, such feeling could only come to consciousness against resistance; it could only make itself known as it overwhelmed the barriers that had been set up to keep it from view. Such disgust is a composite of attraction and shunning, an uncomfortable state of mind that leaves the person who feels it with a considerable resentment for the person who arouses it, as well as a feeling of somehow guiltlessly having been dirtied. The missionaries were thrown chronically into this state by the behavior of the Polynesians, so much so that Charles Stewart counted it as one of the main reasons why it was hard to get a fair view of their character: "a man of nice moral sensibility, and one alive to the purity of affection essential to genuine piety, is exposed, in a disgust at the licentiousness unavoidably obtruded on his notice, to lose sight of all that is pleasing and praiseworthy in the nature and condition of the inhabitants, and to think and speak of them only, as associated, in his mind, with a moral deformity and vileness that, in some respects, can scarce be equalled."[22]

Yet as the missionaries noted the genital displays and the zealous solicitations of the Marquesans, they also noticed that the Marquesans were not themselves disgusted. Instead of being ashamed of their sexual feelings, the Marquesans appeared to be delighted in them, proud of them, and eager to show them off. "They will often take pains," Armstrong once observed, "to show their pollution and licentiousness in our presence ... I scarcely sit down a half hour anywhere to converse with the people that I am not obliged to turn away distressed and disgusted." The unabashed demonstrativeness of the Marquesans made the missionaries' effort to contain their own erotic arousal all the more difficult, and it introduced the extra level of stress in the process of testing. More than once, indeed, the missionaries conclude their denunciations of licentiousness with straightforward admissions of the Marquesans' physical beauty. "Many of these women were truly handsome," Armstrong observed on one occasion, "almost as fair as many American ladies."[23]

It is one thing to be tempted by a recognizable devil; it is quite another to find oneself doubting that the attractive pleasure is in fact devilish. In the Marquesas the missionaries encountered persons whose selves were not formed to the concept that sexual excitement is evil if not contained within monogamous conventions. But to recognize this as a valid possibility of existence would involve a much deeper disturbance than yielding to "sin." If the missionary sinned, by positive action or in the privacy of his thoughts, he could avail himself of the psychic apparatus he had available to restore his moral system to order: he could, in a word, repent. But if he found himself in a state of mind where "sin" and "repentance" ceased to make sense of his experience, his disorientation would run much deeper. He would be invaded by the dread that experience was itself unintelligible.

These themes run through the story of an incident that occurred when the first Protestant missionaries came to the Marquesas. They were brought by the good ship *Duff* in 1791 on the famous voyage that established the highly successful mission at Tahiti. The *Duff* also brought two missionaries to the Marquesas, Mr. Harris and Mr. Crook. Crook stayed on in Tahuata to undertake a long and disappointing labor: our incident concerns the reason why Harris sailed away again with the *Duff*.

Ship Captain James Wilson, who recounted the story, tells us that Harris had misgivings from his first encounter with the Marquesans. While Crook was encouraged by the ceremony of greeting and the general situation in which he found the islanders, Harris "judged the scene before him a solemn one."[24] In describing Harris' reactions Wilson conveys a clear impression that the man was severely shaken: it seemed as though "fear had taken possession of his mind," as though he had "entirely . . . lost his firmness and ardor." As a result, Harris declined to go ashore with Crook to make further investigations, giving as his pretext the need to spend more time packing aboard ship. This decision Wilson condemned, holding that Harris should have made the most of his opportunity to learn "the real state of the island" before he would be forced to a final decision by the departure of the *Duff*. At length Harris could postpone the confrontation no longer, but after six days ashore he returned to the ship with Crook, still voicing his misgivings. Even so, he agreed to make a further trial of the place and again went ashore. Four days later they found him hiding in the hills, having been robbed of his belongings "in a most pitiable plight, and like one out of his senses."[25]

As Wilson was able to reconstruct the story, Harris and Crook had been invited by the chief of the coastal tribe to make a journey inland, which Harris refused to do. So Crook went alone with the chief, who left his wife with Harris "to be treated as if she were his own" until they should return. This action Wilson interpreted as a sign of hospitality, which indeed it was. When Harris declined the wife's favors, however, she "became doubtful of his sex," and in the company of some other women she entered Harris' hut during the night, where they "satisfied themselves concerning that point, but not in such a peaceable way but that they awoke him." Harris thereupon left the hut with his trunk of belongings and went down to the beach, where he was further terrified by a band of males and dashed off to the hills, leaving them to plunder his goods.[26]

To Wilson it was apparent that Harris had failed the test set before him by savagery, and he interprets the episode of disorientation as a pathetic display of faint-heartedness. "Discovering so many strangers, he was greatly terrified; and, perceiving what they had been doing, was determined to leave a place where the people were so abandoned and given up to wickedness: a cause which should have excited a contrary resolution."[27] To Wilson, Harris had given as his excuse for departing precisely the reason for his having come in the first place. The expression "abandoned and given up to wickedness" defined for Wilson the kind of strangeness that the Marquesans represented; and it is likely that Harris had no better language for the dread that had unmanned him. From our point of view it is apparent that Harris' disorientation bespeaks a deeper threat, one that attacked his moral constitution. When he awoke to find the women examining his penis, his already overburdened repressive mechanisms threatened to give way altogether in a collapse that would flood his consciousness with impulses he had no way to manage.[28]

Captain Wilson's condemnation of Harris points to an irony which gives us a glimpse of the deeper processes at work here. Harris had discovered the Marquesans to be "given up to wickedness," but in a form that prompted him to leave instead of staying to redeem them. What was intolerable, manifestly, was not the degree of wickedness that the Marquesans exhibited, but the effect of that wickedness on Harris himself. In response to his confused emotions, Harris becomes vehemently convinced that the Marquesans are "savage," because this ascription helps him to restore himself to order. One may speculate with some confidence, therefore, that there was an element of the unspeakable in Harris' experience: he had been through something that he was literally unable to articulate because the terms in which he understood himself and the world could not be made to apply to it.

The apocalyptic character of Harris' experience is also instructive. To those who recounted the story, Harris' mental collapse testified to the spiritual trial that awaited any civilized man who approached the savage to do him good. It was a trial in which he would be taken to a spiritual extremity, to the boundary beyond which madness lies. Reduced to his essential resources in the savage environment, without the external props that maintain him in his accustomed surroundings, the civilized man is invaded by what Joseph Conrad termed "creepy thoughts."[29] The dramas of testing we will examine have an all-or-nothing character. When the interpretive process that is innate to the self goes to work on materials it cannot render intelligible, the result is an anxiety in which the possibility of order per se seems threatened. As Clifford Geertz points out, we may be able to tolerate the loss of a given interpretation of things, but cannot tolerate the loss of our confidence that things are interpretable.[30] Yet the proximate consternation ignites the ultimate dread, as our visitors to the Marquesans come to the boundaries of those provinces of discourse in which their inward and outward experience made sense and which defined for them not provinces, but reality itself.

To recapitulate: Americans in the Marquesas describe occasions that are structured by the process of maintaining a self that is ordered by a specific system of meanings. In these episodes the encounter with the Marquesan becomes strongly shaped by civilized-savage concepts, as a seemingly absolute threat to the civilized identity is experienced. In this moment the subject calls upon the supreme ordering principle available within his system, reenacting the processes by which civilization was formed from the chaos of the savage. He is reduced to the essentials of his civilized self, and unlike Harris he emerges from the experience reinvigorated, having vindicated civilization as a valid way of being and himself as a worthy exponent of it.

On the day of their arrival at Nukuheva, the wives of the missionaries in Alexander's party aroused much excitement among the islanders, who had seen white males aplenty aboard whalers and merchant vessels but for whom white females were a novelty. Mrs. Parker kept a journal to be sent home to her family, and her entry for that day records the beginning of their struggle with Marquesan eroticism. "They seemed perfectly frantic," she reports; "they expressed their surprise by savage gesture & rude & loud sounds—till our hearts sickened within us."[31] This description does not do justice to the actual behavior of the males (which Alexander referred to as "the lascivious gestures which the men practiced before our wives")[32] because it was emphatically not meant to. To write down in detail what was taking place would be to write pornography; it would stir up defiling reactions in readers at home of the very sort that Mrs. Parker was struggling to quash in herself.

Mary Parker also kept a diary of private reflections where she reveals a turbulence of feeling not apparent in the journal she wrote for her family. In her diary for the same day we find her choking with horror and disgust: "What a savage people—their looks strike terror—I cover my face to keep out the sight—Can they be human? Did humanity ever sink so below the brute? . . . [We are] surrounded by hundreds of these savages, their eyes glaring out on us . . . their words, their gestures shame the very brutes—Gracious God—can these be men and women! It seems impossible!"[33] Trying to explain the scene for her family, she at length recognizes that it cannot be done. "I wish to tell you some things of natives," she writes two days later, "that cannot be told."

She explains to her family why she must turn resolutely away from the direct visual experience, with its power to make her doubt that the Marquesans are human beings at all. "You would say to me come back, set not your foot on their shores should you look at them only—but remembering they are Christ's inheritance and that God is our Protector I know you would say go forward nothing doubting." In order to maintain her belief in the humanness of the islanders, she finds it necessary to focus her attention on the sacred meaning she ascribes to them, rather than on the islanders themselves. When she permits their actual appearance, their noises and their doings, to dominate her consciousness she bluntly declares (in her private diary) that she can see no reason to remain at Taiohae Bay: "For what do we now make our abode among them? No light shines upon the path. So it looks to me."

Yet in communicating with her family, she records a meditative ascent in which she negates this terror and confusion by making spiritual contact with the religious values they held in common. "If I know my heart, this I do—I am not afraid—No not at all—I feel as if I could live on this barbarous shore and toil for this people—Here I can contented live & contented die so long as Jesus lifts on me the light of his countenance. This he does according to his promise—I think on his dear name in peace and with joy—He is with us—and will be always—Even so and my soul in extacy says it is enough." Mary Parker thus achieves a mystical communion with Jesus as she addresses herself to persons who for her are prime representatives of the society that sponsors not only the mission project she is part of, but also the psychic being she must maintain in order to continue. In writing this paragraph she reestablishes the threatened connection between herself and the core of meanings that governs her interpretive schema, and it keeps her mind intact under the prodigious stresses of the moment. The Marquesans cease to appear as incomprehensible monsters, perhaps not even human, and are resolved into inhabitants of a "barbarous shore" which makes them part of "Christ's inheritance." What Mary Parker discovered was that this scheme was alive in her own mind, enough to deliver the ecstasy that transfigured her dread.

Charles Stewart correspondingly informs us that upon his arrival at Nukuheva he took a journey inland to visit a tribe that never before had contact with whites. His purpose was to see "pure heathenism—heathenism as it is before a single ray of Christian light has beamed upon its darkness."[34] There he discovered a festival underway, whose sexual features aroused his disgust. We have already noted the way in which the missionaries' interpretive scheme transformed the Marquesan's smile of pleasure into a ghastly leer; for Stewart, however, there is a further transformation. As evidence of the tyranny of Satan over their lives, the sinfulness of the Marquesans struck Stewart as a victimization for which the Marquesans themselves could hardly be blamed. Stewart's response to the islanders' sexuality can be analyzed thus as a threefold process of distancing, the initial impression being folded more and more securely into the scheme of ideas that grasps it. Sexual pleasure becomes loathsome deformity becomes spiritual misery: in the end Stewart feels sorry for the Marquesans' sexuality. And yet it casts him into a crisis of faith.

Witnessing the festival, which represented for him the absolute of human depravity, Stewart found that he could not stay until the end.

Before the grossness of one half that was forced upon me had passed in view, I was compelled in the thoughts of my very soul to exclaim, "Stop—it is enough" but I had gone beyond the point of escape, and the whole truth in its abominable details was riveted upon me.

There was less of licentiousness in the dance than I had expected;

but in a hundred things else there were such open outrages upon all decency, that I hurried away in a horror of disgust, with a heart too much humbled for the race to which I belong, and too much depressed at the depravity and guilt of man, to think or feel upon any other subject. At first, I could scarce find spirits to interchange a word with my companions, but hastened on before, or fell far behind, that the oppression within me might escape their notice.[35]

Stewart's amusing confession that the dance was not so licentious as he had anticipated is a signal of the stress that animates the ritual of testing he sets before us. Stewart finds himself at the nadir of human sin, looking around at "a hundred things else" to find the moral outrages he had expected to find at the center of the festivity. This discrepancy between what his theological conception of Marquesan life had predicted and the actual dance he witnessed is essential to the spiritual perturbations he reports. Stewart does not interpret the moment as one in which his basic beliefs are discredited, although dread of such a prospect is detectable in his extended discussion. Instead of viewing the "oppression" within him as a struggle against sensual allurements, Stewart describes it as arising from a spiritual anguish typical of the Calvinist tradition in which he stands.

John Calvin taught that God, specifically ordaining all earthly happenings, had predestined "the depravity and guilt of man"; and Calvin further taught that man is not free to escape from the damnation assigned to such wickedness unless God predestines him to do so. Orthodox believers in the sixteenth century assailed this tenet on the ground that it shattered the moral authority of God himself, making him "the author of sin." The Canons of the Synod of Dort (1603), by which this "Arminian" heresy had officially been condemned, stated that even to think of such an imputation was blasphemy. Yet the Synod did not halt the controversy within Calvinist circles over free will, predestination, and divine justice; nor did John Milton's prodigious effort to resolve them in *Paradise Lost*. Succeeding generations of believers, of various doctrinal slants, were fearful of becoming lost in the wandering mazes of this question and typically viewed the very broaching of it as a sign of incipient rebellion against God. Yet the so-called problem of evil cropped up in many forms again and again, so that the spiritual distress concerning it—to say nothing of the theological ingenuities proposed to liquidate it—became a standard feature of orthodox piety well into the nineteenth century.[36]

Stewart perceived in the dance and its accompanying activities an appalling ugliness, sharply discordant with the divine goodness manifested in the beauty of the created order. His belief that this hideous deformity could not be blamed directly on the Marquesans posed for him the chronic enigma of Calvinist belief, and his depiction of the spiritual struggle that ensued shows how he fought off the temptation to blasphemy.

> So completely was I prostrated, that for the first time in my life I believe—not in a spirit of rebellion I trust, but with a feeling of deep anguish—I looked to heaven and exclaimed, "Oh! why—why was sin ever permitted to enter a world otherwise so fair! why has it been allowed to mar the highest glory of man, till in all countries and among all classes, it in too many instances degrades him to the level of the brute!"—Thou, O God, knowest, for with thee is all wisdom—and blessed be thy name, with thee too are all goodness and truth—and "justice and judgment are ever the habitations of thy throne!"[37]

Stewart's concluding invocation should not be taken as a complacent recital of conventional pious phrases, despite its redundant character. The insistence with which he ascribes "wisdom . . . goodness and truth . . . justice and judgment" to God reveals how energetically he must assert these values in order to suppress suggestions that would lead to the opposite, the blasphemous conclusion. The language of his prayer is certainly conventional, as is his depiction of the spiritual distress that the prayer was intended to relieve. Yet what strikes us is the extraordinary extent to which Stewart's mentality was formed by an apprehension of reality that these conventions rehearse, transforming a confrontation with Marquesan eroticism into an effort to quell passionate doubts concerning the justice of God. In the moment of crisis he acknowledges, indeed, that he is ignorant of the state of his soul, declaring only his trust that he had not given way to rebellion, when he found himself asking "why . . . why . . . why" sin had been "permitted" to ruin the human race. Neither does Stewart claim to have achieved a solution to this ancient theological riddle; instead he implicitly grants that the divine mysteries can only be accepted in faith and turns to address the Godhead directly with an admission of his human ignorance and frailty: "Thou, O God, knowest."

Stewart's presentation of this scene thus dramatizes the struggle of the Christian reduced to his last resources in the battle against the powers of darkness, daring those powers in the realm of their greatest influence. His state of inner distress before God was the spiritual condition that he and his fellow-believers considered to be the baseline from which the redemption of the soul progresses. In returning to that stance of entire contrition, Stewart does not weaken his faith, but rejuvenates it through an experience that communicated to him the absolute reality of his moral situation, that of a redeemed sinner. In urging that Christian missions be sent to the Marquesas, he reveals the belief that the islanders could pass from their wretchedness into the joy of his salvation, which he like Mary Parker had tested once again and found sufficient.

David Porter also recounts an experience in which his identity as a civilized man is consummated over against the savagery he encountered in attempting to transform Marquesan life. Stewart believed that the interactions that make for civilization are spiritual in nature, so that he is able to reenact them in his own psychic life. For Porter, however, the determinative processes are brought about by practical arrangements: military operations, trade relations, treaty agreements, and the like. The drama of his testing occurs, therefore, in the course of his effort to bring universal peace to the island by solidifying the "friendship" that he had established between himself and the several tribes. Making his way through the activities that this objective required of him, Porter encounters situations that posed the question whether his civilized and civilizing purposes would prevail. As frustrations begin to accumulate, Porter has reason to discard his initial confidence that the Marquesans are so well suited by nature for social progress as hardly to deserve the name of savages, and to doubt correspondingly whether he himself can measure up to the demands placed on the civilizer.

We have observed that Mary Parker and Charles Stewart relied in crisis on the power of God; they found the strength to reaffirm their civilized identities through confessions of helplessness and dependence. David Porter did not believe that the world is controlled by a mysterious divinity that is active in all earthly happenings. He conceived civilization to have been erected as men used their intellectual powers to discern and exploit the objective structure of things. The personal characteristic that Porter valued as the essence of the civilized was therefore rational self-possession, the ability to persist in finding solutions to practical problems. The superstitions that clog the mind of the savage, as well as the florid instability of his emotional life, were qualities noted by Porter as tending to keep him in his savage state.

Porter dramatizes the opposition of these qualities at the crisis of his enterprise, when his own power to keep his nerve is strained to the utmost. It happens after his initial defeat at the hands of the Typees. Fearing that the islanders might now form a coalition to rid themselves of him, he immediately organized a party of two hundred men to make another attack the next day. Then he discovered that his boats were too leaky to carry the party he needed and decided to undertake an attack overland, setting out by moonlight that evening. By midnight Porter had attained a high narrow ridge, overlooking the valley of the Typees, but his men were too exhausted to go further.

Porter's description of the night on this treacherous summit dramatizes the rational soul in its supreme hour of trial. He could hear the pounding of Typee drums in the valley below and learned that they were celebrating their victory, calling upon their gods to bring rain so as to spoil his muskets. Burdened with weariness and considering his position relatively secure, Porter relaxed his vigilant rational consciousness to the extent of just drifting off to sleep. Then it began to rain, to the tune of increased drumming and shouts of savage joy from the valley. Porter's description of his physical situation clearly depicts the character of his spiritual plight.

I had little hopes that a musket would be kept dry or a cartridge saved. Never, in the course of my life, did I spend a more anxious or disagreeable night, and I believe there were few with me who had ever seen its equal. A cold and piercing wind accompanied the deluge, for I can call it nothing else, and chilled us to the heart; without room to keep ourselves warm by moving about, fearful of stirring, lest we might be precipitated into eternity down the steep sides of the mountains, for the ridge had now become so slippery we could scarcely keep our feet—we all anxiously looked for morning.[38]

This description communicates Porter's dread at having entered an alien environment, where his cognitive apparatus is unworkable. The coming of the rain in apparent response to the drumming of the Typees is the central element of the picture, and is supported by other imagery that completes the suggestion of a total threat against Porter's way of being. The rain comes in a "deluge" as though the gods indeed were angry, and it chills Porter's men "to the very heart." The slippery footing quickly makes it impossible for Porter to take any action at all, for fear of being precipitated into "eternity." These religious elements in the language indicate the depth at which Porter's faith is being tested. In Porter's world, the Godhead maintains an objective order of fact such that human rationality can make sense of it. But here spooky irrational forces seem to have taken command, suggesting a world in which Porter's rationality is inapplicable. Porter refers elsewhere to the Marquesan religion as an affair of dolls and baby-houses; aroused by savage priestcraft, the gods of Nukuheva now confront him with an unanticipated deadly challenge. Thus the stage is set for Porter's evocation of the steadiness that the enlightened problem solver displays in crisis: he holds himself very quiet and very still, maintaining his balance on a slippery precipice in the hope that dawn will flood his world with warmth and light.

These sharply focused dramas of testing, common to exponents of very different versions of the idea of civilization, reveal processes that are at work outside such critical moments. The extended narratives provided by Stewart and Porter, as well as the journals and letters of the missionaries, portray a continuous engagement whose thematic structure reflects the versions of civilization that shaped the actors' response to their circumstances. There is no reason to doubt that Porter actually got rained on during the night, as he reports, or that Stewart saw a dance or that Mrs. Parker witnessed the sexual solicitations of Marquesans; these things were not *invented* as exemplifications of the

Drawn by Capt. Porter.   Engrav'd by W.Strickland.

Taawattaa.

the Priest.

meanings we have detected; they were *experienced* as such. Each of these episodes was meant by its author as a straightforward account of what took place, not as a fanciful construction presented to serve a theme. And yet the common dramatic structure that they share makes it evident that in each case a selective adaptation of the happenings has taken place. It is not a matter of secretly trimming the facts, but of where the focus of attention lies, what issues take the foreground of consciousness and which are left aside.

Perhaps the most revealing of the three test sequences is Mrs. Parker's account of her "extacy," in which she declares frankly that she is leaving out certain matters, deliberately not seeing certain things. If she were to look upon the Marquesans only, she says, she might lose her grip on the reason for having come there. There is no effort here to suppress data clandestinely; the suppression takes place automatically in accordance with the way her mind works. She makes explicit reference, indeed, to the shaping and selecting process that gives the more sophisticated accounts their structure. David Porter, by contrast, gives little account of his subjective processes, but his description of his physical situation and strategic plight conforms closely to the thematic emphases that shaped his consciousness of what was going on.

In these crises, fact and meaning have been fused by the psychic stress that arises when a scheme of meanings threatens to break down, a fusion in which imposed meanings are seen to be inherent in the nature of reality. The civilized person in the Marquesas wonders whether his civilized values can survive without the myriad assistance of familiar social forms. But here, where his culture seems absent, it is most decisively active and present. Without the tangible helps of civilized society he is able to make contact with the essentials, the truly indestructible features, of his civilized identity. In the crisis that consummates this process his values invest themselves absolutely in the nature of things, and can no longer be imagined to be mere prejudices that he brought with him from home.

Reality itself appears to generate meanings in such moments of incarnation, so that the perceiving subject takes himself to have observed or received them. The description of theophanies, in which the Godhead discloses itself to human kind, is a commonplace of religious discourse, since it is essential to religious belief that a scheme of meanings is in fact inherent in reality. Intrinsic to aesthetic experience, too, are fusions in which physical objects and circumstances become charged with meaning, such that the work of art generates a world unto itself in which we can participate for a time with total absorption. Here we find an analogous psychosocial process, where world-informing meanings are vindicated in ecstatic moments whose overwhelming reality strikes home to the subject a vision in which the structure of the self is attuned to the structure of the world. The self is produced and sustained at least in part by such occasions of imprinting in which human beings, the meaning makers who are themselves made by meanings, receive the stamp of a culturally transmitted conception so deeply that it becomes and remains "second nature."

The moral self-dramatization focused in these climactic moments of spiritual testing is implicit throughout the narratives in which they occur. All the facts presented are invested with a structure of meaning that reaches beyond the circumstances described to embrace the meaning of civilized society. The moment, or the extended narration, in which central civilized values are attested as inherent in personal experience is a profoundly communal moment, no matter how private the circumstances in which it occurs. The hardy spirit in his lonely outpost of civilization is a figure who stands at the presumptive boundary of an entire society, inviting his fellows to locate themselves in accordance with the general configuration of the whole that his personal position implies.

It is important, however, to distinguish between the living moment of interior drama, in which the civilizer on the shores of Nukuheva finds his identity reconfirmed, and the shaped narrative in which this reconfirmation is displayed before the public. We have observed that Mary Parker's journal revealed much more inward uncertainty than did her letters home, and the narratives of Stewart and Porter represent an even greater degree of formal clarity. This does not mean only that these narratives foreshorten and simplify the activities they describe; it is also true that the activities themselves could be understood to "say something" that the American public was willing to hear. Alexander's mission by contrast, fraught with anomalies and defeat, simply formed a less suitable topic for book-length treatment than Stewart's voyage or Porter's exploits. Resurrecting Alexander's mission I am concerned in this book to recount a drama in which ambiguous confrontations are explored for their hidden meanings. Porter and Stewart were made of sterner stuff; they found their deeper selves touched by heroic dramas in which savagery was vanquished.

We see in these missionary and imperialist undertakings a drama of symbolic action in which the structural potencies and anxieties of civilized persons are revealed. In it the principal actors vie with each other for the lead, each seeking to establish himself as a true exemplar of the civilized condition. Charles Stewart's journey to see pure heathenism in the valley of the Typees was an exemplary gesture, as was Porter's march of destruction through it; the narratives they wrote completed the gestures by making them visible to an American public invited to accept one and then the other as a hero. And the entire business was carried on in the context of a culture that thought itself to be exemplary, that is, a model of the future for the whole world to look to.

The action of our drama, ostensibly occurring in the Marquesas, takes place within a symbolic world. The drama itself contributes to the maintenance of that world, at times asserting it so forcibly as to attain a hallucinatory self-enclosure; it becomes a hall of mirrors in which the omnipresent image of human history as a movement upward through stages of improvement is focused and refocused, adapted, inverted, and periodically reconfirmed. At those points where the conception threatens to give way in the face of an anomalous experience, the most strenuous efforts are mounted to keep it intact, efforts that may have the effect of rendering the conception even more durable and energetic than it was before its interpretive power was tested. If these efforts do not succeed, however, the result may well be a dreadful mental collapse and an incapacity to take up any coherent program of action. The amusing elements in the story of Harris should not distract us from its horrifying core, the heart of darkness that is no less destructive for being inherent in the social constitution of the self. Yet Americans in Polynesia encountered on every hand circumstances not amenable to the scheme of order they brought with them, anomalies whose larger meaning was subversive to their mental coherence.

One of the most troublesome anomalies was the beachcomber, the citizen of the civilized world who had chosen to take up residence among the islanders. We have noted David Porter's shock at the discovery that certain of his own men had deserted, and his even greater shock at finding that his faithful interpreter Wilson had been working against him. As a throwback who had somehow flouted the progressive direction of history, the beachcomber was manifestly anomalous. But the dynamics of self-definition, as programmed by this concept, made him even more problematical. As civilized men tested their identities against the savage, they viewed the line of contact between themselves and the islanders as a line of battle, a no man's land between alien forces. Yet the beachcomber somehow lives there, on the boundary line between two incompatible realms. He is a more distressing figure than the hapless Harris because he loses his identity without going mad, thus suggesting that the civilized self is not grounded upon the absolute structure of things.

Herman Melville was for a time a beachcomber and learned something of what it meant to become a target for the anxieties of civilized persons. He also learned that the position of the beachcomber provided a narrative standpoint from which to look upon latent features of white activities in Polynesia, a perspective from which the question of perspective itself becomes visible.

The encounter with the Marquesans was enacted by Porter and Stewart to reaffirm the idea of civilization as a structural element in American identity, much as established rituals have the function of reanimating and preserving the meanings about which they are ordered. Yet because such meanings were staked here, in the symbolic import of the encounter, a Marquesan adventure could also be speculative and indeed subversive. The idea of civilization could be made the object of reflection in the very circumstances where its power to structure experience prior to reflection is supposed to be vindicated. Around the beachcomber standpoint could be organized a passage of action and writing that would probe the system of meaning dramatized by other Americans in the Marquesas.

6 / What It Means To Be a Cannibal

MELVILLE DID NOT encounter the Marquesans as an official representative of the United States government or of the American Board of Commissioners for Foreign Missions. Instead of being a self-conscious emissary of civilization, with the legitimacy of a recognized official function, he arrived at Taiohae Bay as a common sailor on a whaling vessel. In childhood and youth he had been reared in affluence, as the second son of a well-to-do New York merchant, but his father's bankruptcy and death followed by the Panic of 1837 reduced the family to virtual poverty and left Herman at the age of twenty-one with no better expedient than to take employment as a whaling sailor; in this way he could support himself, wait for better times, and see something of the larger world. When his whaler reached the Marquesas, Melville deserted her and with a companion named Tobias Greene fled inland hoping to take up residence with a friendly tribe until the ship should depart. He looked upon the Marquesan fastnesses not as a target for the improving work of civilization, but as a refuge from his life of hard usage aboard ship.

Porter and the mission of 1833 each established a civilized base of operations in the Marquesan wilderness from which to mount forays into the surrounding darkness. The grimly rectilinear design of the mission compound expressed the missionaries' belief that the work of elevating the savage would require the maintenance of an unceasing conflict between the demands of righteous order and the luxuriant squalor in which Satan's captives languished. Porter carried on his civilizing work in a graceful semicircle of houses built by the Marquesans after the Marquesan fashion, a design expressing aptly the interplay of rational and technical skills that formed one aspect of Porter's conception of the relationship that civilized men should establish with their savage wards. The armed fort overlooking this center of industry completes the embodiment of Porter's vision. In each case we see a city on a hill, standing in a dynamic tension against its wilderness surroundings.

When Melville arrived in the Marquesas, yet another civilizing effort was in progress. A French flotilla, under the command of Admiral Du Petit Thouars, was completing the annexation of the Marquesas for France, establishing a colonial dominion that continues today. Melville forsook the tenuous beachhead of civilization at Taiohae Bay that the French were then appropriating because he needed to get beyond the reach of the captain of his whaler, or of anyone his captain might pay to capture and return him. Melville lived among the Marquesans on Marquesan terms; he had for a time contracted out of the legal, social, and economic systems of the West. He soon found himself held prisoner by the dreaded Typees, who were to resist the French as they had resisted Porter, with great vehemence and resourcefulness.

Until very recently the role of the beachcomber in the unfolding drama of Western encroachment into Polynesia has been defined much as the respectable Westerners of the period wished to define it, as a nasty scum carried on the advancing tide of civilization. Despite their sharp differences on other matters, the traders, whalers, explorers, missionaries, and government officials who played their several parts in establishing Western dominion all agreed that the beachcomber was a worthless rascal at best and at worst a fiend incarnate. As it became apparent that the Polynesians themselves suffered great evils as the result of Western contact, the exponents of civilization in the area turned with a single voice upon the beachcomber, even as they bandied various accusations among themselves. It is evident, however, that the white man who "went native" was pilloried so remorselessly in part because of the threat he offered to respectable white interests.

We have noted the horror with which David Porter came to realize the part Wilson played in the successful Marquesan effort to oust the garrison he left behind. A beachcomber named Morrison, correspondingly, acted as an interpreter for Charles Stewart and then was discovered to have advised the Marquesans that they should murder Alexander's missionary party for the sake of their belongings. Alexander himself reveals the wariness that bitter experience taught the missionaries; on his own journey of reconnaissance to the Marquesas, he scolds Stewart for having represented Morrison as a sandalwood trader, pointing out that he was tattooed from head to foot, wore the native garb, and was nothing better than a savage. "More is to be feared by the mission from his teaching," Alexander anticipated, "than from any other quarter."[1] The kind of teaching of which the beachcomber was capable is indicated in Edmund Fanning's description of his visit to the Marquesas, when he learned of a plot against him hatched by a resident white. The cold-blooded monster, as Fanning terms him, had informed the islanders that they could destroy Fanning's ship by attaching a line beneath the water, cutting the anchor cables, and towing him onto the rocks. Then they could easily overpower the crew and, having destroyed every trace of the ship and its occupants, would have no need to fear reprisals. Fanning escaped this fate, but not without recognizing that even a relatively ignorant white man possessed knowledge that the Marquesans could put to distinctively Marquesan purposes.[2]

When Melville blundered into the valley of the Typees, he found himself dependent upon the islanders for his survival and completely at their mercy. Although he professes his inability to understand why the Typees were unwilling to let him return to Nukuheva, he notices certain benefits they hoped to derive from his presence. They quizzed him intensively on the strength of the French armed squadron in Taiohae Bay so as to calculate their chances against an assault. The chief also asked Melville to repair a broken musket and was greatly disappointed when he proved unable to do so. He regarded me, Melville reports, "as if he half suspected I was some inferior sort of white man, who after all did not know much more than a Typee."[3]

More significant for Melville's estimation of Marquesan life, however, is the vantage that his place among them compelled him to take. Since he was entirely in their hands, it was necessary for him to view their customs with an eye to his own survival. To David Porter the islanders' desire to exchange names was a source of harmless amusement, which was somewhat useful in cementing his imperial alliances. Melville, by contrast, clutched at it eagerly as a scrap of vital reassurance. His attitude toward Mehevi, the Typee chief he encountered on the first day of his captivity, was the reverse of condescending: "I forthwith determined to secure, if possible, the good will of this individual, as I easily perceived he was a man of great authority in his tribe, and one who might exert a powerful influence upon our subsequent fate" (79). After Melville discovers that Mehevi was the principal chief, whom he calls the King of the Typees, his satisfaction is immense. "I could not avoid congratulating myself that Mehevi had from the first taken me as it were under his royal protection, and that he still continued to entertain for me the warmest regard, as far at least as I was enabled to judge from appearances. For the future I determined to pay most assiduous court to him, hoping that eventually through his kindness I might obtain my liberty" (187).

His beachcomber perspective permitted Melville to notice aspects of Marquesan life that had been invisible to Western observers who enjoyed official backing, and to identify the source of certain false impressions they had broadcast.

These learned tourists [like Porter and Stewart] generally obtain the greater part of their information from the retired old South-Sea rovers, who have domesticated themselves among the barbarous tribes of the Pacific. Jack . . . invariably officiates as showman of the island on which he has settled, and having mastered a few dozen words of the language, is supposed to know all about the people who speak it. A natural desire to make himself of consequence in the eyes of the strangers, prompts him to lay claim to a much greater knowledge of such matters than he actually possesses. In reply to incessant queries, he communicates not only all he knows but a good deal more, and if there be any information deficient still he is at no loss to supply it. The avidity with which his anecdotes are noted down tickles his vanity, and his powers of invention increase with the credulity of his auditors. He knows just the sort of information wanted, and furnishes it to any extent. (170)

It is important to observe, however, that Melville here joins in the general condemnation of those who had gone native as sources of information, claiming a respectability for his own point of view to which the beachcomber was not entitled. Melville thus establishes an interpretive stance as narrator of *Typee* which incorporates the beachcomber perspective into something more complex; he blends it, in fact, with another standpoint with which it might seem to have little in common, that of the sophisticated gentleman-at-large.

Melville establishes his aristocratic credentials by displaying control of a cultivated picturesque rhetoric that demands from the reader a response on grounds of shared cultural superiority. As a creator of Melville's interpretive stance, this rhetoric is pervasive; it is felt throughout the work, even as Melville presents himself as changing his viewpoint in the course of the Marquesan experience. Melville reveals his awareness of the power of idiom to establish social identity quite early, as he introduces the delicate question of his flight from the *Acushnet*. "To use the concise, point-blank phrase of the sailors, I had made up my mind to 'run away.' Now as a meaning is generally attached to these two words no way flattering to the individual to whom they are applied, it behooves me, for the sake of my own character, to offer some explanation of my conduct" (20). Melville is at pains to inform the reader, here as elsewhere in the opening chapters, that he had "moved in a different sphere of life" (32) from that of the sailor and runaway.

A note of loftiness can be detected, accordingly, in Melville's opening condemnations of the misdoings of whites in the Marquesas. When he tell us that the inhabitants of Taiohae "have become somewhat corrupted, owing to their recent commerce with Europeans . . . [but remain] very nearly in the same state of nature in which they were first beheld by white men" (11), we are meant to catch the philosophical echoes of "state of nature" as well as to appreciate the judicious restraint audible in the term "somewhat corrupted." His contempt for the French annexation,

elaborated at points with violent moral passion, is also framed as
an offense to his taste. He speaks of the French warships at Taiohae "floating in that lovely bay, the green eminences of the shore
looking down so tranquilly upon them, as if rebuking the stern-
ness of their aspect. To my eye nothing could be more out of
keeping than the presence of these vessels"(12). Melville here
employs a picturesque style in a manner reminiscent of Charles
Stewart (whose *Visit to the South Seas* he consulted in writing the
descriptive passages in *Typee*),[4] where landscapes and seascapes
are made to convey ethical impressions to the cultivated suscep-
tibility. Yet instead of claiming, as Stewart had done, that possession of high culture and devotion to missions were complementary features of the civilized character, Melville uses the
elevated style to suggest that they are opposed to each other.
Looking down from his position of self-possessed aloofness in
the opening chapter of *Typee*, Melville informs the reader that
"Protestant Missions appear to have despaired of reclaiming
these islands from heathenism," offering in explanation the story
of a missionary who fled the Marquesas after the islanders had
stripped his wife naked, which Melville presents as "a somewhat
amusing incident . . . which I cannot avoid relating" (6).[5]

The presence communicated by Melville's rhetoric is of a person so civilized that he can hold civilization itself up for criticism. When he says that "humanity weeps over the ruin thus remorselessly inflicted upon . . . [the islanders] by their European
civilizers" (15), we are meant to detect in the term "humanity" a
standard of conduct and a community of moral sentiment which
lie beyond what those who call themselves "civilizers" display.
Observe the subtlety with which Melville both lays claim to and
repudiates a civilized identity in the following comment: "A high
degree of refinement, however, does not seem to subdue our
wicked propensities so much after all; and were civilization itself
to be estimated by some of its results, it would seem perhaps
better for what we call the barbarous parts of the world to remain
unchanged" (17). Melville's subjunctive "were" preserves the
option of refraining from the judgment that "civilization itself"
should be estimated by its "results," and he is likewise careful to
specify that he has only "some" of those results in mind. In
speaking likewise, of *"what we call* the barbarous parts of the

world" (emphasis added), he unobtrusively raises the baseline
issue of interpretive perspective. If we ask the downright question whether the person who speaks this sentence believes that
civilization is good or bad, we become aware that he is delicately
holding in abeyance the issue of whether the term "civilization"
applies to himself or to human society at all.[6]

The narrative voice that addresses us in *Typee* is characterized
throughout by this kind of subtle ambivalent balancing, and the
tensions apparent in that voice are related to the uncertain identity of its apparent source, the man who is both a cultured gentleman and a beachcomber.

Yet Melville was assuredly both, and in deserting the *Acushnet*
in the Marquesas he was extending his contact with a place that
figured in the upper-class traditions of his family as much as in
his current hard times. Among Melville's numerous seafaring
kinsmen was Captain John DeWolf II, a close friend of G. H. von
Langsdorff, a Russian naturalist who visited the Marquesas with
Krusenstern in 1804, and there is ample evidence to show that
Melville's early familiarity with DeWolf would have taught him
about the Marquesas as part of the great world of adventure and
exploration in which his uncle had moved. There was also a
cousin, Thomas Melville, with whom Herman was very well acquainted in youth, who had served as a midshipman aboard the
Vincennes on the voyage that brought Charles Stewart to Nukuheva and had even accompanied Stewart on his excursion into
Typee Valley.[7] There is good reason to believe, then, that before
he ever set foot on the shore of Taiohae Bay Melville had vivid
impressions of the Marquesas, as a target for the purposes of scientific explorers, American warships, and missionaries.

Yet he came himself in drastically reduced circumstances, and
he brought with him the complex psychology of a failed patrician. In the early years of the nineteenth century, the bustling in-
dustrial and mercantile economy of the United States began to
make it possible for men of very modest beginnings to achieve
great fortunes, so that the social arena was formed in which the
classic rags-to-riches story emerged as a parable of striving. At
the same time, however, the tenure of the upper classes was rendered precarious so that, with considerably less popular appeal,
there also emerged the characteristic opposite story of riches to

rags. "In this republican country," Nathaniel Hawthorne once commented, "amid the fluctuating waves of our social life, somebody is always at the drowning-point. The tragedy is enacted with as continual a repetition as that of a popular drama on a holiday; and, nevertheless, is felt as deeply, perhaps, as when an hereditary noble sinks below his order."[8] Thinking at least in part of the decline in fortune suffered by his own family, Hawthorne put his finger on an experience that lies in the personal background of quite a number of American writers. Emerson, Melville, and Faulkner all grew up with traditions of lost prominence; Cooper and James found it possible to live on inherited wealth and still were alienated from mercantile America. Accompanying the dilettante and the gentleman-tramp as figures of this scheme of vicissitudes is the noble savage, as a creature dispossessed by the same graceless, pious, and businesslike arrivists that have dispossessed the patrician himself: the noble yet defenseless soul trampled upon by self-righteous civilizers.

Melville's impulse to view the islanders as poignant victims, like his view of the island itself as a refuge from the cruelties of civilized life, thus bears affinities with the treatment Faulkner gives to Sam Fathers and with the noble savages in the Leatherstocking Tales. But Melville's treatment is less decisively ritualized; it preserves critical ambivalences that draw him into deeper and deeper efforts to fathom what his own position truly is, while self-protectively assuming a jaunty demeanor that keeps the internal conflicts at work as an engaging counterpoint instead of letting them harden into contradictions. Melville thus becomes in a sense more marginal than the beachcomber himself, inhabiting a realm where self-definition is inherently unstable because the terms upon which it is possible have been disrupted from within. As he tries to come to terms with his Marquesan experience, he finds the concept of civilization coming to pieces in his hands; yet he has no alternative concept with which to replace it.

Before such profound dislocations become problematical, however, Melville offers a picture that nicely sums up the complexities of his interpretive stance, comparing Western and Marquesan ways from a "third viewpoint," the vantage of a man viewing the peculiarities of both cultures from a tenuous position somewhere outside both. One of the characteristic features of South Sea narratives, well represented in Porter and Stewart, is the "portrait" of a typical islander. Melville recasts this convention toward the beginning of *Typee* where he offers a dual portrait, placing the French admiral in full-dress uniform beside a Marquesan patriarch for purposes of comparison. "They were both tall and noble-looking men; but in other respects how strikingly contrasted! Du Petit Thouars exhibited upon his person all the paraphernalia of his naval rank. He wore a richly decorated admiral's frock-coat, a laced chapeau bras, and upon his breast were a variety of ribbons and orders; while the simple islander, with the exception of a slight cincture about his loins, appeared in all the nakedness of nature" (29). Melville goes on to reflect, characteristically, that the superior refinement and splendor of the Frenchman may have been purchased at an exorbitant sacrifice of the happiness still enjoyed by the simple native; but what deserves emphasis in this depiction is the location of the observer himself, not a member of the civilized or the savage order, but standing ironically aside and holding a "golden-hued bunch of bananas . . . of which I occasionally partook," Melville concludes, "while making the aforesaid philosophical reflections" (29).

Instead of striding before us as an intrepid naval hero with an Enlightenment world view and imperial ambitions, or as a stalwart knight of faith chancing the domain of the Enemy, Melville presents himself as a man eating bananas. The whimsey by which he deflates his own "philosophical reflections" bespeaks a temperament that would prefer to be defined by negations, by a recognition of the formal attitudes in which it does not partake, the schools of thought to which it does not belong. Melville's joking self-effacement here, as throughout the book, arises from his consciousness of the farcical ironies that develop amid the interplay of discordant interpretive perspectives. But he was aware that such ironies can also be tragic, so that the informal and companionable figure of the man eating bananas sometimes gives way to more turbulent self-representations. Melville also speaks to us as a man ravaged by the terrors that his preconceptions inspired, or enraptured by the felicity of the Typees' social state, or seething with fury against the violence done to Polynesians by Westerners in the arrogance of their civilized delusions. In the role of gentleman-beachcomber, that is to say, Melville elaborates a distinctively Romantic perspective on Western undertakings in Polynesia. All of his narrative personae, from the nonchalant to the righteously aroused, present varying expressions of the meditative outsider, who at the bottom of his heart does not know what world he belongs to. Instead of applying a coherent interpretive framework to Marquesan society, Melville struggles with passionate impulses and moral convictions that refuse to be ordered in a general design. Porter and Stewart passed through crises of meaning in which civilization was identified with the white man and the opposing savage was embodied in the Marquesans. In *Typee* the crisis of meaning is located within Melville himself: he finds his mind radically divided between horror and profound admiration for the islanders, as it is also divided between hatred for civilization and a frantic desire to return to it.

Melville thus makes visible the inner misgivings that were circumscribed and controlled in the civilized self. The anxieties attendant upon the encounter with an alien way of being become an explicit theme in Melville's account, instead of being quelled in rituals of civilized self-affirmation. His narrative reflects a Romantic preoccupation with the vicissitudes of the inner life and conforms as closely to a civilized convention as any of the meditations of Porter and Stewart. Yet conformity to a convention of thought does not necessarily lead to error; what it generates is a selective focus upon certain aspects of an experience that may appear insignificant within other conventions. David Porter's outlook, for example, prompted him to give meticulous and detailed accounts of the technical achievements of the Marquesans. The missionaries, with their eagerness to communicate the Word of God, became skilled in the Marquesan language. What we find in Melville is a change of focus: he is fascinated as much by white responses to the Marquesans as by the Marquesans themselves. He shifts the emphasis so that it rests upon the encounter, the experience of contact, rather than upon the Marquesans as a thing observed.

In so doing, Melville becomes fascinated by the ways in which factual information is taken up by exponents of various inter-

pretive perspectives and made into a symbolic carrier of the
world view they embrace. Melville's gift for language served this
interest well, permitting him to catch the tone, the logic, and the
characteristic vocabulary of the disparate modes of response and
analysis that others had presented. The exceptional fidelity with
which he could render the rhetorical stances of other civilized
men prompted him to recognize that the visions they pro-
pounded were frequently more compelling as rhetoric than as
representations of truth. In *Typee* this knack enables Melville to
convey impressions of the ways in which various schemes of interpretation make sense, make nonsense, and wreak havoc in
Polynesia.

Melville at the same time claimed as factual a number of representations that were simply untrue. It has been determined
conclusively, for example, that he was not in the Marquesas for
as long as he claimed: the four months' residence he insisted
upon has been cut back to one or two months. A number of the
more memorable incidents of his stay can be distinguished as
outright fabrications in the light of what is now known of Marquesan life, while others appear highly dubious. Melville also
consistently implies that he wrote up his account from personal
memories, not acknowledging the large extent to which he used
Stewart's *Visit* and other narratives of Polynesian travel. He
claims, in fact, that he "never happened to meet with" (6) Porter's *Journal*, but there is incontestable literary evidence to show
that he had.[9]

Melville's conscious departures from fact include fictional extensions of actual incidents, fabrications of incidents, and outright lies. They have imposed upon students of Polynesia a job of
guesswork so harassing that at least one has dismissed *Typee* as
"a completely romantic fantasy."[10] More patient scholars have
acknowledged that there are some items in Melville's account
that are of use to an ethnographer, particularly in those sections
where his report corresponds to what can be determined inde-
pendently to be likely or true.

Concerned with his way of construing the meaning of his confrontation with the Marquesans, however, we can find certain of
the fictional elements in *Typee* just as revealing as any quantity of
objective ethnography that might be salvaged from it. Melville's

fictionalizing might be taken, indeed, as a conscious extension of the process we have seen at work in Porter and Stewart, according to which the impulse to validate a conviction about the nature of the savage throws information into thematic patterns and sometimes leads to misapprehensions of fact. Porter, we found, insisted that the Marquesans could not be cannibals because such a practice did not make sense within his way of estimating their character. The missionaries, on the other hand, harped upon the Marquesans' cannibalism as the key to their essential character. In both cases cannibalism was taken as a symbolic indicator of radical savagery within the general system of interpretation that made civilization and savagery appear suitable for the purpose of describing the white man's confrontation with the Marquesan.

Melville's fictional devices aid in his general analysis of this confrontation. Admitting that the Marquesans are cannibals, Melville explores a number of questions about what that fact means. Does it mean that their culture as a whole is depraved? Does it mean that white men have an obligation to assume control of their lives? As Melville pursues such questions he finds that he cannot contain his own insights within the categories of civilized and savage that were available to him, or within any other consistent analytic concepts. Melville's eagerness to get at the truth of these issues is incontestable, as is his impatience with the distortions he saw in the accounts of others. Trying to tell the truth through the artifices of fiction became a central preoccupation of his career as it unfolded, and his introduction to *Typee* seeks to forestall the incredulity of certain readers in terms that sketch an early response to the difficulties of doing so. "He has stated such matters [those appearing incredible] just as they occurred, and leaves every one to form his own opinion concerning them; trusting that his anxious desire to speak the unvarnished truth will gain for him the confidence of his readers" (xiv). So we must analyze Melville's fictional constructions in order to get at the truth he wanted to convey, without being beguiled by his claim to have stated things just as they occurred.

Melville remains the gentleman-beachcomber, then, the humorous knowledgeable provocative shrewd cultivated fluent untrustworthy figure in whom the typical uncertainties of civilized

men are made uncomfortably visible. Unlike Stewart and Porter, who wear clerical and military regalia quite in keeping with their identities, Melville appears before us in disguise. He is a connoisseur of the anxieties and instabilities of view that develop as received traditions of thought encounter realities to which they apply only in part; and his presentation of self persistently hints at an inward reality that must remain unpresented.

Melville's narrative of his residence among the Typees sharpens the conflicts and ambivalences detectable in the stance he takes at the outset, as he moves from his aloof spectator's role to one of anxious involvement.[11] The Typees once again force a confrontation that tests the civilized presence to its core. Porter, Stewart, and the missionaries found that they had to come to terms with the Typees, and in doing so they came to terms—for better or worse—with themselves. Melville arranges an analogous confrontation by establishing the Typees early as an ominous presence amid the romantic loveliness of Nukuheva. Among the "strangely jumbled anticipations" (5) that come to haunt him when he learns that the whaler is steering for the Marquesas, Melville gives special prominence to the "particular and most unqualified repugnance" he felt for the Typees. "Even before visiting the Marquesas, I had heard from men who had touched at the group on former voyages some revolting stories in connection with these savages" (25). He knows from the outset, that is, that his vision of Nukuheva as an island paradise paradoxically contains elements of horror, and the first step is taken toward his showdown with the meaning of this paradox when he falls into the Typees' hands.

Melville constructs the narrative in *Typee* to dramatize the experience of living in a situation whose social bearings are uncertain. It is a narrative of shifting perspectives in which the narrator passes through four distinct phases that are dominated by sharply contrasting estimates of the character of Marquesan life. After his initial phase of romantic attraction for life with a "friendly" tribe, Melville's narrator is horrified, then delighted, and finally perplexed by the Typees. The account of his residence among the Typees turns, in fact, on situations in which overwhelmingly powerful interpretive responses are successively revealed to have been mistaken, as the narrator, whom Melville calls Tommo, vainly attempts to arrive at a stable conception of the islanders.

Tommo's first reaction to the Typees is governed by impressions of their character he had received from earlier voyagers, and Melville takes care to underscore their vehemence: "we were now placed in those very circumstances from the bare thought of which I had recoiled with such abhorrence but a few days before. What might be our fearful destiny? To be sure, as yet we had been treated with no violence; nay, had been even kindly and hospitably entertained. But what dependence could be placed upon the fickle passions which sway the bosom of a savage? . . . Might it not be that beneath these fair appearances the islanders covered some perfidious design, and that their friendly reception of us might only precede some horrible catastrophe?" (76).

During the early part of his stay in the valley these ghastly imaginings form part of an attack of melancholy that Tommo is at a loss to understand. At the center of his anxiety is a lameness in his leg that quickly becomes so severe as to prevent him from walking without aid. "I still continued to languish under a complaint the origin and nature of which were still a mystery. Cut off as I was from all intercourse with the civilized world, and feeling the inefficiency of anything the natives could do to relieve me; knowing too, that so long as I remained in my present condition, it would be impossible for me to leave the valley, whatever opportunity might present itself; and apprehensive that ere long we might be exposed to some caprice on the part of the islanders, I now gave up all hopes of recovery, and became a prey to the most gloomy thoughts" (104). The emphasis here is not upon Tommo's view of the islanders, but upon his own dejection; yet it is evident that the dominant theme of his despondence is the thought of being cut off forever from the civilized world in the midst of capricious and inexplicable savages. His melancholy, that is to say, takes form around the polarity of "civilized-savage," with the conventional moral valuations.

The superiority of civilization, for Tommo, is focused here of course on a rather limited issue, namely his expectation that civilized medicine would be able to heal his leg. But the leg ailment itself is depicted by Melville as a signal of Tommo's deeper disorientation. The leg begins to hurt as Tommo and Toby get lost in the Nukuheva highlands. During this part of the story Melville initiates a dramatic struggle that occupies Tommo for the remainder of the book, his effort to maintain resolution and presence of mind in the midst of a disconcerting environment. The leg pains originate at the crisis of this journey, on a night when their hunger, exhaustion, and disorientation are made horrible by an icy rainstorm. Melville's description of the moment emphasizes the threat to his self-possession: "the accumulated horrors of that night, the death-like coldness of the place, the appalling darkness and the dismal sense of our forlorn condition, almost unmanned me" (46).

The dismay Tommo feels at the outset of his stay in the valley grows more intense when Toby disappears and he is given conflicting accounts by the Typees to explain it. One says that Toby is gone forever, another claims that he will return in three days with medicines: when Toby does not return, Tommo is left uncertain whether the Typees had eaten him, whether he had made off without any intention of returning, or what other fate might have befallen him.

Tommo's melancholy therefore appears to him as a concatenation of mysteries. The disappearance of Toby, the malady in his leg, the actions of the Typees, and his own responses all appear unaccountable. In retrospect he is struck by the tenacity of this frame of mind and by the images of Typee character to which it was connected.

In looking back to this period, and calling to remembrance the numberless proofs of kindness and respect which I received from the natives of the valley, I can scarcely understand how it was that, in the midst of so many consolatory circumstances, my mind should still have been consumed by the most dismal forebodings, and have remained a prey to the profoundest melancholy. It is true that the suspicious circumstances which had attended the disappearance of Toby were enough of themselves to excite distrust with regard to the savages, in whose power I felt myself to be entirely placed, especially when it was combined with the knowledge that these very men, kind and respectful as they were to me, were, after all, nothing better than a set of cannibals. (118)

Tommo's dread of the islanders, his regarding them as "nothing better than a set of cannibals," is thus specified as a function of his psychological condition. Instead of standing clear as an objective insight into the character of the Marquesans, the impulse to fix on the practice of cannibalism as typifying their character is presented as a feature of Tommo's state of mind. We have observed that other visitors to the Marquesas present strong feelings, whether of delight or abhorrence, as aroused by characteristics of Marquesan life that are conceived to be inherent. Stewart is disgusted by sexual customs because, he avers, they are disgusting customs. In Melville the same process occurs; but in his characterization of Tommo he finds an alternative way of viewing interpretive responses in which the disposition of the viewer's mind is given greatly increased powers.

The picture of Typee life that Tommo conveys is thus represented as one feature of his general effort to accommodate himself to a social environment for which he lacks adequate conceptual equipment. The civilized-savage polarity gives form to a complex response that is called into play by the apparent requirements of his situation, but it does not permit him to take his bearings satisfactorily. Tommo remains anxious and confused until his initial conception of Typee life is replaced by another.

And this replacement occurs, notably, through the emergence of a new consciousness rather than as the result of acquiring new information or ideas. As though exhausted by the effort to maintain his erroneous preconceptions, Tommo sinks "insensibly into the kind of apathy which ensues after some violent outbreak of despair," whereupon his leg suddenly heals and he begins "to experience an elasticity of mind" that places him "beyond the reach of those dismal forebodings" (123). He no longer views the valley of the Typees as a hellish cage where his captors are indulgently fattening him for a cannibal feast. "When I looked around the verdant recess in which I was buried, and gazed up to the summits of the lofty eminence that hemmed me in, I was well disposed to think that I was in the 'Happy Valley' and that beyond those heights there was nought but a world of care and anxiety" (124). Passing from a state in which he is wrung with horror at the prospect of never returning to civilization, Tommo

is overwhelmed with delight at the felicities of the savage life. A
new set of interpretive presuppositions slips into place, a set that
reverses his earlier valuations of civilized and savage.

He continues to assume that disparate societies may be located
on a single scale, but now he refuses to place his own culture at
the top. "I was fain to confess that, despite the disadvantages of
his condition, the Polynesian savage, surrounded by all the luxu-
rious provisions of nature, enjoyed an infinitely happier, though
certainly a less intellectual existence, than the self-complacent
European . . . In a primitive state of society, the enjoyments of
life, though few and simple, are spread over a great extent, and
are unalloyed; but Civilization, for every advantage she imparts,
holds a hundred evils in reserve" (124). Melville at this point
does not doubt that civilized-savage forms a suitable description
of the varying states of society; like other exponents of the noble
savage, he adopts a rhetorical inversion of the essential concept.

Having dramatized the experience of transcending a mistaken
set of conceptions, Melville now claims the advantage of having
discovered how confining and misleading they can be. He presents a striking series of contrasts between his vision of native felicity and the distorted conception the missionaries had circulated. "Entering their valley, as I did, under the most erroneous
impressions of their character, I was soon led to exclaim in
amazement; 'Are these the ferocious savages, the blood-thirsty
cannibals of whom I have heard such frightful tales! They deal
more kindly with each other, and are more humane, than many
who study essays on virtue and benevolence, and who repeat
every night that beautiful prayer breathed first by the lips of the
divine and gentle Jesus.' I will frankly declare, that after passing
a few weeks in this valley of the Marquesas, I formed a higher
estimate of human nature than I had ever before entertained"
(203).

A primary tenet of the missionaries' Calvinistic view held that
man's innate unruliness made it necessary that society be regulated by firm legal controls. In observing that the Marquesans
had little in the way of formal institutions of government,
Stewart concluded that they were preserved from anarchy by the
"tyranny of superstition" administered by the priests. The evident social harmony of the Typees, flourishing in the absence of

a legal system, gave Melville an opportunity to denounce missionary doctrine on this point and to bring forward the moral
schema he now uses to evaluate Marquesan life.

> There were no legal provisions whatever for the well-being and con-
> servation of society, the enlightened end of civilized legislation. And
> yet everything went on in the valley with a harmony and smoothness
> unparalleled, I will venture to assert, in the most select, refined, and
> pious associations of mortals in Christendom. How are we to explain
> this enigma? . . . They seemed to be governed by that sort of tacit
> common-sense law which, say what they will of the inborn lawless-
> ness of the human race, has its precepts graven on every breast. The
> grand principles of virtue and honor, however they may be distorted
> by arbitrary codes, are the same all the world over: and where these
> principles are concerned, the right or wrong of any action appears
> the same to the uncultivated as to the enlightened mind. It is to this
> indwelling, this universally diffused perception of what is *just* and
> *noble,* that the integrity of the Marquesans in their intercourse with
> each other is to be attributed. (200–201).

Thus Melville enunciates the Romantic moral outlook that
governs the second phase of Tommo's sojourn among the
Typees; it is an outlook analogous to the view of David Porter,
holding that man has an innate knowledge of good and evil. The
distinctive Romantic note is audible in Melville's claim that this
knowledge may be distorted, if not wholly effaced, by "arbitrary
codes," and the attendant claim that such distortions are more
common in civilized life than among primitive men. "Civilization
does not engross all the virtues of humanity," he asserts; "she
has not even her full share of them" (202). Melville's attribution
of greater simplicity to the life of the Marquesan leads him to the
view that civilized man has departed more widely from his innate moral sense, into arbitrary forms and requirements of behavior.

Melville accordingly depicts Tommo's infatuation with the
Typees as a period in which he gains fuller insight by entering
unreservedly into their life. This unforced immediacy of experience becomes possible once the "arbitrary codes" that govern
thought and feeling in his own society have been transcended.
The more Tommo detaches himself from his accustomed mode
of life, the more he discovers that the Typees are virtuous and

carefree. "I flung myself . . . into all the social pleasures of the valley, and sought to bury all regrets, and all remembrances of my previous existence, in the wild enjoyments it afforded. In my various wanderings through the vale, and as I became better acquainted with the character of its inhabitants, I was more and more struck with the light-hearted joyousness that everywhere prevailed" (144).

Melville does not declare that the effort to understand an alien culture must include a degree of sympathetic participation in its life. But in Tommo's period of enthusiasm for the Typees he dramatizes such a spirit of imaginative accommodation. Tommo finds himself intrigued, for example, by a coffin-canoe in which an effigy of the dead chieftain can be seen wielding a paddle. "The place had a peculiar charm for me; I hardly know why; but so it was . . . I loved to yield myself up to the fanciful superstition of the islanders, and could almost believe that the grim warrior was bound heavenward. In this mood when I turned to depart I bade him 'God speed, and a pleasant voyage.' Aye, paddle away, brave chieftain, to the land of spirits! To the material eye thou makest but little progress; but with the eye of faith, I see thy canoe cleaving the bright waves, which die away on those dimly looming shores of Paradise" (173). The Marquesans, to be sure, knew of no distinction between the "material eye" and the "eye of faith," and indeed Melville's use of this language is manifestly intended to parody the symbolic constructions that were placed upon experience by Christian believers. The passage nowhere claims to explain the true meaning of the shrine; Melville simply observes that civilized and primitive men respond in comparable ways to the experience of death. The idea that a man could paddle to heaven shows that "however ignorant man may be, he still feels within him his immortal spirit yearning after the unknown future" (173). Yet the path Melville takes toward this assertion is quite distinctive. Instead of judging the rationality of this observance and finding it infantile (like Porter) or weighting its meaning for missionary doctrine (like Stewart), Melville comes to a sense of its meaning through an intuitive receptivity. As he yields himself to the fanciful superstition, its power as an expressive human act begins to take hold of him.

Melville's enthusiasm for this way of achieving an understanding of Typee life is figured in one of his manifestly fictional passages. Melville introduces us early to Fayaway, the Typee maiden who becomes Tommo's paramour, and in the idyllic period of Tommo's stay he constructs a scene in which the pair go boating together on a lake. On one of their excursions Fayaway, "seemed all at once to be struck with some happy idea. With a wild exclamation of delight, she disengaged from her person the ample robe of tappa which was knotted over her shoulder . . . and spreading it out like a sail, stood erect with upraised arms in the head of the canoe" (134). One does not want to place too great a burden of epistemological meaning on this passage, but it is perfectly clear that the central gesture is of the object examined disclosing itself freely to the viewer. There were no lakes in the valley of the Typees, and it is improbable that the islanders would have permitted an exception to the taboo that forbade women to enter boats. Yet Melville's enraptured fantasy crystallizes his interpretation of Typee Valley as an unspoiled Eden: a primal paradise that will reveal its marvelous secrets if man will lay aside his civilized pretensions and enter into the spirit of the savage.

Having viewed the Typees as figures of evil and then as figures of goodness, Tommo moves on to yet another frame of mind, in which his responses are mixed. As this takes place the civilized-savage convention begins to break down because the Typees lose their status as exemplars of the moral abstractions it organizes.

Melville draws the idyllic period of Tommo's stay in the valley to a close by emphasizing aspects of Typee life that he still finds enigmatic. He points out that his intimate acquaintance with the Typees did not permit him to penetrate the meaning of the taboo system: "I perceived every hour the effects of this all-controlling power, without in the least comprehending it" (221). In a similar spirit Tommo confesses his bewilderment at the religious institutions of the valley, which he claims to have had ample opportunity to observe. "I saw everything," he reports, "but could comprehend nothing" (177).

Tommo's anxieties are provoked when the islanders indicate their passionate desire that he submit to tattooing, a practice (he says) that "always appeared inexplicable to me" (221). In this situation the incomprehension is heartily mutual, however, and

Tommo finds himself confronting the Marquesan chief across a line of opposition that neither of them knows how to account for. "When the king first expressed his wish to me, I made known to him my utter abhorrence of the measure, and worked myself into such a state of excitement, that he absolutely stared at me in amazement. It evidently surpassed his majesty's comprehension how any sober-minded and sensible individual could entertain the least possible objection to so beautifying an operation" (219). As he meditates further on the incessant demands of the Typees, Tommo comes to the conclusion that tattooing was connected with their religion, so that the natives were apparently "resolved to make a convert of me" (220). Instead of finding a life of psychic freedom among the Typees where "the grand principles of virtue and honor" hold sway amenably with his own deepest impulses, Tommo now has to contend with efforts to draw him into an alien and confining social structure. The persistently unintelligible character of Marquesan life, before perceived as a realm of romantic mystery that might be plumbed by intuition, now confronts him as a closed system that leaves him miserably alone. Instead of joining in the communal life wholeheartedly, he is compelled once again to calculate his reactions in order to increase the chances of escape. "The pleasures I had previously enjoyed no longer afforded me delight, and all my former desire to escape from the valley now revived with additional force" (220).

Thus awash in misgivings, Tommo is vulnerable once again to virtually unmanageable terrors. The Marquesans displayed reverence for departed kinsmen by keeping their skulls wrapped in a package of tappa and hung from the ridgepole of the familial hut. When Tommo finds his hosts examining these articles, he instantly assumes that they are the skulls of slain and eaten enemies, and avows his certainty that one of the skulls he saw was that of a white man, perhaps even of his lost companion Toby. This misinterpretation increases Tommo's alarm; "Was I destined to perish like him—like him, perhaps to be devoured, and my head to be preserved as a fearful memento of the event? My imagination ran riot in these horrid speculations, and I felt certain that the worst possible evils would befal me" (233). When he finds evidence that an actual cannibal feast had followed upon a successful skirmish with the Happahs, Tommo's reversal of sentiment is completed. "The last horrid revelation had now been made, and the full sense of my condition rushed upon my mind with a force I had never before experienced" (238).

In this third phase of his response to the Typees, however, Tommo does not simply resume the attitudes he had adopted at the outset of his stay. Instead of looking upon the Marquesans as uniformly representing the savage state, he makes discriminations of a simple kind that have large implications for his final viewpoint. Certain of the Typees sympathize with Tommo's desire to escape, Melville tells us, compassionately recognizing his desire to return to his own. Old Marheyo, the ancient head of the family with which Tommo stayed, is brought forward to represent this group, while a ferocious one-eyed chieftain named Mow-mow represents those who wish to keep him in captivity. This division of the Marquesans into competing factions reflects Melville's moral responses to both the evil and the virtuous in Marquesan character, and corresponds to the internal conflict that grips Tommo down to the instant at which he makes good his escape. Mow-mow and his cohorts swim out to capsize the boat in which he is departing, and as Mow-mow comes within arm's reach Tommo strikes him down, yet not without inner turmoil. "Even at the moment I felt horror at the act I was about to commit; but it was no time for pity or compunction, and with a true aim, and exerting all my strength, I dashed the boat-hook at him" (252).

Tommo's uncertainties and the disagreements of the islanders complement each other nicely in giving excitement to the narrative of escape; both characterization and incident are now invested with the counterpointed internal tensions we have noted in the narrative voice itself. Yet this play of ambivalences in Melville's way of depicting the Marquesans was to create difficulties when he sought to pronounce a moral judgment upon the Western encroachment into Polynesia. Melville's attitude cannot be understood simply as the opinion that the islanders had good traits and bad traits. Scarcely any visitor to the Marquesas ever came to a different conclusion. What makes for the distinctive instability of Melville's position is that his experience of the

Typees had rendered doubtful the way in which this judgment, once arrived at, ought to be construed.

As Melville explains his impressions of the relationship that was developing between whites and Polynesians, it becomes apparent that he does not view Marquesan society as a unit standing lower on the scale of societies than the white. Within such an understanding, the virtues of the Marquesans could be acknowledged as belonging to the savage state without undermining the transcendent moral superiority enjoyed by occupants of the civilized condition.[12] Instead Melville found that goodness and evil were irregularly distributed in an uncertain pattern across the cultural boundary that separates whites from Polynesians. Affirming that man enjoys an "innate perception of what is just and noble," Melville does not explain in detail how it is variously distorted and sustained by the social practices of different societies; yet he makes unmistakably clear his judgment that civilization is not a morally superior state of society.

Melville recognized that Marquesan cannibalism struck the occidental imagination as a sign of savagery in its fullest and most lurid form. Porter and Stewart did not view it merely as a "vice" but as the evidence of a sordid level of existence, long since transcended by civilized men. Melville accordingly finds it necessary to argue that the practice is not incompatible with the achievement of advanced moral qualities: "horrible and fearful as the custom is, immeasurably as it is to be abhorred and condemned, still I assert that those who indulge in it are in other respects humane and virtuous" (205). Instead of triggering the interpretive mechanism that would relegate the Marquesan to the status of a savage, the practice of cannibalism should be looked upon simply as one trait among others. Melville asks, moreover, whether "the mere eating of human flesh so very far exceeds in barbarity" the harsher forms of punishment routinely visited upon criminals in civilized lands. Melville fixes upon the clearest evidence of occidental technical superiority in order to advance the assertion that civilization sets a standard for wickedness rather than virtue: "The fiend-like skill we display in the invention of all manner of death-dealing engines, the vindictiveness with which we carry on our wars, and the misery and desolation that follow in their train, are enough of themselves to distinguish the white civilized man as the most ferocious animal on the face of the earth" (125). The Swiftian intensity of this indictment cuts through the conventional meaning of civilized, and indeed gains strength by incorporating the word into its declaration that the extreme moral abhorrence usually reserved for the savage is more appropriate as a response to the civilized man.

Melville recognizes that the ethical responses he has recorded place him in opposition to the missionary movement. As bringers of civilization, the missionaries conceived themselves to be undertaking a historic role, which had been defined for them by traditions that featured the savage an inherently suited for improvement under their ministrations. Yet Melville sensed that the entire undertaking was geared to erroneous moral analyses and ascriptions. "The term 'Savage' is, I conceive, often misapplied, and indeed when I consider the vices, cruelties, and enormities of every kind that spring up in the tainted atmosphere of a feverish civilization, I am inclined to think that so far as the relative wickedness of the parties is concerned, four or five Marquesan Islanders sent to the United States as Missionaries might be quite as useful as an equal number of Americans despatched to the Islands in a similar capacity" (125–126).

But if the effort to civilize cannot be grounded on the relative ethical qualities of the civilizers and their subjects, how then can it be justified? And what is to be made of the American conviction that savages are morally inferior? At certain points Melville affirms that Polynesian savages are a creation of Western policy: "How often is the term 'savages' incorrectly applied! None really deserving of it were ever yet discovered by voyagers or by travellers. They have discovered heathens and barbarians, whom by horrible cruelties they have exasperated into savages" (27). A close look at this passage reveals, however, that Melville has not broken out of the conceptual framework whose validity he is implicitly challenging. He points out that the term "savages" is *incorrectly applied,* suggesting that it may have some proper applications among primitive people (though none has been discovered). And his substitution of the terms "heathens and barbarians" likewise suggests a morally inferior social state in need of assistance from above.

Melville cannot abandon the idea that civilized men ought

somehow to do good for the uncivilized, and yet when he looks at the practical reality of what is taking place in Polynesia, he is struck by the ironical way in which benevolent abstractions appear to be vindicated by circumstances that are in fact dreadful. "Let the savages be civilized," he affirms, "but civilize them with benefits, and not with evils; and let heathenism be destroyed, but not by destroying the heathen. The Anglo-Saxon hive have extirpated Paganism from the greater part of the North American continent; but with it they have likewise extirpated the greater portion of the Red race. Civilization is gradually sweeping from the earth the lingering vestiges of Paganism, and at the same time the shrinking forms of its unhappy worshippers" (195).

What Melville sees in the interaction between missionaries and islanders in the South Seas is a process where the grand abstractions espoused by the missionaries produce a distortion of native life that justifies and facilitates a system of economic oppression whose results appear to vindicate the abstractions that sponsor them. Melville's outline of this perverse and frightening logic begins as he taunts Calvinistic belief concerning the Fall of Man by pointing out that the Marquesans can feed themselves without heavy labor: "The penalty of the Fall presses very lightly upon the valley of Typee ... I scarcely saw any piece of work performed there which caused the sweat to stand upon a single brow." But he then contrasts this happy condition with the demoralization and social collapse suffered by islanders with whom the missionaries have had their way, observing that the Christianizers themselves impose this ostensibly divine penalty and then collect its proceeds:

> Among the islands of Polynesia, no sooner are the images overturned, the temples demolished, and the idolaters converted into *nominal* Christians, than disease, vice, and premature death make their appearance. The depopulated land is then recruited from the rapacious hordes of enlightened individuals who settle themselves within its borders, and clamorously announce the progress of the Truth ... The spontaneous fruits of the earth, which God in his wisdom had ordained for the support of the indolent natives, remorselessly seized upon and appropriated by the stranger, are devoured before the eyes of the starving inhabitants, or sent on board the numerous vessels which now touch at their shores.

When the famished wretches are cut off in this manner from their
natural supplies, they are told by their benefactors to work and earn
their support by the sweat of their brows! (195–196)

The doctrine of the Fall, however ludicrous its provisions seem
when applied to the original felicity of the islander, becomes
grimly appropriate to his condition once the establishment of
Western commercial enterprises makes it necessary for him to
choose between starvation and earning bread by sweating for it.
Melville observes, that is to say, the dynamic role of theory in the
social process that transforms the island populations into a labor
force.

   More than once, then, Melville glimpses the idea that occidental activities in Polynesia produce savages. The misery and moral
squalor that the civilizers ostensibly meant to relieve is in fact
generated by them. As Melville pursues this line of reflection, it
appears to him that the true meaning of civilization, as a process
arranged by whites for the transformation of Polynesians, is in-
distinguishable from degradation. The Polynesians, he affirms,
have been "civilized into draught horses, and evangelized into
beasts of burden" (196). He observes that the relation between
whites and Polynesians is not one in which the Polynesian is
drawn upward through contact with superior virtue; it is a subjugation both physically and spiritually in which the islanders
are made to conform to the concepts of savagery that the white
man imposes.

   In observing that the worst abuses of the missionary enterprise
could be made to look consistent with the theory on which the
whole was based, Melville described a self-sustaining structure
of prejudice that threatened to gather his own viewpoint into its
scheme of interpretation. In mounting his attack against the civilizers, Melville became uneasily aware of his position as a critical
outsider and had to come to terms with a serious dilemma. How
was he to obtain any argumentative leverage against a social
program whose conception arose directly from a theory of civilization that virtually all of his readers shared? His paradoxical
identity as gentleman-beachcomber might give him opportunities to parody and deflate the pretensions of Americans in Polynesia, but it did not give him a philosophical foundation for the

moral indictment that he wanted to bring. Having at least provisionally crossed the cultural boundary between the American and the Polynesian, Melville found that the predilections and convictions of his own culture seemed to gather into a solid front against his own perceptions.

This problem was particularly troublesome because Melville himself shared the presuppositions whose perverse influence he had noted. His attack on the missionaries is riddled with disclaimers that betray his own uncertainty even as they reveal his effort to find some grounds plausible to civilized Christian readers for offering his violent condemnation of the missionary enterprise. As Melville pursues his claim that the Typees ought to preserve their freedom from civilized influences, he avails himself of persuasive devices which affirm that civilized life does indeed have superior virtues. "Better will it be for them for ever to remain the happy and innocent heathens and barbarians that they now are, than, like the wretched inhabitants of the Sandwich Islands, to enjoy the mere name of Christians without experiencing any of the vital operations of true religion, whilst, at the same time, they are made the victims of the worst vices and evils of civilized life" (181–182).

Here as elsewhere Melville's language subtly preserves possibilities of meaning that are larger than he is prepared to spell out in full, so that what look like contradictions contain the seed of a more comprehensive understanding. Implying that Christianity offers "the vital operations of true religion," he does not explain how it can fail to have a salutary effect upon the Typees. Nor does he explain how it can follow that "in every case where Civilization has in any way been introduced among those whom we call savages, she has scattered her vices, and withheld her blessings" (198). Yet in associating "true religion" with "vital operations," instead of identifying it with a body of sacred and inalterable ideas, he leaves open the possibility of concluding that Christianity is not *the only* true religion, and that its exemplars hence cannot properly measure the moral condition of those who have a different culture by locating them on a civilized scale of values. Preserving such critical ambiguities while not pursuing their implications, Melville works his way into his subject in a manner that lays open a whole range of intellectual and spiritual conflicts whose source was in the idea of civilization itself as a mode of apprehending self and society. Only provisionally does Melville transcend this idea in *Typee;* instead he testifies to the inner tensions that characterized those who embraced it. Faced by the question, finally, of how the missionary movement could have failed, Melville does not pursue the radical implications of his insight. He lays the blame on practical mismanagement.

Taken in the context of his outcries against the missionary cause, and his countless joking sallies against Western religious beliefs, Melville's summation of the issue might be mistaken for a calculated sarcasm: "Lest the slightest misconception should arise from anything thrown out in this chapter, or indeed in any other part of the volume, let me here observe, that against the cause of missions in the abstract no Christian can possibly be opposed: it is in truth a just and holy cause." The undertaking, he observes, "however it may be blessed of Heaven, is in itself but human; and subject, like everything else to errors and abuses" (197). Melville thus focuses his attack on targets that his readers would readily comprehend, on the moral failures of individual missionaries and on their mismanagement of an enterprise he asserts in principle to be glorious. This shift in perspective is more nearly a strategic equivocation intended to accommodate the predilections of religious readers than a veiled gibe intended to parody them. But the larger reason for Melville's shifting viewpoint remains obscure if we do not recognize the extent to which he himself personally shared such civilized conceptions and was inwardly fearful of the way they might apply to him.

Melville knew perfectly well that as a runaway sailor he would instantly be identified as of dubious moral worth by friends of the missionary cause: he strains hard to forestall attacks on his character. His role as beachcomber placed him squarely on the target area that received unanimous cannonading from all respectable students of Polynesian life, so that he now stresses the gentlemen aspect of his presentation of self and stretches it far enough to permit him to bid for a place in the ranks of the righteous. "As wise a man as Shakespeare has said, that the bearer of evil tidings hath but a losing office; and so I suppose will it prove with me, in communicating to the trusting friends of the Hawaiian Mission what has been disclosed in various portions of this narrative. I am persuaded, however, that as these disclosures will by their very nature attract attention, so they will lead to something which will not be without ultimate benefit to the cause of Christianity in the Sandwich Islands" (198–199). The balanced sobriety of Melville's syntax and his allusion to Shakespeare deserve attention here. They are claims to authority that are as telling as his declaration of support for "the cause of Christianity."

Melville's self-defensive maneuvers are so deft and so insistent because the inner anxieties he felt as a gentleman-beachcomber corresponded to the uncertainties that such a role provoked in the society of which he was a part. Because Melville himself shared the general outlook that rendered his position anomalous, the dramatization of his interior uncertainties explores the tensions of the "civilized self" at large. His rhetoric, his narrative, and his formal pronouncements cooperate to produce an expression of the anomalies that Westerners generally sought to banish from awareness for the sake of maintaining psychic coherence. Thus, instead of vindicating the idea of civilization, Melville subverts it.

Yet this subversion makes possible a special form of recreation. Like the other visitors to the Marquesas, Melville dramatizes the experience as a test in which the civilized identity survives the threat of disintegration. *Typee* moves along a course that remains perilously close to the brink of sheer confusion. We have found Melville working with contradictory points of view, discontinuous states of mind, resounding moral declarations crosscut by equivocal disclaimers, and moments of hapless incomprehension. It is now time to recognize that Melville's skillful flirting with such vexations has the effect of rendering tolerable the conflicts which it provokes. Melville is able in effect to dismantle the civilized self and give its constituents play, toying with its root anxieties without giving way to the chaos that threatens to erupt. In his rhetorical stratagems and in the dramas of interaction that he sets forth, Melville flexibly manipulates structural principles (the meanings embodied in the terms "civilized" and "savage") that were rigid fixtures in the personalities of Porter and the missionaries.

We have observed that other narratives of Marquesan encoun-

ters have implicit thematic structures that correspond to conceptions of civilization and to the requirements of the civilized self
as a dynamic process. In *Typee* this endemic ordering process is
raised to a higher level of explicitness even as Melville heightens
the tensions that are controlled by it. William Alexander, on the
basis of extended firsthand experience of the Marquesans, ac-
cused Charles Stewart of writing a "religious novel" about them
instead of giving a straightforward factual account; yet we have
seen that even the daily journal entries of missionaries in the
field are filled with incidents that are shaped in accordance with a
general vision. Melville lays hold directly upon the verbal resources, the devices of style and narrative design, by which such
general schemes of order assert themselves in narratives meant
to be resolutely factual. The fusion of fact and meaning in Melville's treatment, accordingly, does not occur in isolated critical
incidents or moments of ecstasy. Like the inherent tensions of
the civilized self and the rhetorical stratagems employed to contain them, so the symbolic quality of incident and character is
raised to a higher tension in Melville's treatment, with the result
that a verbal texture is created that has a life of its own. Melville's book is, in short, a work of art.

Typee, the book itself, is Melville's city on a hill. It does not
point beyond itself to an establishment at Nukuheva where the
ordering processes of civilization are at work in the midst of a
threatening confusion. Instead of reporting upon an activity that
is occurring elsewhere, it is itself the achievement. Producing the
disorder that it overcomes, Melville's art reanimates the self by
dramatizing its resources and liabilities; instead of locating that
drama in a remote social project, *Typee* places it directly before
the reader and engages him in it by provoking and exploiting his
responses. As such, the book is not so much a container of
meanings as a generator of them. It is a meaning maker that itself
prompts interpretive efforts and reveals new qualities as the
identities of interpreters shift with the times and as they vary
within a given era.

As a work of literary art, Melville's *Typee* extracts from their
setting in daily life certain root paradigms and structural principles that govern the world of social experience and the styles of
selfhood available within it, transposing them into an aesthetic

domain where they can be made the objects rather than the ground rules of thought and feeling. Art thus implicitly relativizes all its materials, and is sometimes attacked when it intrudes upon subjects that are held to be sacred absolutes. Yet Melville's art accentuates, in *Typee* and elsewhere, this subversive and critical activity. The ordering of things he achieves, what I have called his city on a hill, is not a fixed architectonic arrangement embracing the work as a whole. It is rather a deeply rhetorical ordering, in which the reader is carried forward by a voice that continuously delivers engaging and coherent imaginative experiences. Like a skillfully managed sailing vessel, Melville's ongoing discourse maintains headway amid the various winds of doctrine from which it draws power.[13] "City on a hill" is indeed far too static a metaphor, and too landlocked, to do justice to Melville's voyages into mystery.

The voice that addresses us in *Typee* is manifestly civilized, yet leaves unresolved the contraditions and inner tensions it discovers in the civilized way of being. The conversation into which we are drawn is one that remains coherent even as what seem indispensable conditions of coherence are abandoned; we are called upon to experience a recreation of self on terms richer than those presupposed by the nineteenth-century scheme of ideas that provides Melville's idiom. We are beneficiaries of Melville's critical art inasmuch as his example has encouraged endeavors of learning that have allowed us to transcend that nineteenth-century frame of reference and, second, because his craft still explores uncharted waters.[14] As a triumph of utterance, *Typee* conveys the discovery that an established system of values can be made to suggest the possibility of a larger and more adequate vision. It is salutary for us to renew this discovery and to participate in the journey through mystery where it can be renewed, since we have here no abiding city.

Melville wanted to do something more, however, than provide an exalted recreation. Like other visitors to the Marquesas, Melville emerges with a concrete social mission: instead of dreaming of a transformation in the life of the Marquesans, he wants to alter the outlook of his fellow countrymen. The target of his reformist zeal is America, not Nukuheva. Yet Melville quickly discovered that Americans, like Marquesans, were not eager for moral reconstruction.

Although *Typee* was an immediate success, it stirred up a noisy controversy about Melville's "veracity" that shows he had thrown his readers on their civilized defenses. We have noticed that Charles Stewart sought to synthesize the attitudes of the cultured gentlemen with those of the missionary, arguing that the work of civilization belongs to both. Melville split the complementary aspects of Stewart's vision and synthesized the gentleman with the beachcomber, arguing that the work of civilization is a destructive delusion. His veracity was then doubted both because of his synthesis and his argument. British skeptics held that Melville's style clearly indicated he was a gentleman, so he could never have been a beachcomber, while friends of the missionary cause in America pointed out that he was professedly a beachcomber and hence a lewd deceiver, whether he was a gentleman or not.

Melville did not find it difficult to shrug off the critics who doubted he had ever been to the Marquesas, especially after his friend Toby came forward in the midst of the furor to validate his story. Against British skeptics, after all, Melville could point out that "an American can be a gentleman, & have read the Waverly Novels, tho every digit may have been in the tarbucket." Taking his stand on the distinctive features of democratic civilization in America, he had a strong position from which to fight for credibility even as his British publisher continued to demand "documentary evidence" of his voyage.[15]

His response to the counterattack from American exponents of the missionary cause, however, was much less secure. Within six months of the publication of *Typee* he was prevailed upon to accept an expurgation in which his moral analyses and proposals were removed. The story of this expurgation makes sharply visible the processes whose workings we have detected in the minds of civilized persons who did not give their anxieties play. The scheme of order laid out for psychic experience by the concept of civilization was administered by a censoring process that can be seen at work here in both its individual and social dimensions. When Stewart and Porter quashed their own misgivings and reaffirmed their commitment to a civilized consciousness, they engaged in a deeply communal act. And when Melville's opponents began to bring arguments against *Typee* and to put pressure on his publisher about the book, they touched off misgivings in Melville himself that brought him to agree—at least for a time—that the expurgations were appropriate.

Soon after *Typee* was published, a pair of favorable reviews welcomed Melville's way of handling ethical issues. Nathaniel Hawthorne, in particular, praised him for his openness to alien ways of life in terms that suggest his awareness that others would find it objectionable. He found in Melville "that freedom of view—it would be too harsh to call it laxity of principle—which renders him tolerant of codes of morals that may be little in accordance with our own; a spirit proper enough to a young and adventurous sailor, and which makes his book the more wholesome to our staid landsmen."[16] Margaret Fuller also expresses her agreement with Melville's strictures on the missionary enterprise, and whimsically commended the book to the "sewing societies, now engaged in providing funds for such enterprises."[17] In retrospect the praise of Hawthorne and Fuller for a successful first book makes it hard to conceive that anyone of significance could attack Melville as a threat to civilization. But these writers were not spokesmen for the dominant values of America in the era of revivalism and the benevolent empire. Like Melville himself, they were marginal figures who in varying ways offered challenges to the regnant ethos, while hoping to remain at peace with it. As their reviews make clear, they were both nervously aware that Melville had run the risk of offending the champions of Christianity and civilization, individuals whose role as leaders of opinion was conferred upon them because of their ability to articulate and exemplify values broadly accepted in America.[18]

The opening blast came from the *New-York Evangelist* and fixed on the issue that was to remain central to the dispute, the evident moral confusion and degeneracy of *Typee*'s scapegrace author. "He had life among Marquesan cannibals to his liking; a plenty of what pleases the vicious appetite of a sailor, or of sensual human nature generally." Melville's character, like that of the Marquesans themselves, was to be estimated by evangelical commentators in accordance with the doctrine of original sin. In

addition to making understandable Melville's abounding "slurs
and flings against missionaries and civilization," the doctrine
carried implications for the literary quality of the book. To the
orthodox, man's imagination was infected by original sin as
much as any other aspect of his nature, and provided an avenue
by which the impious could traduce the principles of Christian
readers. "We have long noted it as true in criticism," the *Evangelist* asserted, "that what makes a large class of books bad, im-
moral, and consequently injurious, is not so much what is plainly
expressed, as what is left to be imagined by the reader."[19]

The evangelical advocates of Christian truth issued warnings
against reading any sort of fiction. Such works "insult the understanding of the reader by representing as truth what is con-
fessedly false, and by assuming that the great object of reading is
amusement rather than instruction." If indulged, "a habit of
reading for *amusement* simply becomes so fixed that science loses
all its charms." The exercise of imagination that a work like *Typee*
stimulates is here arraigned as a beguiling seduction that enfee-
bles the mind, subverting its capacity to discriminate truth from
falsehood. Fictions mix up these two drastically opposed moral
categories in a way that opens a pathway toward precipitous
moral collapse. "Indiscriminate novel reading" is "intoxicating
and poisonous, and excites a thirst for what is maddening and
destructive." The deadliest elixir is to be found in *"foul and exciting romance"* which "familiarizes the reader with characters, sentiments and events, that should be known only to the police.
Licentious scenes and obscene imagery are unblushingly introduced, and the imagination polluted by suggestions & descriptions revolting to the pure in heart."[20] It is evident that this writer
is concerned mainly about erotic excitements; but the orthodox
clung, as noted, to a general moral schema in which sexuality offered only one of a coordinated set of threats against correct
mental processes. It is not merely licentiousness that will result
from continual intoxication under the stimulants of romance, but
a generalized moral vertigo, what the writer calls "mental delirium tremens." At stake in the *Evangelist's* suspicion that *Typee* is
"sheer romance" is the effort of orthodox believers to keep their
systems of interpreting moral reality firmly in place. The imaginative freedom of romance, which permits alternative ways of

viewing experience to be indulged, threatens to undermine the absolute authority that the orthodox ascribed to their moral vision. The deviant forms of thought and behavior represented by romances may describe things that really happen among men, but they should only be acknowledged in the act of arresting and condemning them: they "should be known only to the police."

We have already noted that the policing of inner responses was a feature of the psychodynamic processes by which the idea of civilization maintained its grip on the identities of Americans. If thoughts and feelings emerge within the civilized self that threaten to discredit the premises on which it makes sense of experience, an effort will be made to remove them from consciousness. The "mental delirium tremens" against which the *Evangelist* warns is that very state against which Porter, Stewart, and Mary Parker braced themselves, the state of losing one's bearings in the midst of an experience suddenly grown enigmatical. The internal policing that led the missionaries to term erotic responses "revolting" thus had its frank public counterpart in the effort to control the realm of literature.

The most sophisticated and powerful of the attacks on *Typee* came from the *Christian Parlor Magazine*, which had been established to preserve Christian readers against "the overwhelming flood of impure and corrupting literature."[21] Instead of merely reciting orthodox perspectives, this reviewer applied them with care to the text of Melville's book. He attempts to counteract *Typee*'s romantic poisons by including sarcastic parodies of its flights of fancy: "Come, oh celestial Spirit of Primitive Bliss! and waft me on thy golden pinions to the lovely abodes of the Typeeans! . . . Come, oh yearning soul of the angelic FAYAWAY! let me henceforth be the chosen partner of thy tabued pleasures!"[22]

Behind the engaging surface of Melville's account, the critic discovers striking symptoms of the mental deterioration that can infect unwary readers. Melville's evocations of the interior tensions of the civilized self, his way of provoking and entertaining the state of "mental delirium tremens" without losing his aesthetic or ethical equilibrium, are taken by the reviewer as evidence of mere befuddlement. In its comparisons of the civilized and savage state, and particularly in its commentary on missions, *Typee* "is filled with the most palpable and absurd contradictions," violations of common logic that are "so carelessly put together as to occur in consecutive paragraphs." Conceding that the coming of civilized men may have brought certain evils in its train, the writer demands to know exactly what Melville wants: would he "consent to have the Polynesians relapse again to what they were one hundred years since—withdraw the foreign population—recall the missionaries—burn up the Bible and the various works in the dialects of the Pacific?" The critic thus cuts through Melville's disclaimers and fixes attention on the radical character of his objections. Pushing the essential thrust of Melville's attack to its logical end, the writer declares that if Melville is not prepared to see the Polynesian restored in every way to his original state, he "deserves the scorn of an intelligent community" (75, 79).

Melville had illustrated his claim that the Polynesians were being "civilized into draft horses and evangelized into beasts of burden" with an extended caricature of a missionary's wife, obese and sanctimonious, being taken to church services in a little go-cart drawn by two of the islanders. The reviewer does not take this as Melville intended it, as a figure for the entire relationship between the missionaries and the objects of their ostensible benevolence. He defends it, rather, as a perfectly reasonable social practice. "But why need our author go to the Pacific to find 'evangelised draught horses?' . . . He may find 'civilized beasts of burden,' in the shape of public porters, drawing heavily loaded hand-carts after them in every city of the United States!" This well-attested civilized practice is simply a part of the general program of social uplift that the missionaries have pioneered; it inculcates the virtue of honest labor. "Better to earn a subsistence by industry as porters than to slaughter and devour each other" (80).

The critic consistently applies the thesis that Melville had challenged but had been unwilling altogether to repudiate, that of the essential moral superiority of civilized life and of its inevitable tendency to elevate the native. Melville had objected to the "prettily furnished coral-rock villas" of the missionaries as luxuries obtained at the expense of native misery. To the critic these residences provide a contrast with native huts that is useful to the work. "They are an advanced standard which the natives are encouraged to reach." He quotes in corroboration the statement of the famed missionary martyr, Williams: *"It was my determination when I originally left England to have as respectable a dwelling as I could erect;* for the missionary does not go to barbarize himself, but to civilize the heathen. He ought not, therefore, to sink down to their standard, but to elevate them to his" (80).

The reviewer scarcely knows what to make of the fact that Melville concedes the Marquesans to be cannibals, while holding that they are "in other respects humane and virtuous." The far more cursory review in the *Evangelist* had picked out this remark in order to suggest Melville's moral disorientation. The *Christian Parlor* critic also asserts that such a statement cannot make sense, declaring that he would be very curious to see Melville's "system of ethics" (82). Here as elsewhere the reviewer strikes right home to those statements that indicate most clearly Melville's mixed viewpoint, and scores heavily with the charge that no "system" can be made of it.

The reviewer demands to know why Melville felt such an "insatiable desire to escape from the abodes of bliss and return to the vices and miseries of civilization." Such a desire, he assumes, must have a moral principle behind it of sufficient validity to be applied to Marquesan and American culture alike. He concludes that Melville must have returned to America in order to act as one of the "four or five Marquesan missionaries" that he said might be as useful as the Americans were in Polynesia. "Native missionaries are generally the best pioneers in evangelising and enlightening a people; and here, American 'Savage!' is one of our own countrymen, from the renowned valley of Typee in the Marquesas, who has sacrificed his happiness with an unparalleled devotion to your welfare to convert you to Typeeism! All hail! Apostle of Cannibalism!" (77). Far from concluding that he or other Americans might indeed have something to learn from Melville, he takes the hypothetical possibility as the basis for a *reductio ad absurdum.* Since societies exist in various "states" along a scale of progressive civilization and refinement, it follows that America must be less developed than the Marquesas if it is not more developed. The American savage to which the reviewer refers is not Melville himself, but the typical American. Melville had attempted to break the spell that caused Americans to look upon a cannibal as a candidate for wholesale moral renovation on civilized terms. Now he found himself styled an "Apostle of Cannibalism."

It cannot be known for sure whether the *Christian Parlor* review was part of a coordinated effort to put pressure on Melville's publisher; and it really doesn't matter, since when influential people are uniformly offended no superintendent conspiracy is necessary in order to concert their actions. The *Christian Parlor* three times makes pointed reference to the fact that *Typee* was published in Wiley and Putnam's Library of American Books, noting that this distinguished placement gives it considerable "respectability and influence." The *Evangelist* reviewer likewise had expressed his sorrow at finding such a volume among Wiley's offerings, and suggested by way of extenuation that perhaps it had not been read before it was sent to the printer. In early July of 1847, along with the *Christian Parlor* review, an attack on *Typee* appeared in the prestigious *New Englander*, which begins by noting that "we were not disposed at first to say anything against this volume" and then goes on to attack Melville as "utterly incapable, from moral obtuseness, of an accurate statement."[23] Late in July, Wiley received a very substantial book order from Rufus Anderson, the secretary of the American Board of Commissioners for Foreign Missions, to which he had added a postscript: "I have read *Melville's 'Typee,'* with great regret that it bears the respectable name & sanction of your House."[24]

By the time Anderson's note arrived, however, John Wiley had already taken action. He had succeeded in obtaining Melville's agreement to a thoroughgoing expurgation in which all the anti-missionary passages were removed, together with many of his saltier incidental observations. The line of argument that Wiley took with Melville may be audible in the description of the planned changes that Melville wrote on the day they held their discussion:

> The revision will only extend to the exclusion of those parts not naturally connected with the narrative, and some slight purifications of style. I am pursuaded that the interest of the book almost wholly consists in the *intrinsick merit of the narrative alone*—& that other portions, however interesting they may be in themselves, only serve to impede the story. The book is certainly calculated for popular read-

ing, or for none at all.—If the first, why then, all passages which are calculated to offend the tastes, or offer violance to the feelings of any large class of readers are certainly objectionable.

   —Proceeding on this principle then I have rejected every thing, in revising the book, which refers to the missionaries . . . Certain "sea-freedoms" also have been modifyed in the expression.[25]

It is noteworthy that this description of the changes implies no acquiescence in the criticisms that orthodox reviewers had brought against *Typee*. Melville was prepared to accept alterations justified on the ground of literary unity and improved sales; too great an emphasis on the nature of the "feelings" he had offended might well have prompted him to recoil altogether and refuse to make the changes.

Rufus Anderson and the orthodox upholders of missions did not represent "civilization" or "America" in any statistical sense: they were the heralds of a vision that had attained a significant hold on the American identity. Their importance lies not in their having spoken for the American public in attacking Melville, but in their having sought to do so. The evidence from sales of *Typee*, and from the bulk of the reviews, is that the general public was delighted by the book to such an extent as to suggest quite clearly that the missionary vision of Polynesian savagery (and of American civilization) was losing a grip on the popular mind that had been virtually unchallenged for some fifteen years.[26] The censoring of Melville's book would not have been necessary if the missionary scheme of values had been identical with the American character: in that case the policing would have occurred unconsciously in Melville's own mind, or the book would never have been published. But evangelical and benevolent Protestant America now faced a situation in which its authority to speak for America as a whole was increasingly dubious. If we take "the Christian parlor" as the metaphorical midpoint of the civilization whose outer boundary was defined by the missionaries in the Pacific, then we can recognize an analogy between the "overwhelming flood of impure and corrupting literature" that now threatened to swamp the parlor and the savage horde that had engulfed the mission compound at Taiohae Bay. The action taken against Melville was a defensive gesture bespeaking powerful uncertainties and tensions concerning the identity of the American community, not an edict from a monolithic establishment.

Melville for his part reacted with disgust when he realized that what he had been prevailed upon to accept amounted to an expurgation.[27] His uncertainties had prompted him to make peace with the spokesmen for the righteous, so long as he was able to suppress in himself the awareness of doing that. His sense of his own identity was somewhat indistinct, but he was emphatically hostile to having it determined by missionaries and their sponsors. In the role of gentleman-beachcomber, moreover, he had struck a responsive chord in an American public that had consumed a steady diet of solemn pronouncements on the need for moral transformation in Polynesians who were the targets of missionary work, and in Americans who ought to support that work more conscientiously. The immense success of evangelicalism and the benevolent empire had generated a readership for Melville prepared to find amusement in rebellions against pious canons of respectability, so long as the expressions of rebellion were evidently meant for amusement.

The revisions of *Typee* had the effect of rendering the work more "romantic" in the sense of detaching it from weighty ethical and philosophical concerns, so that one ironical result of the orthodox attack on the book was to help create Melville as a public figure who exemplified the willingness of Americans to take the civilized identity as a theme of humor and to indulge in fantasies of escape from its burdens into imaginary savage domains.

Melville himself was determined, however, to stand by his graver insights and set about to write a new novel of South Sea adventure, where he renewed his attack on the mssions in terms sufficiently strong to establish a clear repudiation of Wiley's criticisms. Melville's title for the new work adequately signifies how firmly he had chosen to entrench himself in the marginal perspective; he called it *Omoo*, which, as he explains, is a Marquesan word meaning "rover." Melville's refusal to yield to the canons of civilized respectability forms part of the larger intellectual adventure of his works, as does his increasing refusal to accept the public demand that romance be kept free of ethical and philosophical probings. Melville pursued unstable and ambiguous perspectives into deeper and deeper ranges of meditation as his career unfolded, to a point at which he unsettled the presuppositions of his age with sufficient energy and acuteness to alienate readers who had been delighted by *Typee* in its unexpurgated form.

Melville's skirmish with the spokesmen for the work of civilization in Polynesia hardened his determination to oppose them, but did not bring him any renewed hope for the Polynesians. In *Typee* he issues passionate appeals as though believing that the terrible degradation of the islanders might somehow be reversed. But in *Omoo* he tersely notes their worsening condition and declares that nothing can be done to help them. "Their prospects are hopeless. Nor can the most devoted efforts, now exempt them from furnishing a marked illustration of a principle which history has always exemplified. Years ago brought to a stand, where all that is corrupt in barbarism and civilization unite, to the exclusion of the virtues of either state; like other uncivilized beings, brought into contact with Europeans, they must here remain stationary until utterly extinct."[28]

This prediction did not prove to be literally true in the case of the Tahitians with whom *Omoo* is concerned. After a period of decline, the native population of those islands began again to increase, although the Tahitians who survived were not the Tahitians of old. If a society is characterized by the traditions and systems of meaning by which its members conduct their lives and render their experience intelligible, then the Tahitians did indeed become extinct. In the Marquesas, Melville's anticipation of racial eradication came much nearer fulfillment.

An American traveler retracing Melville's steps in the Marquesas in the early twentieth century found a dozen people in the valley of the Typees, who still emphatically thought of themselves as Typees even as they listened to verses from a Marquesan translation of the Gospel of John.[29] The traveler noted with virtual unbelief the tenacity with which Marquesans clung to their ancestral valleys, refusing to mingle in the cosmopolitan motley of Taiohae Bay until only one or two members of the valley tribe remained. The grip exerted on these people by a specific community presents itself as a striking analogue to the system of self-definition that enclosed and supported the American visitors to this island, albeit lacking the expansive world-wide scope of the civilized identity.

Concluding
Metascientific
Postscript

PHILIP MASON has observed that a remarkable number of stories which provide parables of social interaction take place on islands,[1] perhaps because the surrounding ocean establishes a limit that suggests the boundary between one society and another, or the boundary between the social realm itself and some contrasting domain, like that of nature or the infinite. Characters encounter each other on islands as elements in a social matrix, much perhaps as they encounter transcendent presences in a religious matrix on mountains. Mason's own study of the colonial mentality focuses on Prospero's island in *The Tempest*, where he finds an interplay among Prospero, Ariel, Caliban, and Miranda which corresponds to the perceptions and responses visible in the behavior of colonial administrators. So conceived, these figures are held in what might be called a correlative network, where each implies and presupposes the others, much as Robinson Crusoe and his man Friday—actors in another island drama—interact as elements in a common scheme. Gulliver, the Yahoos, and the Houyhnhnms likewise form a distinctive constellation, keyed to Swift's outraged conservative principles; and a comparable interactive structure might be found among Captain Hook, Tinkerbell, and Peter Pan. In each of these cases an imaginary island is made the locale of a story in which the characters enact a psychodrama, representing attitudes that belong together as features of a distinctive vision of social experience.

In this book, too, the principal figures are located within a system of social interactions. The spiritual liberator, the political educator, the interpreter, the beachcomber, and the censor are presented as figures typical of the drama whose leading parts are played by the civilized man and the savage. Yet the island on which these interactions took place is not imaginary, the persons who acted in them were real, and the actions and utterances I have recounted are all factual, so far as historical study can now ascertain them.

The question remains whether this kind of interpretive study is not merely an exercise in artfulness, spinning another tale of a legendary island, rather than getting directly at a true subject matter. I have argued that Porter, Melville, and the missionaries took the island of Nukuheva as a stage on which to enact their versions of Civilized America, assuming the Nukuhevans into an imagery that rather poorly represented the lives they actually led. The histrionic stand each adopted meant that, even where correct information was conveyed, it was conditioned by the rhetorical gesture and thus confirmed widespread misconceptions. Looking upon the Marquesans implicitly as parts of themselves, these Americans did not do justice to the distinctive form of humanity that the Marquesans really presented. Yet something of a comparable sort might be said for my study too, where events are selected and arranged in accordance with a dramatic format.

My key contention is that the drama here described was inherent in the doings of the actors, not imposed upon them. It is not necessary—and it is hardly sensible—to claim that human activity is exclusively conditioned by the systems of meaning that give it coherence and direction. But the forms that do condition it in this fashion are central realities of human experience. Such systems of meaning are ingredient to human being; not merely the inevitable spinoff of political and economic activity, and certainly not eternal givens, their production and maintenance is a root concern of human society. This feature of a social activity— the aspect in which it appears as a carrier and generator of meanings—deserves study in itself, and since such study requires the examination of meaning-laden activity, it naturally takes up dramatic frameworks for its organizing principles. In

The Grammar of Motives Kenneth Burke argues that the method of "dramatism" is suitable to discussing the dialectics of meaning, and he orders his material according to elements of drama, providing chapters on Act, Scene, Agent, Agency, and Purpose.[2] What I have produced is an interpretive schema adapted more closely to a specific case in point, with the purpose of bringing out its special features clearly. To get at the humanity that is expressed as persons make apparent the meanings by which they conduct their lives, it is important to stay as close as possible to minute particulars. This is not a matter of conveying what is sometimes called the "flavor" of events, but of capturing the true texture of a dramatic interaction made up of elements that have their meaning in relation to other elements within the same texture. It is the extraordinary delicacy of this interplay that makes the specific circumstance telling.

The drama recounted in this book has set forth a running contrast between masterful histrionic gestures and scenes of unresolved confusion. Stewart's trumpet blast calling for a mission, Porter's ceremony of possession-taking, and Melville's flight into the Marquesan fastnesses all evoked attitudes that were broadly shared in the audiences for which they were performed. Yet in each case the clear-cut action gives way to disorder: the mission collapses, Porter's Madison Ville is demolished, and Melville ends up in an ambivalent conflict with his publisher. The bold gesture propounds a human arrangement that subsequent happenings do not bear out, an ironical mischancing that is typical of the circumstance in which psychosocial identity is maintained.

The embracing dramatic gesture of going to the boundary of the civilized world, encountering there the antitype of the civilized self, and returning to tell the story is exemplary by reason of its rhetorical character as much as by its statistical representativeness. Porter is a characteristic figure of Enlightenment America; the missionaries are typical of the era of Benevolence; and there were many with a taste for Romance in the audience before whom Melville played his part. Yet the implied audience of each gesture is not a coterie or even a majority, but "civilization" and "America as a civilized nation."

This is true in defiance of several realities of which the proponents were fully aware. They were all aware that America was not the only civilized nation. Porter was animated by the desire to assert a place for the United States amid the great nations of the world, acknowledging British and French ascendancy; and Melville was pleased to have *Typee* published first in England since he was then able more easily to locate an American publisher. And they would vehemently have agreed that not all Americans could be called civilized, since each implicitly or explicitly blamed important groups of Americans for failing to attain a civilized standard. Each of these figures struggled against competing interests and hostile points of view in the occidental culture they addressed, even as they jostled with each other for the spotlight. The exemplary gesture has its meaning, necessarily, against such a background of conflicting ascriptions and claims.

"Civilization" never referred to a fixed coherent order. It was a social theory on which the attempt was made to compose a welter of activities and roles, of interests and institutional structures, of deep cultural memories and pressing practical demands. The candidate for the exemplary role casts himself as a figure against such a ground, seeking to call forth a sympathetic vibration, so that the tumult of forms may be seen for a time to take on intelligible shape. The idea of civilization provided the idiom in which this interaction took place. Instead of describing the individual or the society, it was a term in which the connection between them was expressed. An element in a dialectic rather than a verbal tag connected to a thing, the idea was very powerful in early nineteenth-century America and retains significance in weakened form today. When an American president declares, for example, that the "whole civilized world" is shocked by the behavior of an African nationalist, he is invoking the vivid old language for a feature of our national self-understanding still very much alive in terms like "development" and "modernization." Yet whether the image projected is civilized or has some other content, there is always an ironic relationship between the pose that is struck, the exemplary self that is fashioned, and the social circumstance in which it is embraced as typical.

The same irony is present also in the relation between the fashioned self and the experience that the exemplary individual undergoes. The civilized image is maintained as a psychological achievement against opposition, and against a welter of seemingly extraneous moments, tangents of millions of circles in which the exemplar does not move.

I have spoken of the Marquesan encounters as dramas of self-definition; yet these have meaning only insofar as we recognize that any human encounter involves such a drama, selves interacting in accordance with the conceptions that inform them. Highly specialized interactions, between persons of profoundly disparate cultures, merely focus aspects of a process that is going on all the time. We have observed that Melville, Porter, and the missionaries learned something from their encounters, and that the something each learned was a correlate of the self he maintained. Persons and groups understand things in configurations that correspond to features of individual and corporate self-understanding, since the self is maintained by a scheme of stresses and exclusions that renders certain features of experience readily available to thought and removes others from the domain of interest, if not from consciousness altogether. The reception of new knowledge compels new social and psychological structures, which is one reason why it frequently encounters resistance. It is also true that the effort to achieve a fundamentally enlarged understanding is a spiritual enterprise that requires the cultivation of a style of selfhood in which the circumstances given consideration can register.

The job of understanding people like the Marquesans is now a highly developed professional activity, for which there is a process of initiation in which the novice seeks the kind of selfhood that is needed. Yet contemporary anthropological field technique is a cultural achievement whose dynamic underpinnings may be lost to view because of the general acceptance it has gained.

The experiences of Bronislaw Malinowski provide an instructive example of the relation between the self and knowledge, and also the relation between the exemplary public role and its hectored immediate context. Malinowski argued that the anthropologist must involve himself intimately in the society under consideration, so as "to grasp the native's point of view, his relation to life, to realize *his* vision of *his* world."[3] His work gave immense

authority to a vision of the anthropological fieldworker as gaining a spiritual empathy with the lives of those he studies, coming
to interact with ease according to the patterns of life found
among them.

This conception of the fieldworker, and of Malinowski himself, was staggered by the publication in 1967 of the personal
diary he kept during his own most productive period of fieldwork, so much so that several commentators within the discipline of anthropology responded with sentiments like those
Rufus Anderson expressed concerning *Typee:* they wished it had
never been published. Malinowski's sexual obsessions, his
seemingly racist attitudes, and his besetting hypochondria all
seemed impossible to reconcile with the attitude of sympathetic
objectivity he had promulgated. Yet the tumult of Malinowski's
inner life was in large part a result of the fact that he was not
merely coming to terms with a strange people, but was pioneering a new form of selfhood.[4]

Malinowski repeatedly affirms that the task of confronting the
alienness of the Trobriand environment, to open himself to its
disconcerting strangeness, must be accompanied by an effort to
maintain contact with his own inner reality: "The exoticism
breaks through lightly, through the veil of familiar things . . . An
exoticism strong enough to spoil normal apperception, but too
weak to create a new category of mood. Went into the bush. For
a moment I was frightened. Had to compose myself. Tried to
look into my own heart. 'What is my inner life?' No reason to be
satisfied with myself. The work I am doing is a kind of opiate
rather than a creative expression. I am not trying to link it with
deeper sources. To organize it."[5] The organization of his work,
Malinowski observes, will arise from a creative inner life, in
which new categories of mood can be articulated to make sense
of a circumstance that at the moment remains hidden behind a
veil of the familiar. His exasperation with the "niggers," his self-
disgust over masturbation and "pawing" the native girls, his perhaps even greater self-disgust over reading novels, and his bouts
of listlessness and despair are all vented into this diary as a way
of keeping close track of the new self he was forging, giving it
continuity even as it came to birth. The diary is a record of the
exultation he felt at achieving new possibilities of knowledge and

a junk heap for the trash that accumulated while he was constructing the self that made new knowledge possible.

The writing of this anguished personal document supported, paradoxically, Malinowski's effort to maintain objectivity; it reveals that the "self as implement of study" he was creating had psychodynamic underpinnings, like any other form of the self. "I should clearly and distinctly feel *myself*," he affirms, "apart from the present conditions of my life, which in themselves mean nothing to me. Metaphysically speaking, the tendency to disperse oneself, to chatter, to make conquests, marks the degeneration of the creative tendency to reflect reality in one's own soul" (112). As a receptacle for Malinowski's repugnance and contempt, the diary served his need to keep the self distinct, not to permit its being peddled out in his relationships with Trobrianders and local whites. If the self is to "reflect reality" it must hold local affiliations firmly at a distance, permitting no involvement to take precedence over study.

The self that Malinowski was forming does not appear in this diary, but stands behind the lucid and forceful voice that addresses us in his great enthnographic treatises: the example presented by those treatises and the presence communicated by that voice have had a broader and more powerful influence on the subsequent unfolding of the discipline than any of his conclusions or theories. Malinowski's abundantly well-attested charisma was rooted in his successful completion of an exemplary action which provided a new version of the boundary line that encloses the occidental community. The boundary line he dramatically exemplified does not separate the advanced from the retarded in a moral, cultural, or civil sense, but marks off the knowers from the unknown, and has called into action a vital constituency within Western society which insists that those earlier considered savage or primitive in truth represent alien versions of humanity to be understood on their own terms without being located on any Western moral scale.

Yet in Malinowski's work itself there is a curious mingling of attitudes that shows how decisively the question of audience enters into the way in which peoples under study are described. Malinowski did not address himself to the discipline of anthropology as it now exists, but to the general community of learned people in Europe and America, and he instructed them concerning what he called in the foreword to *Argonauts of the Western Pacific* "savage humanity." As E. R. Leach has observed, Malinowski frequently refers to "the savage" as occupying a stage of cultural evolution beneath that of the European, while conducting his potent evangelical campaign on behalf of a scientific appreciation of "the native point of view."[6] This happens in part because the campaign required it. He was arguing before the European and American intellectual community at large for the view that the "scientific self" he embodied was an appropriate way for truly civilized people to relate to small-scale societies like the Trobrianders'. This argument required, if it was to carry conviction, that the new form of the self be identified with the highest achievements of Western man, which when Malinowski did his major work was still summed up generally in the term "civilization." And the argument Malinowski brought forward was all the more forceful and sophisticated because it was in part an argument with himself.

The dynamic structure of the self becomes visible at its borders, where limits are fixed that mark it off from the not-self. For the civilized self, that border is occupied by the savage; but in Malinowski's diary we find him struggling with a new set of limits, the limits of the self-as-knower. He recognizes, for example, that the ideal of wholly objective observation cannot be reached because the self can never act wholly as an observer, since even in the act of observation it shapes the realities with which it deals.

Writing of retrospective diary suggests many reflections: a diary is a 'history' of events which are entirely accessible to the observer, and yet writing a diary requires profound knowledge and thorough training; change from theoretical point of view; experience in writing leads to entirely different results even if the observer remains the same—let alone if there are different observers! Consequently, we cannot speak of objectively existing facts: theory creates facts. Consequently there is no such thing as "history" as an independent science. History is observation of facts in keeping with a certain theory; an application of this theory to the facts as time gives birth to them. —The life that lies behind me is opalescent, a shimmer of many colors. Some things strike and attract me. Others are dead. (114)

The movements of Malinowski's thought in this passage, as elsewhere in the diary, cut quickly into axiomatic issues. What appears here a criticism of history as a science is equally applicable
to anthropology or any other program of learning, and certainly
to the work that Malinowski was then doing, not merely in writing the diary but in observing the events in the daily lives of the
Trobrianders ("entirely accessible to the observer") that he is
seeking to understand. The profound knowledge he refers to includes knowledge of the shimmering opalescent moment when
fact and theory reveal their interdependencies and new theories
can be given birth that will administer the birth of new facts.
What stands as the final challenge to the self-as-knower is simply the unknowable, the enigma blocking the path which also
lures the explorer to envision revolutionary new possibilities.
The impediments to achieving knowledge that are built into the
process of knowing both daunt and invigorate the knower; they
limit and empower the scientific self, releasing its energies by
supplying a determinate identity.

In the Trobriand environment, struggling to maintain the scientific self as a new version of the civilized self, Malinowski confronts the ultimate recalcitrance against which that self must be
tested, and he sees the Trobrianders both as objects for disin-
terested study and as savages. But now savagery stands in part
for the not-known, and even for the not-knowable. In like manner, Claude Lévi-Strauss in his search for the ultimate untouched
savages discovered when he found them that they were "only too
savage." This did not mean for him that they were bloodthirsty
or licentious, simple or candid, childlike or degenerate: it meant
simply that they threatened to defeat his powers of understanding.[7]

The supreme trial of Malinowski's period in the Trobriands
took place, however, in a situation where personal emotions
overwhelmed him, emotions of the sort that had to be kept at
bay if the self was to be maintained as an instrument of investigation. In addition to the guilt and doubts that dogged Malinowski because of failures to maintain his working attitudes
consistently (the frequent digressions into erotic byplay and the
reading of novels), there were also feelings of guilt that arose because of the conflict between the scientific obligation he was

seeking to put first and other obligations that likewise clamored for primacy. Malinowski was plagued by remorse over the difficulties his own family was suffering because of World War I, in which he would himself have fought but for his scientific work. "My God, my God," he bursts out on one occasion, "how terrible it is to live in a continuous ethical conflict. My failure to think seriously about Mother, Staś [a friend from boyhood], Poland—about their sufferings there and about Poland's ordeal—is disgusting!" (165). He also stewed endlessly over a woman referred to in the diary as N.S., whom he had decided to reject for the sake of E.R.M., whom he was later to marry. Fearing that N.S. might commit suicide and fearing that he would be to blame, Malinowski confounded himself over whether and how to break the news to her concerning his changed commitments. These feelings of moral complicity, arising from a structure of ethical obligations that had a firm grip on his character, became associated with a situation that developed among the Trobrianders. He learns that Inekoya, the wife of one of his informants, has fallen ill:

> I went to see: she had another hemorrhage, groaned horribly, and was apparently dying. I thought of the horrible torment of a hemorrhage and of N.S. and suddenly felt that I was deserting her. I also felt that I wanted to be with her at any cost, to allay her sufferings. Strong reaction. I also thought of E.R.M. and in my nervous disarray I told myself: "*the shadow of death is between us and it will separate us.*" My betrayal of N.S. confronted me in all its starkness.—Over the hut in which my lamp was glowing, tall palms, thick white clouds, through which the moonlight filtered. Kabwaku sings melodiously and clearly.—Death—all this is like an ebb tide, a flowing off into nothingness, extinction. Through all this, the cruel *customs* of the *niggers*—who were again washing her, preparing her for death. (191–192)

Malinowski now approaches the rock bottom of his existence, where those concerns with the greatest power to destroy the new integrity he is constructing have their moment of full influence, radically testing the self that is in the making. The self-as-scientific-observer is not present among the people he studies in order to do them good. Unlike the civilizer seeking to elevate the savage, the student has no moral program; he visualizes no better future for the subjects of his study than the existence they lead before his eyes. Yet Malinowski clearly feels compassion for Inekoya's sufferings, so that his outburst against "the cruel *customs* of the *niggers*" has to be understood, paradoxically, as an expression of fellow-feeling. Yet this sort of moral involvement is not merely irrelevant to the program of work he is conducting, but is indeed hostile to it. He had come to the Trobriands in order to understand the people, not to improve or denounce them. The moral sentiments aroused by Inekoya's suffering trigger a sense of guilt in Malinowski that is system-specific: it is inseparable from the role of student to which he seeks to give fidelity. Accordingly, all of his causes of remorse now gang up on him, pouring into the structural cleavage in his way of being that has been laid open by the stress of this situation.

When Inekoya dies, the effect on Malinowski is devastating: "*I lose my nerve*. All my despair, after all those killed in the war, hangs over this miserable Melanesian hut" (196). For seven days there are no entries, and when the diary resumes, it is apparent that Malinowski is fighting his way out of a general physical and psychological collapse. He fears that he has tuberculosis, the same disease that killed Inekoya, and welcomes the prospect of death. "Beginning to believe in the hypothesis that I am about to die. I am indifferent. Fever, lack of vitality; rotten physical condition. No desire to live, I don't regret any loss. Feeling this is a good time to die. Alone, calm, *air of finality*" (197).

Malinowski interprets his distress in terms that are consistent with the system of values he is living out. He looks upon himself just as he was schooling himself to look upon others, as an object about which scientific knowledge might be obtained. "That I might die" is a "hypothesis," to be contemplated objectively like any other hypothesis. The scientific heroism that here receives climactic expression is manifested, actually, in the hypochondria that besets Malinowski from the beginning of the diary to the end. Hypochondria is a symbolic transference in which psychological distresses are experienced as physical ailments. Once this transference has been effected, Malinowski is in a position to find remedy in medical procedures and drugs: products, that is, of the scientific enterprise. It is noteworthy that Malinowski hates the novels that he reads in order to counteract the psychic stresses of his work, and derives as much misery as solace from his interpersonal transactions, both those available in the Trobriands and those he carries on by letter with E.R.M. and other correspondents. But he never loses faith in his exercises or in his collection of powders, elixirs, and pills.

The turning point in this crisis, after which his improvement is steady, comes when he finds a drug to cure him: "Collapse in the afternoon. Wrote to Billy. Took an enema—this relieved me at once. The calomel and general purge. Effervescent salts, which turns out to be my salvation" (197). Instead of spiritual remedies for problems of the spirit, Malinowski encloses such problems in a physical form, so that a product of scientific work can give him salvation. The ethical complications that crop up as the role of participant-observer is forged gather here into one terrible thunderhead of suffering from which he eventually emerges intact, the newly fashioned self having survived the trials of its boundary line.

The most powerful source of support for the structure of meanings that Malinowski was struggling to consolidate as a new form of the self came from the very task to which that self was adapted, from his scientific work. Again and again Malinowski spurs himself to stay on the job, to let nothing interfere, to defeat lethargy, to devote himself unstintingly; and he does so because the doing of the work had a ritualistic import. Not only would its outcome, in the form of knowledge, justify the labor and the sacrifices, but the actual daily application engaged the structure of meanings within the self that Malinowski was trying to incarnate: it gave tangible expression to an otherwise nebulous and theoretical scheme of values. He prods himself to stay on the job not because the job itself was distasteful, but because it represented an avenue by which he could transcend his uncertainties and energetically live out the self he was becoming. "Preserve the essential inner personality through all difficulties and vicissitudes," he writes. "I must never sacrifice moral principles or essential work to 'posing,' to convivial *Stimmung,* etc. My main task now must be: work. *Ergo:* work!" (268).

What Malinowski undertook alone as a heroic pioneer is now a routine process of initiation into a well-established academic guild. It is generally understood that the stresses of anthropological fieldwork result from a situation in which an alien social context renders unworkable most of the orientations that the fieldworker brings from his or her home culture, and that the resulting confusions must be sustained and survived if effective work is to be done. It is emphatically not the case, as is sometimes implied, that the fieldworker must discard *all* Western attitudes in order to understand the alien culture. It is necessary, rather, to retain the values that make for the production of knowledge at the expense of other values that happen to conflict with them. Learning to cope with the resultant guilt, which may crop up for example when a fieldworker must take notes in the course of a funeral, is also now a part of the initiatory routine.[8] The encounter with the "savage," whose trials once marked the boundary between civilized and uncivilized life, has become an encounter with the exotic, whose trials mark the passage into a professional identity. The drama of the boundary line, it would seem, has become a liminal drama of the kind that Victor Turner describes as taking place between programmed stages of individual development within a culture.[9]

Yet the role of participant-observer that the fieldworker assumes, where the self and its responses are made an instrument of investigation, is hardly confined to anthropological study. The knack of being involved with people both emotionally and intellectually while maintaining a detached position where one cultivates private objectives is an ambiguous gift with which contemporary experience makes us quite familiar. The view of the self as a bundle of provisional enactments or "presentations" is a favored theme of study, which shows up in analyses of social interaction that take their guiding metaphors from games and game playing. Students of contemporary social experience have increasingly observed behavior in which the self is yielded up for the nonce to the requirements of specific situations, rather than taking its bearings from some fixed moral order. Daniel Lerner has identified such a "mobile sensibility" as characteristic of the modern West, where industrialization, urbanization, and communications have destroyed the authority of parochial societies and their value systems, compelling the awareness that cultural boundaries are not ultimate boundaries.

The distresses resulting from *ad hoc* selfhood in our time have been felt very widely, so much so that therapeutic psychology has focused increasingly on the problems of synthesizing and maintaining a coherent identity; and one of the profounder impulses of modern literature has been to promise that aesthetic experience can restore the sense of wholeness, of integrity, that modern life has rendered so precarious. As Stephen Greenblatt has pointed out, moreover, the "mobile sensibility" of our era has historical origins in modes of behavior visibly forming during the Renaissance, an improvisational style of selfhood whose ethical problems are investigated by Shakespeare. The role model that Malinowski established for anthropological fieldworkers may be seen, accordingly, as one version of a self-style that descends from the sixteenth century and has come to be more and more dominant in the contemporary era. Like the "civilizer" of the nineteenth century, the "objective fieldworker" of today enacts in an intensified form a pattern of interaction by which we have come, for better or worse, to know ourselves.[10]

Yet we know ourselves, and our world, on larger terms as well. Even as the role model of the objective social scientist has gained currency, its apparent moorings in the procedures of the physical sciences have been loosened. The most imposing examples of this shift in the conception of "science" have come from physics, where the studies of John Archibald Wheeler are perhaps the most probing among those suggesting that the participation of the observer in the subject under study is intrinsic to the knowledge attained, and even to the reality of the subject itself, rather than being a mere data gathering preliminary to objective analysis.[11] The paradoxes that Malinowski encountered and conquered in the Trobriands have survived as a continuing preoccupation of theoretical physics. As for the scientific self excluding broader moral imperatives, moreover, "development anthropologists" now seek to make of their knowledge and their participation a means to assist the peoples under study.[12] And my own book attempts to join interpretive anthropologists on the common ground that has been discovered where once was a furiously contested line of battle between science and the humanities.

The ethical complexities confronting the fieldworker, not least of all the problems of ethical integrity, are thus not at bottom different from those faced by any person who is aware of excluding possibilities of being in order to take up a productive role—which makes it possible for exemplars of the anthropological discipline to make of it an avenue toward the deliberation of central human dilemmas. Figures as various as Margaret Mead, Carlos Castaneda, Claude Lévi-Strauss, Weston La Barre, Colin Turnbull, Victor Turner, and Clifford Geertz have all sought to bring exotic happenings to bear upon issues of concern to the intellectual community at large.

And despite the complaints that are sometimes heard against popularizing the discipline, one would be hard pressed to find a guild practitioner sturdy enough to claim that the knowledge obtained is valuable insofar as it is philosophically trivial. Still there is a crucial distinction to be drawn between those who ascribe privileged status to a given tribe or shaman, making up representatives of Essential Man, and those for whom the goal is to make unfamiliar circumstances intelligible. As Geertz has observed, it may be well to construct an image of the savage (noble or not) to embody the essence of a given point of view; but to claim that the exemplary image has been discovered in the flesh is quite another thing.[13]

When Melville made the observation that Marquesan missionaries to the United States might be as valuable as American missionaries in the Marquesas, his enemies pounced on it as evidence of his mental deterioration, and Melville himself hardly meant it seriously. Yet a central impulse of contemporary anthropology is to enable strange peoples to speak to us in their own voices, on the Socratic premise that enlarging the scope of human discourse is an intrinsic good. An enterprise is not tainted merely because the quest for self-knowledge is visible as one of its motives. What matters is the extent, as Mary Douglas has suggested, to which anomaly—the encounter with radically unfamiliar realities—can prompt constructive further efforts instead of being systematically ruled out of consideration.[14]

The collapse of Marquesan society as the result of contact with the West has been the subject of much speculation, since it was so much more drastic than the declines that occurred in other places where a comparable assortment of diseases, firearms, and cultural overlordship was brought in by whites. It seems possible that Marquesan culture was itself peculiarly fragile, unable to adapt to the strange new conditions whites imposed, although the culture was so completely obliterated that reliable answers will probably never be obtained. Yet it is interesting to meditate on the fact that those we term "Marquesans" did not call themselves by that name. Beyond the terms for familial, subtribal, tribal, and regional groupings, the only comprehensive title they accepted was *te tau 'enana*, the men. The archipelago as a whole they referred to as *te henua 'enana*, the land of men, as though assuming—like many other societies large and small—that the culture in which they lived was coterminous with humankind itself.[15]

It is certainly not useful here to impose another moral lesson on the Marquesans, but we may learn from their ethnocentrism something of the reason why the gestures of cultural exemplars may be most problematical when they appear most gloriously to succeed. We have noted that the dynamic character of a given psychosocial identity becomes visible at its borders, where limits are fixed that mark it off from what it is not. The conflicts that occur at this frontier are not avoidable, but are rooted in the contrapuntal process by which the self becomes distinct. Glamorous exemplars like Porter and Stewart enact this conflict in an absolute form, identifying the antagonists as cosmic opposites such that the only acceptable outcome is total victory for the cherished values and unconditional surrender for their antitype.

Yet no version of the self can claim ultimate validity as an embodiment of cosmic absolutes, so that the appeal of such a vivid and compelling gesture contains a fundamental deceit. Porter's march through the valley of the Typees and Stewart's call for a mission encouraged systematic blindness and thus became fountainheads of confusion. Conversely it is true that activities appearing clumsy and abortive to the participants—like Alexander's mission—can be understood as a delicate representation of social complexities that no one present at the scene was prepared to unravel. A rarer gift is what Melville displays, a tolerance for ambiguity sufficient to permit anomalous experience to be made available to consciousness, however inconsistent the resulting attitudes and feelings may appear to be. In the messages that are given and received amid social interactions we do not find an unchanging absolute logos, either in savage or civilized form, which once heard removes the necessity of listening further. We find ourselves taking part in an inexhaustible discourse, a drama without conclusion that ends—when it must— with a postscript.

Notes

Bibliography

Index

Notes

A manuscript source located in Houghton Library at Harvard University is indicated by (Houghton). Those in the Hawaiian Mission Children's Society Library in Honolulu, Hawaii, are identified by (Hawaiian Mission Children's Society).

1. Characters in Search of an Audience

1. Bronislaw Malinowski, *A Diary in the Strict Sense of the Term*, trans. Norbert Guterman (New York, 1967), pp. 254–255.

2. See Audrey Richards, "In Darkest Malinowski," *Cambridge Review*, January 19, 1968, pp. 186–189; Clifford Geertz, "Under the Mosquito Net," *New York Review of Books*, September 14, 1967, pp. 12–13; letters from Hortense Powdermaker and Ashley Montague, *New York Review of Books*, November 9, 1967, pp. 36–37; George W. Stocking, Jr., "Empathy and Antipathy in the Heart of Darkness," *Journal of the History of the Behavioral Sciences*, 4 (1968), 189–194; Ian Hogbin, "Review of *A Diary in the Strict Sense of the Term*, *American Anthropologist*," 70 (1968), 575; Murray Wax, "Tenting with Bronislaw Malinowski," *American Sociological Review*, 37 (1972), 1–13.

3. See the lucid commentary of E. R. Leach, "The Epistemological Background to Malinowski's Empiricism," in *Man and Culture: An Evaluation of the Work of Bronislaw Malinowski*, ed. Raymond Firth (London, 1957), p. 137.

4. See Clifford Geertz, *The Interpretation of Cultures* (New York, 1973); Victor W. Turner, *The Ritual Process: Structure and Anti-Structure* (Chicago, 1969) and *Dramas, Fields, and Metaphors: Symbolic Action in Human Society* (Ithaca, 1974); Claude Lévi-Strauss, *The Savage Mind* (Chicago, 1966); James L. Peacock, *Consciousness and Change: Symbolic Anthropology in Evolutionary Perspective* (New York, 1975); Mary Douglas, *Purity and Danger: An Analysis of Concepts of Pollution and Taboo* (New York, 1966).

5. Claude Lévi-Strauss, "The Structural Study of Myth," in *Structural Anthropology*, trans. Claire Jacobson and Brooke Grundfest Schoepf (New York, 1963); see p. 209.

6. Paul Ricoeur, "Structure, Word, Event," in *The Philosophy of Paul Ricoeur*, ed. Charles E. Reagan and David Stewart (Boston, 1978), pp. 109–119; see also "Explanation and Understanding," pp. 149–166. A further discussion of Ricoeur's view on these questions may be found in "The Model of the Text: Meaningful Action Considered as a Text," *New Literary History*, 5 (1973), 91–117. I have confined myself to observations on certain of the philosophical sources of structuralist theory and the limitations they impose. Further discussions, providing commentary on specific structuralist (or post-structuralist) critics, may be found in *Directions for Criticism: Structuralism and Its Alternatives*, ed. Murray Krieger and L. S. Dembo (Madison, 1977); see especially Hayden White, "The Absurdist Moment in Contemporary Literary Theory," pp. 55–110. See also Gerald Graff, *Literature Against Itself: Literary Ideas in Modern Society* (Chicago, 1979).

7. James A. Boon, *From Symbolism to Structuralism: Lévi-Strauss in a Literary Tradition* (New York, 1972).

8. Geertz, "Ritual and Social Change: A Javanese Example," in *The Interpretation of Cultures*, pp. 142–169; Turner, "Religious Paradigms and Political Action: Thomas Becket at the Council of Northampton," in *Dramas, Fields, and Metaphors*, pp. 60–97. This movement within anthropological study is unfolding very swiftly at present. In a searching discussion of recent developments, Geertz treats the notions of "drama" and "text" as applied to social experience. See his "Blurred Genres: The Refiguration of Social Thought," *The American Scholar*, 49 (1980), 165–179.

9. Any discussion of Melville's Polynesian experiences must take its point of departure from Charles Roberts Anderson, *Melville in the South Seas* (1939; rpt New York, 1966). Anderson examines Melville's use of other travel books and the factual content of his Polynesian tales in reference to contemporary documents and modern ethnographic study, showing that *Typee* cannot be taken uncritically as a source of biographical or ethnographic information. These findings have provided a basis for subsequent study in which the aesthetic coherence of *Typee* has been examined and, for the investigation pursued here, where forms of action are seen to have thematic content. Following Anderson, criticism of *Typee* has largely tended to place autobiography and art in separate compartments, with the conclusion that since the book is not a literal transcription of events in Melville's life, it must be art. See, for example, Paul Witherington, "The Art of Melville's *Typee*," *Arizona Quarterly*, 26 (1970), 136–157. Yet *Typee*, like others of Melville's first-person narrations, breaks through this distinction and requires a critical approach that likewise transcends it. A recent critical discussion recognizing this need is Faith Pullin, "Melville's *Typee*: The Failure of Eden," *New Perspectives on Melville*, ed. Faith Pullin (Edinburgh, 1978), pp. 1–28.

10. Henry Nash Smith, *Virgin Land: The American West as Symbol and Myth* (Cambridge, 1950); R. W. B. Lewis, *The American Adam: Innocence, Tragedy and Tradition in the Nineteenth Century* (Chicago, 1955); Leo Marx, *The Machine in the Garden: Technology and the Pastoral Ideal in America* (London, 1964).

11. Charles A. Beard and Mary R. Beard, *The American Spirit: A Study of the Idea of Civilization in the United States* (New York, 1942); Ernest Lee Tuveson, *Millennium and Utopia: A Study in the Background of the Idea of Progress* (Berkeley, 1949) and *Redeemer Nation: The Idea of America's Millennial Role* (Chicago, 1968); Roy Harvey Pearce, *The Savages of America: A Study of the Indian and the Idea of Civilization*, rev. ed. (Baltimore, 1965).

12. Beard and Beard, *The American Spirit*, p. 11.

13. Michael P. Rogin, *Fathers and Children: Andrew Jackson and the Subjugation of the American Indian* (New York, 1975), p. 166.

14. Jerome S. Bruner, "Myth and Identity," in *Myth and Mythmaking*, ed. Henry A. Murray (New York, 1960), p. 281.

15. David Porter, *Journal of a Cruise Made to the Pacific Ocean*, 2 vols. (Philadelphia, 1815), II, 13.

16. Charles Stewart, *A Visit to the South Seas*, 2 vols. (New York, 1831), I, 226-227, 229-231.

17. Herman Melville, *Typee: A Peep at Polynesian Life*, ed. Harrison Hayford, Hershel Parker, and G. Thomas Tanselle (Evanston, 1968), p. 15.

18. The suggestive power of the sentence, "Not the feeblest . . . gratification" is indirectly attested by the fact that the sentence was omitted from the American edition of *Typee*. See "List of Substantive Variants," *Typee*, p. 347. Daniel Williams, "Peeping Tommo: *Typee* as Satire," *Canadian Review of American Studies*, 6 (1975), 36-49, points out several other passages that provide sexual titillation, though he views them as part of an effort on Melville's part to make Tommo—the ostensible narrator—a target of satire.

19. Alfred Schutz, *The Problem of Social Reality, Collected Papers*, I, ed. M. Natanson (The Hague, 1962), 231.

20. Claude Lévi-Strauss, *The Savage Mind* (Chicago, 1966), pp. 1-33.

21. Geertz, "The Cerebral Savage: On the Work of Claude Lévi-Strauss," in *The Interpretation of Cultures*, pp. 345-359; see also "Religion as a Cultural System" pp. 87-125. Arthur O. Lovejoy, *The Great Chain of Being* (1936; rpt. Cambridge, 1976), pp. 3-23. For a good discussion of the role of ideas in social activity, see Peter Winch, *The Idea of a Social Science and Its Relation to Philosophy* (London, 1958).

22. Thomas S. Kuhn, *The Structure of Scientific Revolutions* (Chicago, 1962), pp. 52-65.

23. Population estimates in the Marquesas are uncertain, especially for the earlier time, partly because the population fluctuated sharply as a result of drought and famine before the white man arrived in force. Yet the general pattern of post-contact devastation is unmistakable. For a careful discussion, see Robert Suggs, *The Archeology of Nuku Hiva, Marquesas Islands, French Polynesia,*

Anthropological Papers of the American Museum of Natural History, 49, part 1 (New York, 1961), 190–192.

24. See Louis Rollin, *Les Iles marquises* (Paris, 1929), pp. 264–265; Weston La Barre, *The Ghost Dance: Origins of Religion* (New York, 1970); James Mooney, *The Ghost-Dance Religion and Wounded Knee* (1896; rpt. Toronto, 1973); Peter Worsley, *The Trumpet Shall Sound: A Study of "Cargo" Cults in Melanesia* (London, 1957).

25. James M. Alexander, *The Islands of the Pacific* (New York, 1895), pp. 231–243.

26. Clifford Geertz has given an extended discussion of these misleading metaphors in *The Interpretation of Cultures*, pp. 21–23.

2. City on a Hill

1. William Patterson Alexander to Rufus Anderson, Journal letter, September 4, 1833, to May 13, 1834 (Houghton), entry of September 4, 1833. Cited hereafter as Alexander to Anderson.

2. Rush Welter, *The Mind of America, 1820–1860* (New York, 1975), p. 52. The passage in Matthew from which Winthrop drew his metaphor runs as follows: "Ye are the light of the world. A city that is set on a hill cannot be hid. Neither do men light a candle, and put it under a bushel, but on a candlestick; and it giveth light unto all that are in the house. Let your light so shine before men, that they may see your good works, and glorify your father which is in heaven" (5:14–16).

3. Perry Miller, *Errand into the Wilderness* (Cambridge, 1956), pp. 1–2. See also Loren Baritz, *City on a Hill* (New York, 1964), for a discussion of this idea as it informs the thinking of selected American writers, including Melville.

4. William Appleman Williams, *The Contours of American History* (New York, 1961), pp. 181–183.

5. Roy Harvey Pearce, *The Savages of America: A Study of the Indian and the Idea of Civilization*, rev. ed. (Baltimore, 1965), pp. 53–58. Michael P. Rogin, *Fathers and Children: Andrew Jackson and the Subjugation of the American Indian* (New York, 1975), pp. 179, 206–211. For a further study of the meanings of the Indian and of his destruction, as they developed within the white society of the early nineteenth century, see Bernard W. Sheehan, *Seeds of Extinction: Jeffersonian Philanthropy and the American Indian* (Chapel Hill, 1973).

6. General information concerning the mission is derived from Mary Charlotte Alexander, *William Patterson Alexander in Kentucky, the Marquesas, Hawaii* (Honolulu, 1934); Alexander to Anderson; "Journal written at the island of Nuuhiva" by Richard Armstrong with entries from August 21, 1833, to March 22, 1834; and "Joint communication of Messrs. Alexander, Armstrong & Parker," drafted by Benjamin Wyman Parker, April 10, 1834.

7. Alexander to Anderson, entry of November 30, 1833.

8. Ibid.

9. These are approximate figures. The exact location is "between parallels 7°

50' south of the Equator, and meridians 138° 25' west of Greenwich." E. S. Craighill Handy, *The Native Culture in the Marquesas*, Bernice P. Bishop Museum Bulletin 9 (Honolulu, 1923), p. 6; cited hereafter as Handy. Lawrence John Chubb, *Geology of the Marquesas Islands*, Bernice P. Bishop Museum Bulletin 68 (Honolulu, 1930), pp. 17–18.

10. The accepted spelling for this tribe is "Taipi." I have chosen to use "Typee" because both Porter and Melville used it, and a continual shifting from one spelling to the other would take place if I followed accepted usage in my own writing. Also to avoid confusion I have regularized spellings of Marquesan names that appear in the text, while preserving original usages in citing titles in the notes.

11. Handy, pp. 7–8.

12. Handy, pp. 187–188.

13. Robert Carl Suggs, *The Archeology of Nuku Hiva, Marquesas Islands, French Polynesia*, Anthropological Papers of the American Museum of Natural History, 49, part 1 (New York, 1961), 191.

14. Robert Suggs did the basic research that led to this remarkable finding; see *Archeology*, pp. 180–181.

15. Andrew Sharp, *Ancient Voyagers in Polynesia* (Berkeley, 1964), pp. 132–136, summarizes additional evidence in support of this conclusion, and David Lewis, *We, the Navigators: The Ancient Art of Landfinding in the Pacific* (Wellington, 1972) assembles navigational lore showing how it could have occurred.

16. Suggs, *Archeology*, pp. 180–181.

17. Sharp, *Ancient Voyagers*, pp. 135–136.

18. Suggs, *Archeology*, p. 182.

19. Suggs, *Archeology*, pp. 160, 180, and Handy, pp. 152–154, provide illustrations and further descriptions.

20. Handy, p. 61.

21. Handy, p. 68. Irving Goldman, *Ancient Polynesian Society* (Chicago, 1970), p. 418.

22. See discussions in Goldman, *Ancient Polynesian Society*, pp. 450–452, 462–464.

23. Ibid., pp. 467–473.

24. Handy, pp. 70, 101.

25. Keith F. Otterbein, "Marquesan Polyandry," in *Marriage, Family and Residence*, ed. Paul Bohannan and John Middleton (Garden City, 1968), pp. 287–296.

26. Alexander to Anderson, entry of September 20, 1833.

27. Suggs, *Archeology*, pp. 30–33, 188.

28. Goldman, *Ancient Polynesian Society*, p. 146.

29. Handy, p. 54.

30. Goldman, *Ancient Polynesian Society*, pp. 20–22, 133, 140.

31. Gregory M. Dening, "Tapu and Haka'iki in the Marquesas, 1774–1813," unpubl. diss. (Harvard University, 1971), pp. 209–220. Dening's discussion implies that there was only one *haka-iki* of any significance per tribe, whereas the

diffusion of the term itself suggests that, while one may have been supreme, there were others who were considered *haka-iki* as well. Documents from early visitors to the Marquesas amply demonstrate this multiplicity of chiefs, in relation to a supreme chief. The missionaries of 1833, for example, offered the following: "There are those who are called chiefs and who have by common consent a kind of superiority over other natives. But every man who has a little piece of land or any other small amount of property is a chief. When visiting the different valleys we asked who were the chiefs, they replied by saying I'm a chief & you are a chief & he's a chief. If a chief wishes to have any piece of work done, he must take the same course to accomplish it as the poorest man in the island. He must prepare a feast and with this hire his men to work. He can call on no one to do it for him." "Joint communication of Messrs. Alexander, Armstrong & Parker," drafted by Benjamin Wyman Parker, April 10, 1834.

32. See Goldman, *Ancient Polynesian Society*, pp. 136–137, for *taua, tohuna,* and *toa.*

33. Alexander to Anderson, entry of December 22, 1833.

34. Handy, pp. 317–318, 344–345.

35. Handy, p. 322; Robert Carl Suggs, *Marquesan Sexual Behavior* (New York, 1966), p. 153.

36. Handy, p. 329, and Suggs, *Marquesan Sexual Behavior,* p. 27.

37. Suggs, *Marquesan Sexual Behavior,* pp. 88–89. See also Handy, p. 222, and Goldman, *Ancient Polynesian Society,* p. 565.

38. Handy, p. 217, and Suggs, *Marquesan Sexual Behavior,* p. 89.

39. Richard Armstrong, "A Sketch of Marquesian Character," *The Hawaiian Spectator,* 1 (1838), 12.

40. Alexander, *William Patterson Alexander,* pp. 144, 156.

41. Alexander to Anderson, entry of December 5, 1833.

42. Handy, p. 124.

43. Ralph Linton and Paul S. Wingert, *Arts of the South Seas* (New York, 1946), p. 34.

44. Suggs, *Archeology,* p. 171.

45. Handy, p. 124.

46. Karl G. Heider, *The Dugum Dani: A Papuan Culture in the Highlands of West New Guinea* (Chicago, 1970), pp. 99–133; Roy A. Rappaport, *Pigs for the Ancestors: Ritual in the Ecology of a New Guinea People* (New Haven, 1967), pp. 109–152.

47. *The Marquesan Journal of Edward Robarts, 1797–1824,* ed. Greg Dening (Honolulu, 1974), p. 84. See discussion in Dening, "Tapu and Haka'iki in the Marquesas," pp. 110–111.

48. Handy, p. 9.

49. Alexander to Anderson, entry of September 23, 1833.

50. Alexander to Anderson, entries of September 23, 1833, and January 21, 1834.

51. Alexander to Anderson, entries of November 30, 1833; December 22, 1833; December 28, 1833; March 29, 1834; April 5, 1834.

52. "Joint communication of Messrs. Alexander, Armstrong & Parker," drafted by Benjamin Wyman Parker, April 10, 1834.

53. Alexander to Anderson, entry of April 21, 1834.

54. Alexander, *William Patterson Alexander*, p. 178.

55. James M. Alexander, *The Islands of the Pacific*, rev. ed. (New York, 1908), p. 43. This account, although first published in 1895, forty-two years after the events, deserves credit as a transmitter of authentic earlier documents since James Alexander was the son of William Patterson Alexander.

56. Alexander to Anderson, entry of September 4, 1833.

3. Liberating Satan's Slaves

1. See *Mission, Church and Sect in Oceania*, ed. James A. Boutilier, Daniel T. Hughes, and Sharon W. Tiffany (Ann Arbor, 1978), for a fascinating series of individual studies.

2. Gavan Daws, *Shoal of Time: A History of the Hawaiian Islands* (Honolulu, 1968), pp. 29–43, 54–60.

3. W. Patrick Strauss, *Americans in Polynesia, 1783–1842* (East Lansing, 1963), pp. 55–56.

4. Ibid., pp. 57, 53.

5. Ibid., pp. 44–46; Clifton Jackson Phillips, *Protestant America and the Pagan World* (Cambridge, 1969), pp. 24–27.

6. Strauss, *Americans in Polynesia*, pp. 156–159.

7. This expansion is clearly marked in the opening sections of the official reports of the ABCFM, where members of the board are listed. In 1821 this section features a modest list of "agents of the Board" in various states who can accept contributions. By 1823 there are three categories of members listed: "Members under the act of Incorporation," "Corresponding Members," and "Honorary Members." In 1830 the board lists 711 persons in these categories, including governors, senators, college presidents, federal and state judges, and other dignitaries.

8. There is a very extensive literature on early nineteenth-century revivalism and the benevolent societies. Perry Miller provides a comprehensive account in "The Evangelical Basis," *The Life of the Mind in America from the Revolution to the Civil War* (New York, 1965), pp. 3–95. An excellent treatment providing guides to further reading is Sydney E. Ahlstrom, *A Religious History of the American People* (New Haven, 1972), especially "The Golden Day of Democratic Evangelicalism," pp. 385–509. On the ABCFM in the context of the benevolent empire, see Phillips, *Protestant America and the Pagan World*, pp. 235–253. See also Clifford S. Griffin, *Their Brothers' Keepers: Moral Stewardship in the United States, 1800–1865* (New Brunswick, 1960).

9. Strauss, *Americans in Polynesia*, p. 157.

10. Ibid., p. 64.

11. See *Report of the American Board of Commissioners for Foreign Missions . . . 1830*, pp. 58–71; *Report of the American Board . . . 1831*, p. 58. See also Mary

Charlotte Alexander, *William Patterson Alexander in Kentucky, the Marquesas, Hawaii* (Honolulu, 1934), p. 49.

12. Armstrong and Alexander sailed from New Bedford, Massachusetts, on November 26, 1831; see Alexander, *William Patterson Alexander*, p. 49. Charles Stewart's *A Visit to the South Seas* was reviewed in *North American Review*, 30 (October 1831), 484-506.

13. Charles S. Stewart, *A Visit to the South Seas*, 2 vols. (New York, 1831), I, 214. Subsequent references to volume I of this work appear in the text.

14. See Roy Harvey Pearce, *The Savages of America*, rev. ed. (Baltimore, 1965), pp. 82-83; Ernest Tuveson, *Millennium and Utopia* (Berkeley, 1949), pp. 195-203, and *Redeemer Nation* (Chicago, 1968), pp. 59-68.

15. "A review of the letters of the Rev. C. S. Stewart respecting the Sandwich Islands contained in his book entitled: 'A visit to the South Seas, etc.' " (Houghton).

16. Alexander to Anderson, Honolulu, November 28, 1832 (Houghton).

17. Alexander, *William Patterson Alexander*, p. 91.

18. Ibid., p. 121.

19. Alexander to Anderson, entry of April 5, 1834.

20. Alexander, *William Patterson Alexander*, p. 134; *Minutes of the General Meeting of the Sandwich Islands Mission*, Lahaina, June 5, 1833, to June 26, 1833; Strauss, p. 66.

21. Alexander to Anderson, entry of September 28, 1833.

22. Ibid., September 15, 1833.

23. Ibid.

24. Strauss, p. 48.

25. Alexander, *William Patterson Alexander*, p. 118.

26. "Journal written at the island of Nuuhiva" by Richard Armstrong, with entries from August 21, 1833, to March 22, 1834 (Houghton), entry of December 15, 1833.

27. Alexander to Anderson, entry of December 28, 1833.

28. Ibid., January 21, 1834.

29. Gregory M. Dening, "Tapu and Haka'iki in the Marquesas, 1774-1813," unpubl. diss. (Harvard University, 1971), p. 198; "Joint communication of Messrs. Alexander, Armstrong & Parker," drafted by Benjamin Wyman Parker, April 10, 1834 (Houghton).

30. H. E. Maude, *Of Islands and Men: Studies in Pacific History* (Melbourne, 1968), pp. 156-157.

31. Alexander to Anderson, entry of March 20, 1834.

32. James M. Alexander, *The Islands of the Pacific*, rev. ed. (New York, 1908), p. 38; Alexander to Anderson, entry of March 29, 1834.

33. "Joint communication of Messrs. Alexander, Armstrong & Parker," April 10, 1834 (Houghton).

34. Richard Armstrong to Rev. B. B. Wisner, Honolulu, August 28, 1834 (Houghton).

35. Mary E. Parker, "About the Marquesas, and the Little I know of Events

that Transpired there Fifty Years Ago," *Jubilee Celebration of the Arrival of the Missionary Reinforcement of 1837, held April 9th, 10th & 11th, 1887,* published by the Hawaiian Mission Children's Society (Honolulu, 1887), p. 199.

4. Educating Nature's Children

1. David F. Long, *Nothing Too Daring: A biography of Commodore David Porter, 1783–1843* (Annapolis, 1970), p. 124.

2. Ibid., pp. 79–80, 108, 98–104.

3. See, for example, Reginald Horsman, "Western War Aims, 1811–1812," in *American History: Recent Interpretations, Book I, to 1877,* ed. Abraham S. Eisenstadt (New York, 1962), pp. 252–267.

4. David Porter, *Journal of a Cruise Made to the Pacific Ocean,* 2 vols. (Philadelphia, 1815), II, 9. Subsequent references to volume I of this work appear in text.

5. Charles A. Beard and Mary R. Beard, *The American Spirit: A Study of the Idea of Civilization in the United States* (1942; rpt. New York, 1962), pp. 75–79, 94–152.

6. Hoxie Neal Fairchild, *The Noble Savage: A Study in Romantic Naturalism* (New York, 1928), pp. 104–111, discusses Hawkesworth's transformation of Cook's report.

7. W. Patrick Strauss, *Americans in Polynesia, 1783–1842* (East Lansing, 1963), pp. 149, 151–152.

8. Henry F. May, *The Enlightenment in America* (New York, 1976), pp. 275, 307–336.

9. "Captain David Porter's Proposed Expedition to the Pacific and Japan, 1815," ed. Allan B. Cole, *Pacific Historical Review,* 9 (1940), 63.

10. Ibid., pp. 64–65.

11. In *Fathers and Children: Andrew Jackson and the Subjugation of the American Indian* (New York, 1975), Michael Rogin finds this metaphor at the center of white responses to the "savage" Indian, in accordance with his general program of tracing in Freudian terms the dominance of early familial relationships in the formation of adult attitudes and responses. In the approach taken in this book the central metaphor is the hierarchical scale, with several subsidiary metaphors (including the metaphor of childhood) to signify relative positions on the scale. But Porter's view is closer to "child and teacher" as a variant of "pupil and teacher" than to the intensely familial "child and father" that Rogin finds in Jackson's and his contemporaries' attitudes toward Indians.

Familial relationships, as Marquesan society reminds us, cannot be taken as transcultural absolutes, and the primal influence they exert upon character formation is itself shaped by the systems of meaning by which a given culture organizes its experience, which include the systems that pattern kin relations. Such systems bequeath chronic unconscious conflicts, I believe, that can be as severe concerning the specific religious, political, and cultural constituents of identity as those well-recognized conflicts in sexual and familial relationships. The union of depth psychology with historical study will not reach its full potential until this aspect of psychological experience is better understood.

12. The missionary in question was William Crook of the London Missionary Society, who came to Tahuata in 1797 and went to Taiohae Bay in May 1798. See James Wilson, *A Missionary Voyage to the Southern Pacific Ocean . . . in the Ship Duff* (London, 1799), pp. 128–148, and Edmund Fanning. *Voyages Round the World . . . between the Years 1792 and 1832* (New York, 1833), pp. 156–214.

13. See Roy Rappaport, *Pigs for the Ancestors* (New Haven, 1967), p. 119, and Karl G. Heider, *The Dugum Dani* (Chicago, 1970), p. 110.

14. See Pierre Maranda, "Marquesan Social Structure: An Ethnohistorical Contribution," *Ethnohistory*, 11 (Fall 1964), 342–345, for a discussion of Marquesan exchange relations. See Irving Goldman, *Ancient Polynesian Society* (Chicago, 1970), p. 510, and E. S. Craighill Handy, *The Native Culture in the Marquesas* (Honolulu, 1923), p. 43.

15. J. Shillibeer, *A Narrative of the Briton's Voyage to Pitcairn's Island* (London, 1817), pp. 69, 71.

16. Herman Melville, *Typee: A Peep at Polynesian Life*, ed. Harrison Hayford, Hershel Parker, and G. Thomas Tanselle (Evanston, 1968), p. 26.

17. David Porter, "Transactions at Nooaheevah, after Captain Porter's Departure: Compiled from the Journal of Lt. Gamble." This account appears as chapter 19 in the 1822 edition of Porter's *Journal*: David Porter, *Journal of a Cruise Made to the Pacific Ocean* (New York, 1822), II, 181.

18. Ibid., p. 194.

19. Ibid., pp. 181, 195.

5. Heart of Darkness

1. Clifford Geertz, "The Impact of the Concept of Culture on the Concept of Man," in *The Interpretation of Cultures* (New York, 1973), p. 46. See also "Thick Description: Toward an Interpretive Theory of Culture," pp. 3–30, and "The Growth of Culture and the Evolution of Mind," pp. 55–83.

2. Kai T. Erikson, *Wayward Puritans: A Study in the Sociology of Deviance* (New York, 1966), pp. 6–7.

3. Quoted in Margaret T. Hodgen, *Early Anthropology in the Sixteenth and Seventeenth Centuries* (Philadelphia, 1964), p. 386. See also Arthur O. Lovejoy, *The Great Chain of Being* (Cambridge, 1936), which is the classic study of this idea.

4. Hodgen, *Early Anthropology*, pp. 418–419.

5. Ernest Lee Tuveson, *Millennium and Utopia: A Study in the Background of the Idea of Progress* (Berkeley, 1949), pp. 113–152.

6. Charles A. Beard and Mary R. Beard, *The American Spirit: A Study of the Idea of Civilization in the United States* (1942; rpt. New York, 1962), p. 63.

7. Ernest Lee Tuveson, *Redeemer Nation: The Idea of America's Millennial Role* (Chicago, 1968), pp. 64–66. See also Rush Welter, *The Mind of America, 1820–1860* (New York, 1975), pp. 3–4, as well as appendix A, p. 395, for a comment on Tuveson's discussion.

8. Welter, *The Mind of America*, pp. 3–25.

9. Beard and Beard, *The American Spirit*, pp. 99–100.

10. Welter, *The Mind of America*, p. 321.

11. Quoted in Michael P. Rogin, *Fathers and Children* (New York, 1975), p. 116. For a treatment of McKenney as a humanitarian, see Herman J. Viola, *Thomas L. McKenney, Architect of America's Early Indian Policy, 1816–1830* (Chicago, 1974).

12. For an extended discussion of the analogies between Freud's account of the unconscious and the attitudes of colonial administrators toward their non-Western wards, see O. Mannoni, *Prospero and Caliban: The psychology of colonization*, trans. Pamela Powesland (New York, 1956), and Philip Mason, *Prospero's Magic: Some Thoughts on Class and Race* (London, 1962).

13. See Victor W. Turner, *The Forest of Symbols: Aspects of Ndembu Ritual* (Ithaca, 1967); *The Ritual Process: Structure and Anti-Structure* (Chicago, 1969); *Dramas, Fields and Metaphors: Symbolic Action in Human Society* (Ithaca, 1974), pp. 33–43.

14. Erikson, *Wayward Puritans*, pp. 9–19.

15. James Baird, *Ishmael: A Study in the Symbolic Mode in Primitivism* (1956; rpt. New York, 1960).

16. Charles Stewart, *A Visit to the South Seas* (New York, 1831), I, 222, 279, 311. David Porter, *Journal of a Cruise Made to the Pacific Ocean* (Philadelphia, 1815), I, 118.

17. Wallace Stevens, "Anecdote of the Jar," in *The Collected Poems of Wallace Stevens* (New York, 1954), p. 76.

18. Joseph Conrad, *Heart of Darkness and Secret Sharer*, introduction by Albert J. Guerard (New York, 1958), p. 95.

19. Turner, *The Ritual Process*, p. 47.

20. See Kenneth Burke, *A Grammar of Motives* (Berkeley, 1969), pp. 33–34, and Simone de Beauvoir, *The Second Sex*, trans. H. M. Parshley (1953; rpt. New York, 1961), pp. xvi–xxix.

21. Ernst Kris, *Psychoanalytic Explorations in Art* (New York, 1952), pp. 56–63, 177.

22. Stewart, I, 354–355.

23. "Journal written at the island of Nuuhiva," by Richard Armstrong, with entries from August 21, 1833, to March 22, 1834 (Houghton), entries of October 6, 1833, and December 4, 1833. See also Richard Armstrong, "Journal of a Voyage from Sandwich Islands to Washington Islands, Brigantine Dhaulle, July 2, 1833 to Aug. 21" (Houghton), entry of August 21, 1833.

24. James Wilson, *A Missionary Voyage to the Southern Pacific Ocean . . . in the Ship Duff* (London, 1799), p. 133.

25. Ibid., pp. 133, 137, 141.

26. Ibid., pp. 141, 142.

27. Ibid., p. 142.

28. It is likely that the Marquesan women, instead of being "doubtful of his sex," were simply curious, inasmuch as they were exceptionally interested in genital characteristics. See Robert C. Suggs, *Marquesan Sexual Behavior* (New

York, 1966). Melville indicates that he and his companion were subjected to a similar investigation (*Typee*, p. 77).

29. Conrad, *Heart of Darkness*, p. 96.

30. Clifford Geertz, "Religion as a Cultural System," *The Interpretation of Cultures* (New York, 1973), pp. 99–101.

31. Mary E. Parker, journal letter, November 23, 1832, to August 18, 1833 (Houghton), entry of August 10, 1833.

32. Alexander to Anderson, Taiohae, Nukuheva, August 13, 1833 (Houghton).

33. Mary Elizabeth Parker, "Intimate Diary of Religious Thoughts," 2 vols. in manuscript, vol. I, entry of August 10, 1833 (Hawaiian Mission Children's Society).

34. Stewart, I, 262.

35. Ibid.

36. For a fuller discussion, see my *Moby-Dick and Calvinism: A World Dismantled* (New Brunswick, 1977), pp. 38–41.

37. Stewart, I, 262–263.

38. Porter, *Journal of a Cruise Made to the Pacific Ocean*, 2 vols. (Philadelphia, 1815), II, 99.

6. What It Means To Be a Cannibal

1. Mary Charlotte Alexander, *William Patterson Alexander in Kentucky, the Marquesas, Hawaii* (Honolulu, 1934), p. 117.

2. Edmund Fanning, *Voyages Round the World . . . between the Years 1792 and 1832* (New York, 1833), pp. 133–139.

3. Herman Melville, *Typee: A Peep at Polynesian Life*, ed. Harrison Hayford, Hershel Parker, and G. Thomas Tanselle (Evanston, 1968), p. 185. Subsequent references to this edition appear in text.

4. See Charles Roberts Anderson, *Melville in the South Seas* (1939; rpt. New York, 1966), pp. 70–71.

5. The incident Melville relates did not take place during the American mission of 1833–34, and indeed Melville specifies that the missionaries in question came from Tahiti, which means that they were representatives of the London Missionary Society. An LMS mission was established in Tahuata in October 1834, led by Mr. and Mrs. Rogerson and Mr. Stallworthy. An account of this mission published in 1895 reports that the Rogersons abandoned the effort in 1837 "being convinced that the islands were unfit to be the residence of civilized females," and that Stallworthy remained until 1841. See James M. Alexander, *The Islands of the Pacific* (New York, 1895), pp. 242–243.

6. The idea of civilization has been accepted by students of Melville, who have not recognized that Melville actually holds it in question. D. H. Lawrence, to choose a distinguished example, states that Melville discovers in *Typee* that "one cannot go back" to the condition in which the islanders exist, "centuries and centuries behind us in the life-struggle"; *Studies in Classic American Literature* (1922; rpt. Garden City, 1953), p. 149. With varying emphasis the same

scalar relation between Marquesan life and Western life is present throughout the critical literature on *Typee*. Only quite recently has Faith Pullin observed that Melville makes the idea of civilization a target of his inquiry. See "Melville's *Typee*: The Failure of Eden," in *New Perspectives on Melville*, ed. Faith Pullin (Edinburgh, 1978), pp. 1–28.

7. Charles Roberts Anderson, *Melville in the South Seas* (1939; rpt. New York, 1966), pp. 15–19.

8. Nathaniel Hawthorne, *The House of the Seven Gables* in *The Complete Novels and Selected Tales of Nathaniel Hawthorne*, ed. Norman Holmes Pearson (New York, 1937), p. 265.

9. We have already noted Melville's direct adaptation of Porter's description of his march through the valley of the Typees; see Chapter Three, note 17. See also Anderson, *Melville*, pp. 70–72, 96–98.

10. W. Patrick Strauss, *Americans in Polynesia, 1783–1842* (East Lansing, 1963), p. 149.

11. See Warwick Wadlington, *The Confidence Game in American Literature* (Princeton, 1975), pp. 56–58.

12. Roy Harvey Pearce, *The Savages of America*, rev. ed. (Baltimore, 1965), pp. 84–89, gives a discussion of this way of viewing "savage" virtue.

13. This feature of Melville's characteristic aesthetic quality was noted by Warner Berthoff in *The Example of Melville* (Princeton, 1962) where he discusses the "continuous activity of outgoing imagination" as what holds the particulars of Melville's art together (pp. 5–6). Two recent studies have shifted the focus from the immediate continuous ordering power of the speaking presence and have sought to find coherence in *Typee*'s narrative voice by dividing it into two points of view, that of Tommo in the midst of his experience and Melville in retrospect considering it. For William Dillingham this explains the conflict between those moments in which Typee Valley appears a paradise and those in which it appears dreadful, on the principle that the immediate adversities of Tommo are qualified by the tranquility in which Melville recollected the experience. See *An Artist in the Rigging* (Athens, Georgia, 1972), pp. 10–13. For Edgar Dryden the two voices propound a chaos of individual moments, on the one hand, and the coherent meaning that is perceived as Melville reconsiders what he had been through. See *Melville's Thematics of Form: The Great Art of Telling the Truth* (Baltimore, 1968), pp. 38–40. Yet, as my discussion has shown, there are numerous occasions when Tommo in the immediate moment is joyous and others in which he sees coherence in what is happening; and there are also many occasions when Melville the retrospective commentator is both agonized and confused.

There are in fact other voices in addition to these, and the book exemplifies what Robert Abrams has termed Melville's "capacity to enter sympathetically into, and to temporarily inhabit, multiple speaking voices." Abrams rightly observes that this stylistic quality is closely associated with Melville's "growing awareness of the fundamental elasticity and mutability of his so-called 'identity.' " See *"Typee* and *Omoo*: Herman Melville and the Ungraspable Phantom of Identity," *Arizona Quarterly*, 31 (1975), 33–50.

The best discussion of the aesthetic quality Melville achieves in this mode, including perceptive commentary on its psychosocial bearings, is to be found in Warwick Wadlington's *The Confidence Game in American Literature*. Tracing the moment-by-moment interactions in which the narrative voice engages the reader, Wadlington studies Melville's knack of provoking consideration of the terms on which identity and community are generated and regenerated. "In order to be renovated, his audience's *familiar* premises must be activated in the largely unconscious negotiations of rhetoric; they must be exercised in a way analogous to the narrator's experiences" (p. 51).

14. Proof of Melville's continuing power to provoke thought about the issues of meaning that emerge when one culture confronts another, and hence confronts itself, is to be found in a recent book of essays on such questions, where an extended quotation from *Moby-Dick* is included as a contribution. See *Symbolic Anthropology: A Reader in the Study of Symbols and Meanings*, ed. Janet L. Dolgin, David S. Kemnitzer, and David M. Schneider (New York, 1977).

15. See Melville's letter to John Murray in *The Letters of Herman Melville*, ed. Merrell R. Davis and William H. Gilman (New Haven, 1960), p. 72.

16. Jay Leyda, *The Melville Log: A Documentary Life of Herman Melville*, 2 vols. (New York, 1951), I, 207–208.

17. *The Recognition of Herman Melville*, ed. Hershel Parker (Ann Arbor, 1967), p. 3.

18. See Perry Miller's astute discussion of the way in which Evert Duyckinck's friendly review of *Typee* also took a stand that confirmed Melville's alienation from the majority sentiment. *The Raven and the Whale* (New York, 1956), p. 208.

19. *New-York Evangelist*, 17 (April 9, 1846), 60.

20. "Beware of Bad Books!", *New-York Evangelist*, 18 (January 28, 1847), 13.

21. Hugh W. Hetherington, *Melville's Reviewers: British and American, 1846–1891* (Chapel Hill, 1961), p. 48, n. 56.

22. "Typee: The Traducers of Missions," *Christian Parlor Magazine*, July 1846, p. 75. Subsequent references to this review appear in the text.

23. *The Recognition of Herman Melville*, p. 4.

24. Leyda, *The Melville Log*, I, 224.

25. *The Letters of Herman Melville*, p. 39.

26. See Strauss, *Americans in Polynesia*, p. 156.

27. *The Letters of Herman Melville*, p. 43.

28. Herman Melville, *Omoo: A Narrative of Adventures in the South Seas*, ed. Harrison Hayford, Hershel Parker, and G. Thomas Tanselle (Evanston, 1968), p. 192. Melville here echoes the conclusion, well entrenched by the 1840s, that American Indians could not become civilized, so that the only alternative to their extinction was to isolate them from the white community. Yet Melville is not arguing here in behalf of Indian Removal or of any other policy meant to raise hopes of eventual felicity for the Indians and Polynesians who were the

objects of white benevolence. On the removal program, see Michael P. Rogin, *Fathers and Children* (New York, 1975), pp. 206–248. And see Bernard W. Sheehan, *Seeds of Extinction: Jeffersonian Philanthropy and the American Indian* (Chapel Hill, 1973), pp. 243–275.

29. Frederick O'Brien, *White Shadows in the South Seas* (Garden City, 1919), pp. 308–309.

Concluding Metascientific Postscript

1. Philip Mason, *Prospero's Magic* (London, 1962), p. 90.

2. Kenneth Burke, *A Grammar of Motives* (Berkeley, 1969). Burke's writings generally are a rich source for dramatistic conceptions linking social processes with the life of art.

3. Bronislaw Malinowski, *Argonauts of the Western Pacific* (1922; rpt. New York, 1961), p. 25.

4. George W. Stocking, Jr., argues that the "modern anthropological point of view" owes a great deal to the psychological struggle recorded in the diary. His sensitive and discerning commentary pursues issues akin to those developed here. See "Empathy and Antipathy in the Heart of Darkness," *Journal of the History of the Behavioral Sciences*, 4 (1968), 189–194. For other responses see Chapter 1, n. 2.

5. Bronislaw Malinowski, *A Diary in the Strict Sense of the Term*, trans. Norbert Guterman (New York, 1967), p. 31. Subsequent references to this edition appear in text.

6. E. R. Leach, "The Epistemological Background to Malinowski's Empiricism," in *Man and Culture: An Evaluation of the Work of Bronislaw Malinowski*, ed. Raymond Firth (London, 1957), pp. 119–137.

7. Claude Lévi-Strauss, *Tristes Tropiques*, trans. John and Doreen Weightman (New York, 1974), pp. 332–333.

8. See *Women in the Field: Anthropological Experiences*, ed. Peggy Golde (Chicago, 1970), p. 91; Hortense Powdermaker, *Stranger and Friend: The Way of an Anthropologist* (New York, 1966), pp. 84, 112, 115, 291–292. For a discussion of fieldwork as a *rite de passage* into the discipline—it includes a section on "Ethics and Sanity Maintenance"—see *Marginal Natives: Anthropologists at Work*, ed. Morris Frielich (New York, 1970). This lively book was rendered a good deal more staid, and less revealing, in a republished version, a process reminiscent of what happened to Melville's *Typee*. See *Marginal Natives at Work: Anthropologists in the Field*, ed. Morris Frielich (New York, 1977).

9. Victor W. Turner, *The Ritual Process: Structure and Anti-Structure* (Chicago, 1969), pp. 94–130.

10. See Erving Goffman, *The Presentation of Self in Everyday Life* (Garden City, 1959); Louis A. Zurcher, Jr., *The Mutable Self: A Self-Concept for Social Change* (Beverly Hills, 1977); Eric Berne, *Games People Play* (New York, 1967); Daniel Lerner, *The Passing of Traditional Society: Modernizing the Middle East* (1958; rev. ed., New York, 1964), p. 49; Allan Wheelis, *The Quest for Identity* (New York, 1958); Erik H. Erikson, *Childhood and Society* (New York, 1950) and *Identity,*

Youth and Crisis (New York, 1968); Robert Langbaum, *The Mysteries of Identity: A Theme in Modern Literature* (New York, 1977); Stephen J. Geenblatt, "Improvisation and Power," in *Renaissance Self-Fashioning: From More to Shakespeare* (Chicago, forthcoming).

11. See John Archibald Wheeler, "Genesis and Observership," *Foundational Problems in the Special Sciences,* ed. R. E. Butts and K. J. Hintikka (Dordrecht-Holland, 1977), pp. 3–33, and "Frontiers of Time," scheduled for publication in *Problems in the Foundations of Physics,* ed. G. Toraldo di Francia (Amsterdam, 1979), pp. 395–497.

12. A good example of development anthropology is the Kalahari Peoples Fund in Albuquerque, New Mexico. For a probing discussion of ethical issues bearing on fieldwork, see Clifford Geertz, "Thinking as a Moral Act: Ethical Dimensions of Anthropological Fieldwork in the New States," *Antioch Review,* 28 (1968), 139–158.

13. Clifford Geertz, *The Interpretation of Cultures* (New York, 1973), p. 347.

14. Mary Douglas, *Implicit Meanings: Essays in Anthropology* (London, 1975), p. 226.

15. Robert C. Suggs, *The Island Civilizations of Polynesia* (New York, 1960), p. 110.

Bibliography

Berger, Peter L., and Thomas Luckmann. *The Social Construction of Reality: A Treatise in the Sociology of Knowledge.* Garden City: Doubleday, 1966.

Berne, Eric. *Games People Play: The Psychology of Human Relationships.* New York: Grove, 1967.

Berthoff, Warner. *Fictions and Events: Essays in Criticism and Literary History,* New York: Dutton, 1971.

Boon, James A. *The Anthropological Romance of Bali 1597–1972: Dynamic Perspectives in Marriage and Caste, Politics and Religion.* Cambridge: Cambridge University Press, 1977.

———— *From Symbolism to Structuralism: Lévi-Strauss in a Literary Tradition.* New York: Harper and Row, 1972.

Burke, Kenneth. *A Grammar of Motives.* Berkeley: University of California Press, 1969.

———— *Permanence and Change: An Anatomy of Purpose,* 2nd rev. ed. Los Altos: Hermes Publications, 1954.

———— *The Philosophy of Literary Form: Studies in Symbolic Action,* 2nd ed. Baton Rouge: Louisiana State University Press, 1967.

———— *A Rhetoric of Motives.* Berkeley: University of California Press, 1969.

Cassirer, Ernst. *Language and Myth,* trans. Susan K. Langer. New York: Dover, 1946.

Cohen, Abner. "Symbolic Action and the Structure of the Self." *Symbols and Sentiments: Cross Cultural Studies in Symbolism,* ed. Ioan Lewis. London: Academic Press, 1977.

Douglas, Mary. *Implicit Meanings: Essays in Anthropology.* London: Routledge and Kegan Paul, 1975.

———— *Purity and Danger: An Analysis of Concepts of Pollution and Taboo.* New York: Praeger, 1966.

227

Duncan, Hugh Dalziel. *Language and Literature in Society*. New York: Bedminster Press, 1961.

Erikson, Erik H. *Childhood and Society*. New York: Norton, 1950.

—— *Identity, Youth and Crisis*. New York: Norton, 1968.

Erikson, Kai T. *Wayward Puritans: A Study in the Sociology of Deviance*. New York: Wiley, 1966.

Gadamer, Hans-Georg. *Truth and Method*, trans. and ed. Garrett Barden and John Cumming. New York: Seabury Press, 1975.

Geertz, Clifford. *The Interpretation of Cultures*. New York: Basic Books, 1973.

—— "Thinking as a Moral Act: Ethical Dimensions of Anthropological Fieldwork in the New States." *Antioch Review*, 28 (1968), 139–158.

—— "Art as a Cultural System." *Modern Language Notes*, 91 (1976), 1473–1499.

—— "Found in Translation: On the Social History of the Moral Imagination." *Georgia Review*, 31 (1977), 788–810.

—— "Blurred Genres: The Refiguration of Social Thought," *The American Scholar*, 49 (1980), 165–179.

Goffman, Erving. *The Presentation of Self in Everyday Life*. Garden City: Doubleday, 1959.

Gombrich, E. H. *Art and Illusion: A Study in the Psychology of Pictorial Representation*. Princeton: Princeton University Press, 1960.

Gouldner, Alvin W. "Romanticism and Classicism: Deep Structures in Social Science." *Diogenes*, 82 (1973), 88–107.

Greenblatt, Stephen J. *Renaissance Self-Fashioning: From More to Shakespeare*. Chicago: Chicago University Press, forthcoming.

—— "Marlowe and Renaissance Self-Fashioning." *Two Renaissance Mythmakers: Christopher Marlowe and Ben Jonson*, ed. Alvin Kernan. Baltimore: Johns Hopkins University Press, 1977, pp. 41–69.

—— "Learning to Curse: Aspects of Linguistic Colonialism in the Sixteenth Century." *First Images of America: The Impact of the New World on the Old*, ed. Fredi Ciappelli. Berkeley: University of California Press, 1976.

La Barre, Weston. *The Ghost Dance: Origins of Religion*. London: Allen and Unwin, 1972.

Lévi-Strauss, Claude. *The Savage Mind*. Chicago: University of Chicago Press, 1966.

—— *The Scope of Anthropology*, trans. Sherry Ortner Paul and Robert A. Paul. London: Jonathan Cape, 1967.

—— *Structural Anthropology*, trans. Claire Jacobson and Brooke Grundfest Schoepf. New York: Basic Books, 1963.

—— "Structuralism and Ecology." *Social Science Information*, 12(1) (1972), 7–23.

—— *Totemism*, trans. Rodney Needham. Boston: Beacon Press, 1963.

—— *Tristes Tropiques*, trans. John and Doreen Weightman. New York: Atheneum, 1974.

Mannoni, O. *Prospero and Caliban: The Psychology of Colonization*, trans. Pamela Powesland. New York: Praeger, 1956.

Mason, Philip. *Prospero's Magic. Some Thoughts on Class and Race*. London: Oxford University Press, 1962.

Mead, George H. *Mind, Self, and Society, from the Standpoint of a Social Behaviorist*, ed. with intro. Charles W. Morris. Chicago: University of Chicago Press, 1962.

Meaning in Anthropology, ed. Keith H. Basso and Henry A. Selby. Albuquerque: University of New Mexico Press, 1976.

Myth and Mythmaking, ed. Henry A. Murray. Boston: Beacon Press, 1960.

Myth, Symbol and Culture, ed. Clifford Geertz. New York: Norton, 1971.

Peacock, James L. *Consciousness and Change: Symbolic Anthropology in Evolutionary Perspective*. New York: Wiley, 1975.

Poirier, Richard. *The Performing Self: Compositions and Decompositions in the Languages of Contemporary Life*. New York: Oxford University Press, 1971.

Ricoeur, Paul. "The Model of the Text: Meaningful Action Considered as a Text." *New Literary History*, 5 (1973), 91–117.

―――― *The Philosophy of Paul Ricoeur: An Anthology of His Work*, ed. Charles E. Reagan and David Stewart. Boston: Beacon Press, 1978.

Rules and Meanings: The Anthropology of Everyday Knowledge, ed. Mary Douglas. New York: Penguin Books, 1973.

Sahlins, Marshall. *Culture and Practical Reason*. Chicago: University of Chicago Press, 1976.

Schutz, Alfred. *The Problem of Social Reality*. Vol. I of *Collected Papers*, ed. M. Natanson. The Hague: Nijhoff, 1962.

Smith, M. Brewster. "Perspectives on Selfhood." *American Psychologist*, 33 (1978), 1058–1063.

Stonequist, Everett V. *The Marginal Man: A Study in Personality and Culture Conflict*. New York: Scribner's, 1937.

Symbolic Anthropology: A Reader in the Study of Symbols and Meanings, ed. with intro. Janet L. Dolgin, David S. Kemnitzer, and David M. Schneider. New York: Columbia University Press, 1977.

Turner, Victor W. *Dramas, Fields, and Metaphors: Symbolic Action in Human Society*. Ithaca: Cornell University Press, 1974.

―――― *The Forest of Symbols: Aspects of Ndembu Ritual*. Ithaca: Cornell University Press, 1967.

―――― *The Ritual Process: Structure and Anti-Structure*. Chicago: Aldine, 1969.

Turner, Victor W., and Edith Turner. *Image and Pilgrimage in Christian Culture: Anthropological Perspectives*. New York: Columbia University Press, 1978.

Wadlington, Warwick. *The Confidence Game in American Literature*. Princeton: Princeton University Press, 1975.

Weiner, Annette B. *Women of Value, Men of Renown: New Perspectives in Trobriand Exchange*. Austin: University of Texas Press, 1976.

Wheelis, Allan. *The Quest for Identity*. New York: Norton, 1958.

White, Hayden. "The Absurdist Moment in Contemporary Literary Theory."

Directions for Criticism: Structuralism and its Alternatives, ed. Murray Krieger and L. S. Dembo. Madison: University of Wisconsin Press, 1977.

———— "The Fictions of Factual Representation." The Literature of Fact, ed. Angus Fletcher. New York: Columbia University Press, 1976.

Whorf, Benjamin Lee. Language, Thought and Reality: Selected Writings of Benjamin Lee Whorf, ed. and intro. John B. Carroll. Cambridge: Massachusetts Institute of Technology Press, 1956.

Winch, Peter. The Idea of a Social Science and Its Relation to Philosophy. London: Routledge and Kegan Paul, 1958.

Worsley, Peter. The Trumpet Shall Sound: A Study of "Cargo" Cults in Melanesia. London: MacGibbon and Kee, 1957.

Index

231